AI POWER FUNNELS

A Practical Guide for Using AI
To Systematically Grow Your Online Sales

YLVA BOSEMARK

Ylva Bosemark
AI POWER FUNNELS
A Practical Guide for Using AI
To Systematically Grow Your Online Sales

Ylva Bosemark

Printed Worldwide
First Printing 2023
First Edition 2023

Paperback ISBN: 9798861114783
Hardcover ISBN: 9798861114882

10 9 8 7 6 5 4 3 2 1

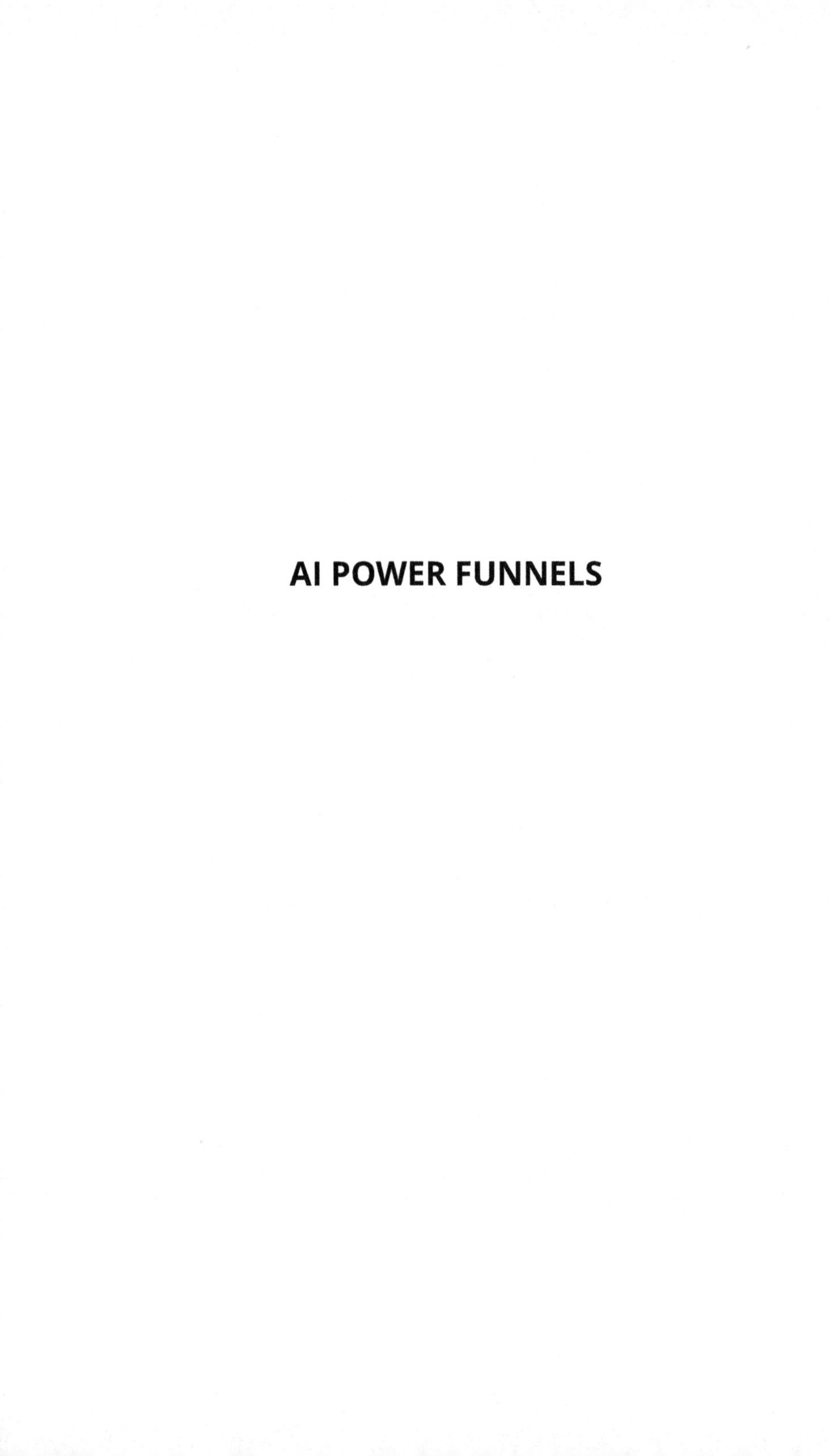

AI POWER FUNNELS

Table of Contents

Foreword

ROB MARKOVICH

I first came across Ylva's online business while at VMware. What started as a search for ways to engage software developer customers at several upcoming community events evolved into an unexpected mentorship.

Her products delighted my customers, but her service and efficiency delighted me, or more specifically, the marketeer in me. Her website seamlessly guided me through customizable corporate merch offers that were sustainable and refreshingly distinct. Her funnels were so seamless that I couldn't help but admire how she drove the sales process—from closing our initial project to driving follow-up business.

As our partnership grew, it became clear that she didn't leave much to chance. She had systematic, repeatable processes in place, and I was intrigued by the mechanics that drove her success. Even years later, as I advised startups and entrepreneurs, I STILL found myself thinking back to how Ylva's streamlined processes could benefit a wider audience. Realizing how valuable her methods could be for entrepreneurs, I encouraged her to write a guidebook that teaches what she learned in practice.

In many ways, I wish I had this book when I became an entrepreneur. I'm an engineer by training and had to endure lots of trial and error (and lost time and money) before I became successful with marketing. When you're working to increase online sales, there are so many possible levers to pull, and it can be daunting to make sense of it all. Without a good understanding of what strategies and workflows really matter, it's like rolling dice in a casino.

If you want to optimize lead generation and lead conversion to increase online sales, there are a few key workflows to focus on—this is what the book refers to as Power Funnels. But this isn't just "another business book." *AI Power Funnels* is a step-by-step roadmap that masterfully breaks down the most important strategies and makes them highly actionable (and it's fun to read the stories she shares). Throughout this book, Ylva teaches you how to leverage AI to minimize guesswork and accelerate results. Instead of being overwhelmed by AI, she shows you how AI can do the work that's overwhelming for you.

A systematic approach gives you the structure to execute a proven plan, unlike haphazard tactics that can hit or miss. Think about a new gym with top-notch equipment. Without a personal trainer with a structured approach to help you achieve your goals, the effectiveness of the gym equipment is squandered. This book is your personal trainer to make the most use of AI-driven Power Funnels (and at a fraction of the cost of a fitness coach).

All this to say, in the ever-evolving realm of online business, you either learn fast to increase sales or risk competition eating your lunch. There is a hard way and an easy way to realize this. Take the easy path and learn from this book.

Rob Markovich

Entrepreneur, Angel Investor, Marketing Executive

Co-founder of Visual Networks (IPO)

Former Chief Marketing Officer for 8 Silicon Valley startups including Wavefront (acquired by VMware), VSS Monitoring (acquired by NetScout), Moogsoft (acquired by Dell), and Empirix (acquired by Infovista).

Preface

In the fast-paced, competitive world of entrepreneurship, we all grapple with one constant dilemma: how can we drive more sales without burning a hole in our pocket (or overloading our calendar)? Conventional business wisdom suggests that spending more money directly fuels sales growth. If you get an inquiry for every 10 clicks on an ad, then investing in more clicks should directly increase inquiries, right?

Here's the flaw. This "spend more to sell more" model is expensive and unsustainable. When the cost of acquiring a sale outweighs the profit generated, the model collapses. Pouring more resources into this model only accelerates losses, costing you time and money.

The solution is smarter digital marketing. Let's shift the flawed paradigm from "spend more" to "optimize more" by looking at step-by-step processes that lean on artificial intelligence (AI) to generate more sales with less time and money.

In this book, I'll show you how AI acts as an *efficiency amplifier*. Rather than replace your efforts, it can compress a task that might take five hours into one. But it's not enough to have AI tools; you need to know how to use them. Just as a craftsman needs to learn the foundations of their trade before receiving apprentices, you need to learn the underlying concepts before integrating AI into your business. There's no way around that step. This book not only teaches you the skills to use AI effectively, but also the shortcuts, hacks, and practical resources to take it to the next level. Every chapter provides action items, resources, and ChatGPT prompts to fit your needs, so you can hit the ground running, ready to compete.

POWER FUNNELS AND WHY THEY MATTER

Power Funnels optimize lead generation and conversion methods to increase sales. This type of workflow combines psychology, methodology, marketing, digital media, and relationship building to supercharge your digital presence.

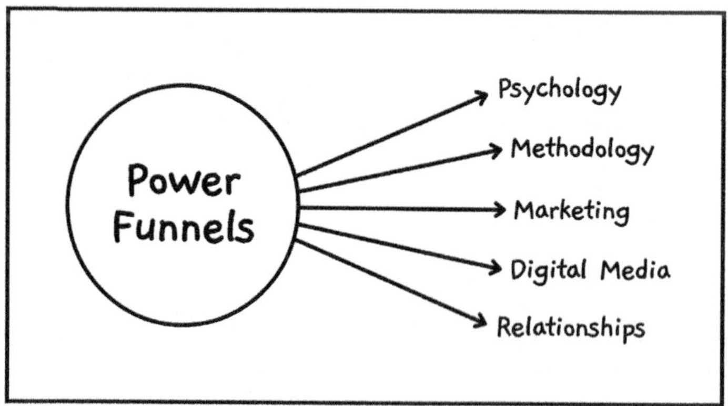

Many entrepreneurs overlook the potency of Power Funnels because of their inherent invisibility. Power Funnels aren't sexy. They aren't the latest trend you can show off to your audience or competitors. They work behind the scenes to form the foundation of a successful digital business. Yet, their invisibility is what makes Power Funnels enduring. They aren't short-lived methods that will lose relevance tomorrow; they're rooted in time-tested principles of human behavior and business strategy.

You'll soon realize that Power Funnels and effective writing go hand in hand. With an online business, your main tools for communicating with your audience are your website, emails, texts, social media posts, and videos. Sure, images and graphics are helpful, but they leave room for interpretation. So, you need to master the process of engaging with customers without having them in front of you. That's where copywriting comes into play. Whether you're crafting a video script, SMS sequence, or sales page, if you can't communicate with your audience successfully, the strategies covered in this book won't meet their full potential. We'll cover a range of topics, like copywriting, customer psychology, AI, and more, but the core premise of this book is simple. You can't improve what you don't understand. Once you learn the science of Power Funnels, you can put processes in place that can be repeated endlessly. This book is a comprehensive guide to uncovering, understanding, and implementing these invisible powerhouses in your digital toolkit—with the help of AI.

WHO CAN BENEFIT FROM THIS BOOK

Whether you're an online service provider, solopreneur, a brick-and-mortar business looking to transition online, or run an e-commerce brand, this book is valuable to you. Aspiring entrepreneurs dipping their toes into the digital landscape will also benefit from this book.

You may come from diverse industries, have different business models, or sell various products and services, but your destination is the same. You want to maximize your online visibility, convert leads, and scale your business without blowing your budget.

THIS BOOK'S APPROACH

The book is divided into two parts. Part I focuses on the sales funnel, the cornerstone of Power Funnels. It digs deep into the six core stages that make up the sales funnel. Part II explores six additional Power Funnels that will take your online sales to the next level.

Part I

SALES FUNNEL FUNDAMENTALS

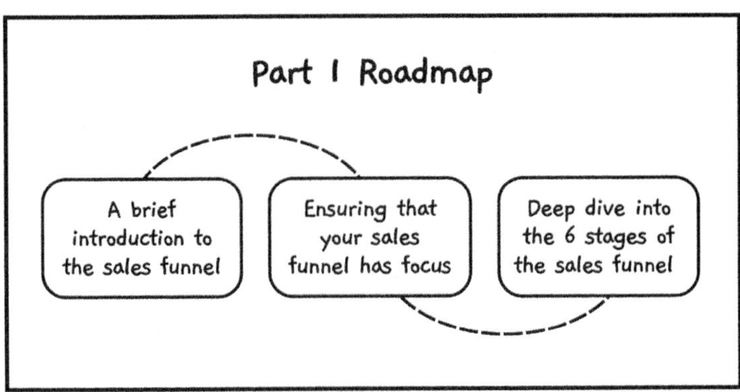

In Part I, we'll deep dive into the backbone of Power Funnels: the sales funnel. The sales funnel is a vital asset to any online business because of its systematic, step-by-step approach to guiding consumers through their purchasing journey. However, it's crucial to understand that the sales funnel doesn't work on its own. If you do not understand your ideal customers and how to serve them, this tool will miss its mark. Power Funnels aren't just about selling; they're about creating lasting customer relationships. So, before we jump into the six stages of the sales funnel, let's talk about what it is and how it can work for you.

First, we'll examine how the sales funnel shapes consumer behavior. Then we'll look at how to focus your funnel to reach the right audience and present your brand effectively. Starting in Chapter 3, we'll explore the six stages that form the heart of the sales funnel—Traffic, Discovery, Nurture, Sales Process, Purchase, and Loyalty. We'll learn how the stages work together to guide potential customers from discovery to loyalty. By the end of Part I, the sales funnel will no longer be an abstract concept. It will become an actionable blueprint you can tailor to streamline your online business.

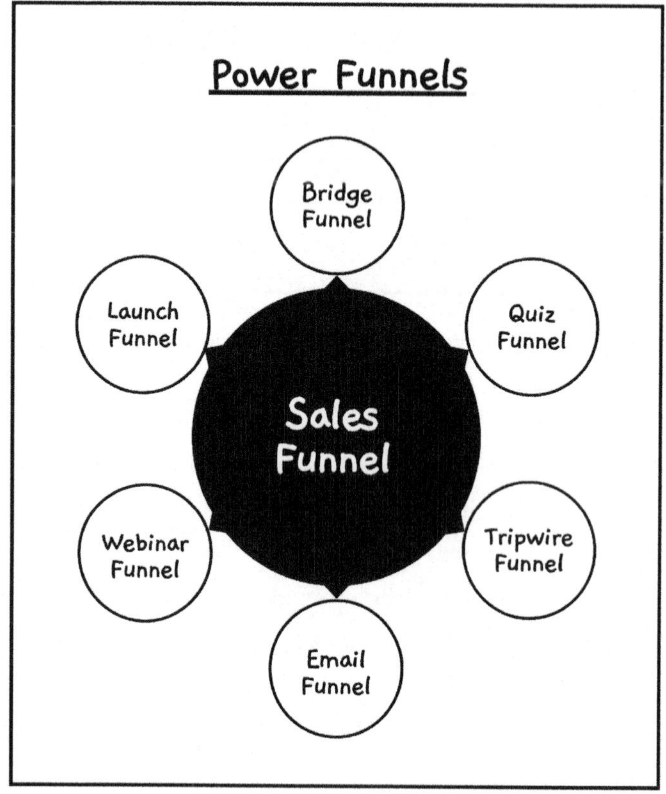

The sales funnel is the most important Power Funnel, and the additional Power Funnels are a force multiplier.

In Part II, we learn the true magic of Power Funnels comes into play when they are arranged in an order that promotes upselling, called Funnel Sequencing. Using the momentum generated from one funnel to drive customers toward the next, you can seamlessly guide them toward higher-value offers. Once you understand how Power Funnels can work together, they help you to acquire (and retain) more customers, make more sales, and most importantly, do it in less time. That is what this book is about.

Let's get started!

1

STONE AGE MINDS

Setting the Stage

We belong to the Homo genus, which emerged about 2.4 million years ago. For roughly 84,000 generations, we spent most of our existence living as hunter-gatherers. Only 7 generations have lived in the industrial age. In fact, over 99 percent of our evolution happened in hunter-gatherer societies, where our wants and needs originated.[1]

Our modern lifestyle, characterized by sedentary habits, air-conditioned homes, e-commerce, and media entertainment, is barely a century old. And the digital age, which has drastically transformed our existence, has only been around for two generations! This seemingly permanent way of life is just a blip in the grand timeline of humanity. The transition from hunters throwing spears to shoppers clicking online orders has taken place insanely fast. Our environment is rapidly changing, and our brains can't keep up. As evolutionary psychologists put it, "Our modern skulls house stone age minds."[2]

This is why we should shift our focus from simply observing consumer purchasing trends to understanding the fundamental *reasons and processes* behind these behaviors. Though buying goods and services is a relatively new concept, the primitive brain circuits that help us choose resources are still running the show. Our methods for selecting which products to buy online mirror those used by our ancestors foraging in the Serengeti plains. For example, when we consistently choose a particular footwear or electronics brand, it echoes our ancestors' preference for familiar sources while foraging for food—choices proven to avoid pain and predict pleasure. Considering the evolutionary backdrop of our behavior, it's important to understand how these primal instincts can be harnessed for your online businesses.

The sales funnel is a key mechanism that taps into these evolutionary instincts and guides customer behavior. Much like the name suggests, a sales funnel looks a lot like...a funnel, wide at the top and narrow at the base. At the top, we have many potential customers who are discovering your brand. As they progress through the funnel, some drop off, and others continue towards the end, where they finally decide to buy. The sales funnel, consisting of six stages, uses psychological principles and relationship-building techniques to increase your sales.

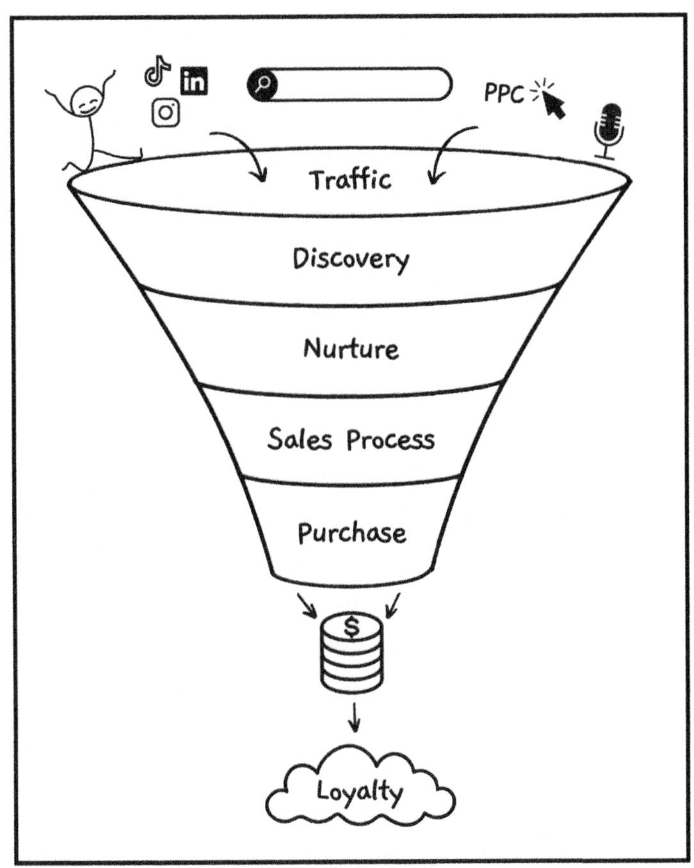

The Sales Funnel

The sales funnel starts when a potential customer first interacts with your brand and continues through each phase to the loyalty phase. The main goal of the funnel is to shape customer perceptions, so they see your brand as the "safest" choice among competitors. The smoother the transition between each stage in the funnel, the more effective it will be in persuading the naturally cautious "Stone Age" mind to continue. As a result, potential customers are more likely to trust your brand, make a purchase, and (most importantly) keep coming back.

The sales funnel's Traffic stage resembles our ancestors' first encounter with new food sources. As we progress down the funnel, the Discover and Nurture stages imitate our ancestors' inspection process when deciding whether an unfamiliar food source is safe to eat. The Sales Process and Purchase stages echo the final steps in the foraging process when our ancestors actually chose to try the new food. Finally, the Loyalty stage of the sales funnel mirrors the Pleistocene humans' repeated choice of familiar, safe food sources. Although this analogy is oversimplified, it helps to frame the context of online shopping behavior. By understanding and tapping into deep-seated instincts, you can craft a sales funnel that guides customers through the buying process and encourages repeat purchases.

THE AIDA MODEL

Now that we've established the basics, let's break down the customer journey into bite-sized stages. The effectiveness of a sales funnel boils down to four key elements, known as AIDA.

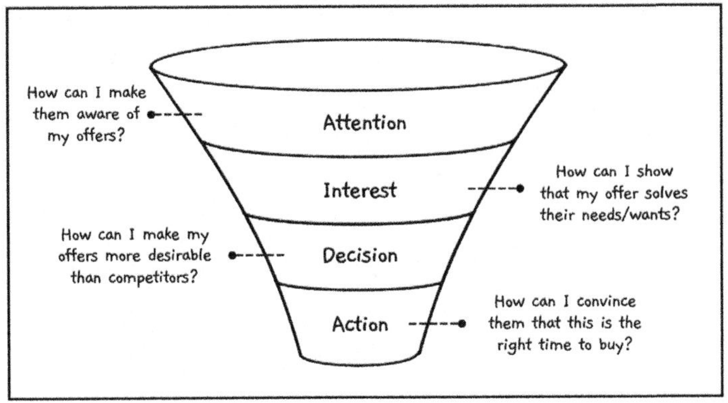

ATTENTION

First Impressions Matter

Imagine this: you're at a social event, and across the room, you spot the love of your life. You can't just rush over there and ask them to marry you. That'd be creepy, not to mention a surefire way to earn a restraining order. First, you need to introduce yourself. That's the Attention stage – making your potential customers aware of your existence in the most appealing way possible.

Whether it's an engaging social media campaign, an informative blog post, or a TikTok video, the Awareness stage is all about making a memorable first impression. It's your chance to say, "Hey, we're here, and we've got something you'll love."

INTEREST

Let's Get to Know Each Other

Now that you've made a good first impression, it's time to keep going. The Interest stage is like the flirting phase of a budding romance. You're getting to know your potential customers, and they're getting to know you. You're trying to spark their interest, pique their curiosity, and make them want to learn more about you.

This stage might involve educational content, like eBooks, webinars, or in-depth blog posts that offer valuable insights related to your product or service. Remember, at this stage, it's not about hard selling. It's about providing value and establishing yourself as a trusted, credible source. It's about letting them get to know you and how your product can solve their problem.

DECISION

Will You Buy My Product?

You've made a good impression, piqued their interest, and earned their trust. Now, it's time for the Decision stage – the nerve-wracking moment when you pop the question. Not the marriage proposal kind of question, but the "So, are you ready to buy our product?" question.

At this stage, you want to make your offer irresistible. You could offer special discounts, free shipping, bonus products, return guarantees, or anything else that adds value to the purchase (more in Chapter 6). Just like getting down on one knee and presenting a sparkling engagement ring, you want to create an irresistible proposition that compels your potential customers to say, "Yes, I want this!"

ACTION

Saying "I Do" To Your Offer

There's one more step to make this connection between your business and your customers even stronger. Action. Think of it as the moment you both take a leap of faith and commit to each other.

In the Action stage of the sales funnel, it's time to seal the deal and turn their interest into concrete action. This is where your potential customers make the final move by clicking that "Buy Now" button, filling out a contact form, or scheduling a consultation.

You want to make this transition as smooth and effortless as a well-practiced dance move. Streamline your website's checkout process, eliminate any unnecessary hurdles (more in Chapter 7), and provide clear instructions on what steps your customers need to take.

Remember, it's not enough to have them say "I do" and then you disappear into the sunset. To cultivate a lasting relationship, you need to follow through on your promises. Deliver exceptional customer service, provide timely support, and go the extra mile to exceed their expectations.

By nurturing these post-action interactions, you create a strong foundation for long-term loyalty and repeat business. Show your customers that you value their trust and you are committed to their satisfaction. Treat them like a cherished partner, and they'll become repeat customers and enthusiastic brand advocates.

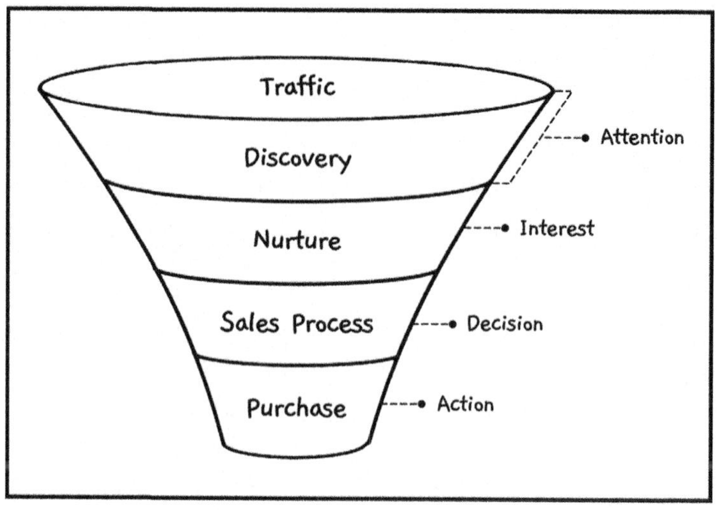

Here's how the sales funnel corresponds to the AIDA model. Note: Loyalty is not included in the AIDA model, but it's a key stage of modern sales funnels.

CHAPTER RESOURCES

Action Items

1. Before jumping into the heart of this book, set at least one specific and measurable goal you want to achieve after finishing it (i.e. increase average order value or customer retention rate by X% etc.).
2. The upcoming chapters lean on ChatGPT and other AI tools to maximize your efforts. If you're not yet familiar with ChatGPT or want to learn more, please skip ahead to Chapter 16 for an overview of ChatGPT and prompt engineering techniques.

Each of the following chapters will provide relevant tools and example ChatGPT prompts under "Chapter Resources" to help you apply the concepts covered in the chapter. The needs and budgets of every business are unique, so each chapter will provide a variety of tools that you can mix and match to fit your specific needs.

2

SADDEST-FRIES AND OAT MILK

Know Your Audience

In 2013, Burger King expanded its menu with a new product called Satisfries.

Satisfries were created as a healthy alternative to traditional french fries, with less fat and fewer calories. When Satisfries were rolled out, Burger King's strategy hinged on a few key assumptions about their customers.

First, they believed customers were seeking healthy alternatives, prompting the creation of a lower-fat, lower-calorie version of their popular french fries. Second, they assumed customers would be willing to pay more for healthier options, evident in the pricing of Satisfries, which were more expensive than regular fries. Burger King also assumed that, if the product tasted good, customers would pick the healthier choice.[3]

Satisfries were a catastrophic failure.

By 2014, just a year after their launch, Satisfries were discontinued and coined "saddest-fries" by disappointed customers. Burger King assumed the US market would prioritize health over factors such as price. However, sales data showed that their customers preferred low prices over healthy alternatives.

The failure boiled down to two mistakes—Burger King's flawed understanding of its target audience and its attempt to cater to every customer's preference. This is one of the most common mistakes among entrepreneurs—trying to be everything to *everyone.*

It's tempting to believe that, by targeting as many people as possible, you'll secure countless customers. Businesses that adopt this approach often water down their marketing efforts, becoming as generic and forgettable as unbuttered toast.

Magical things happen when you put your ideal customers at the center of your business strategy. You're no longer trying to fit a square peg into a round hole; you're offering tailor-made solutions that effortlessly meet your ideal customers' needs and exceed their expectations.

That's why it is critical to develop an ideal customer avatar (ICA)—a fictional persona representing your dream customer—before working on your sales funnel. An ICA helps you understand your customers' preferences and behaviors so you can create a marketing plan that draws them to your brand.

Now, in theory, an ICA is a handy tool. It helps you fine-tune your offerings, polish your copy, and create products your ideal customers actually want. Here's the thing: the industry insists that you have just one ICA to rule them all—the ultimate dreamboat client that becomes your brand's sole obsession. In reality, most brands have several ICAs, including yours.

So, the first, and arguably most important, question you need to ask yourself is: who are my dream customers? They're the ones who not only need what you have to offer but also deeply resonate with your brand and values.

The takeaway here is simple. By trying to reach everyone, *we fail to resonate with anyone.* We fail to make an impact. Let's face it, where do people invest their time and money—on something they like or something they love? As Seth Godin put it, if you want to stand out, be the purple cow.[4]

Humans are wired to spot what's different.

The counter-intuitive desire to be liked by others leads to a lack of clarity and opens the door to a host of problems. Especially in saturated markets, consumers no longer settle for one-size-fits-all solutions. They crave content, products, and services that cater to their unique situations and needs. As humans, we're naturally drawn to brands that speak *directly* to us. Everything else blends into the background.

By embracing your brand's uniqueness, making your purpose crystal clear, and connecting with your audience on a personal level, the competition simply fades away in a sea of the same, same, and…same. Now, you can absolutely give customers that "*Holy shit, this is what I've been looking for!*" moment. So, let's figure out who your ideal customers are.

STEP 1

About Them

Try to answer the following questions to describe 2-3 *distinct* personas, unless your ideal customer avatars are all carbon copies, which would be weird. Feel free to use ChatGPT to help you with this brainstorming process (for more details on ChatGPT and prompt engineering, view Chapter 16). If you answer these questions in a separate document, they can be conveniently referenced later.

Who They Are

1. What are their demographics (age, gender, location, etc.)?
2. What are their hobbies and interests?
3. What motivates and inspires them? This can range from personal growth and making a positive impact to seeking adventure and new experiences.
4. How do they talk? Are they casual and witty, formal and professional, dreamy and aspirational?
5. What are some things they wouldn't like? Are they put off by aggressive sales tactics, excessive use of technology, or lack of authenticity?

Where They Are Located

1. Where do they spend their time online? Are they active on lifestyle blogs, tech forums, or specific social media platforms?
2. What are their preferred communication channels? Do they prefer email, social media, or phone calls to receive updates and stay connected?
3. How do they consume information? Do they enjoy reading blog posts, watching TikTok videos, or listening to podcasts?
4. What influencers do they follow? Who are their role models?
5. What keywords do they search for? What websites do they visit most?

What They Need and Desire

1. What are their pain points and challenges?
2. What are their goals and aspirations? How can my offer help them reach those goals?
3. What things do they value? (i.e. what are they willing to pay a little more for?)
4. How do they make purchasing decisions? Are they influenced by expert recommendations and customer reviews, or do they prefer to research extensively before buying?

Don't worry if you feel stuck or can't answer all the questions perfectly right now. Defining your ICAs is a continuous process of refinement.

Your customers, just like your business, evolve and change over time. So, keep the conversation going and, as you grow, continue to adapt your understanding of your ideal customer avatar.

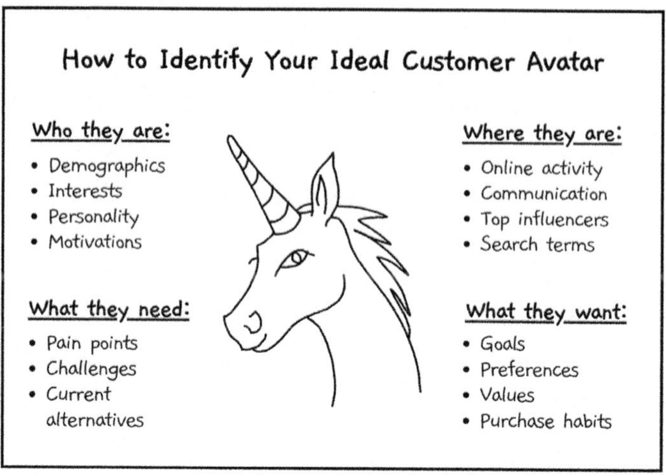

STEP 2

About You

This is the part where most ICA guides drop the ball... they forget to include one vital step. They give you all this info about identifying your ideal customer, but they don't show you how it relates back to your business. Well, that's where the real fireworks happen. When you understand how your ideal customer interacts with your business, you bridge the gap and make meaningful connections.

Now that you have identified your ICAs, take each profile you've created and go back to these questions. Copy and paste them for *each* ICA and give your answers. It's like adding the cherry on top of your ICA sundae.

1. Why would this person be interested in your offers or your brand?
2. What problems are you solving? What benefits are you providing to your ICA?
3. What outcomes do they expect to receive by using your product or service?
4. How does your brand's messaging and tone resonate with your ideal customer's communication style and preferences? Can you make a connection with them on their level?
5. How does your pricing structure align with your ideal customer's perceived value and willingness to invest?
6. What would make this person choose you over a competitor / another similar option?
7. How can you tailor your customer experience to meet the preferences and expectations of your ideal customer?
8. How can you showcase social proof or testimonials from satisfied customers within your ideal customer's specific demographic or industry?

Pro Tip: Feeling unsure about some of the answers to these questions? When in doubt, just ask! Reach out to your past favorite customers (or even someone you'd absolutely love to work with) and tell them you're looking to work with more customers who are just like them. Ask them if they have a few moments to answer a couple of quick questions. Choose a few questions from the list above and jot down their responses in your shiny new ICA document. It's a great way to gather valuable insights straight from the source.

STEP 3

Narrate It

Now, let's combine steps one and two and give your ideal customers some life. In your document, paint a vivid picture of your two to three dream customers by telling a story about each one. Feel free to draw inspiration from real individuals or from your imagination. Let's look at two example avatars for a brand design agency.

ICA #1

Tyler

"Tyler is known for his quick wit, love for stand-up comedy, and impressive collection of quirky shirts. He embraces the world of fantasy novels and can quote his favorite characters easily. Balancing his desire for spontaneity and a longing for a stable routine, he dreams of daring travel adventures while also craving the comforts of a cozy home (the eternal struggle of wanderlust and pajama parties). His personal style is a vibrant mix of modern and eclectic, with a love for unique accessories.

He values authenticity, creativity, and experiences over material possessions — he'd trade a fancy watch for a ticket to an improv show any day. Tyler wants to work with a branding design agency that aligns with his genuine approach and wants guidance in transforming his creative ideas into reality. As we work together,

Tyler would value open and collaborative communication, and he would want the end result to reflect his brand's bold personality."

ICA #2

Aria

"Aria is the queen of multitasking and the master of coffee-fueled creativity. She has a knack for juggling multiple projects and deadlines, all while maintaining a cool and collected demeanor (and a healthy stash of chocolate). When she's not growing her businesses, you can find her singing '80s ballads in her car or binge-watching the latest Netflix series. Her home office is decorated with colorful Post-it notes filled with ideas, reminders, and inspirational quotes.

Aria values collaboration and a sprinkle of quirkiness. She's also looking for a brand design agency that can match her energy and bring fresh perspectives to the table. She'd be thrilled to work with an agency that can capture her playful brand identity."

STEP 4

Detective Work

Once you've finished your ICA profiles, it's time to play detective and uncover the commonalities that bind your dream customers together. This stage is all about identifying the threads that connect them: their passions, preferences, and values. What are their similarities, and how does your offer speak to them?

For example: "Both Tyler and Aria have a strong sense of humor and appreciate the lighter side of life. Tyler's desire for both spontaneity and a stable routine mirrors Aria's ability to juggle multiple projects while maintaining composure. They want guidance to navigate the complexities of their lives and businesses while finding a healthy balance. They also both appreciate unique experiences and value authenticity in their personal and professional lives. Whether it's Tyler's vibrant style or Aria's quirky office, they gravitate towards self-expression and unconventional approaches. As a result, they seek an end result that reflects their individuality and captures the essence of their adventurous spirits. They would be drawn to our brand design agency because they like our genuine approach and ability to capture unique personalities in our work."

Take a moment to visualize a Venn diagram of your dream customers. How much overlap is there? Are there similar key traits or interests that emerge? Paint a clear picture of what draws them to your brand and fuels their enthusiasm.

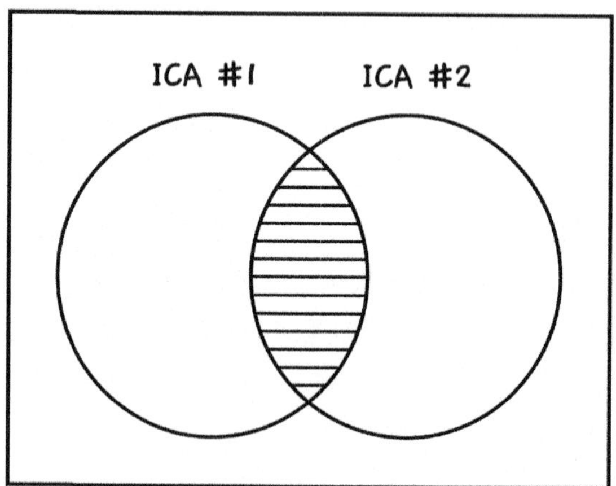

The overlap of your ICAs is like the intersection of a Venn diagram, revealing their shared needs, values, and characteristics.

STEP 5

Circling Back

Now that you have a better idea of who your ICAs are (or might be) and their unique characteristics, it's time to tie them back to the heart of your business. The next time you write a newsletter, update your website, post on social media, create a new offer, design a funnel, or respond to an inquiry, envision yourself speaking directly to these people. Your goal isn't to attract everyone but to captivate *your ideal customer.*

Curious about what this might mean to your business? Let's take a look at some practical ways to put your new ideal customers' avatars into action:

Align Your Offers

- Do your services or offerings truly align with what your ideal customers are looking for?
- Is the new product or service you're considering genuinely in line with your target audience's desires and needs? Have you conducted market research to uncover their wants and needs? (Remember, "If you don't know... ask!" There's nothing more powerful in business than asking people what they want and then delivering exactly that.)
- Which words will resonate with your ideal customers? Do your words clearly communicate that what you offer is designed specifically for people like them?
- How can you customize or further clarify your offerings? (More often than not, people offer too much instead of too little.)

Evaluate Your Content

- What challenges are your ideal customers struggling with, and what topics would they want to learn more about from you? (Creating helpful, relatable, and entertaining content that serves your customers is the ultimate way to build relationships.)
- What type of posts would resonate most with your ideal customers? Jot down 3-4 topics they'd likely enjoy seeing and would incite them to interact. To take it a step further, identify the types of accounts they probably follow on Instagram and observe the content those accounts create.
- Do your social media captions directly speak to your ideal customers? Does your tone of voice align with the type of customer you're hoping to attract? One idea: Imagine you're writing to just one of the customers you've envisioned as a friend. How would you communicate with that person?

Check Your Website

- Does your website have a similar aesthetic to other brands where your ideal customer invests? Is it aligned with where they spend their time or money, online or in-store? (If not, and there's a valid reason, such as your customer valuing functionality over aesthetics, that's fine! Just ensure it's a deliberate choice.)
- Would your ideal customer feel at home on your site? Would the fonts, layout, and styling make them want to spend more time there (and therefore, more time with you)?

- Are your offers, values, and benefits clearly communicated on your website? Is it evident who you're serving and how you can help?

Write Compelling Copy

- Which aspects of your story, expertise, or personality would most appeal to your ideal customer?
- Does any part of your website copy make your ideal customer exclaim, "HOLY CRAP, THIS IS ME"? If not, how can you tailor it to evoke that reaction?
- Are you emphasizing the benefits of working with or purchasing from you that your ideal customer would most appreciate?
- Once again, consider whether your brand's tone of voice would appeal to your ideal customer. Should it be more formal, serious, witty, or aspirational? Establish some guidelines to ensure your brand's voice aligns with your desired audience.

Oatly Spam

Engaging your target audience is both an art and a science as you research your ICAs and use them to create a captivating campaign tailored to them. A memorable example of a company that mastered this fine balance is Oatly (yes, the oatmilk company). In February 2023, Oatly took the internet by storm when they launched their newsletter. While a newsletter launch might seem unremarkable at face value, Oatly turned it into a viral sensation.

First, Oatly decided to name its newsletter "Spam," a bold move that turned many heads. Then, contrary to expectations, they promoted their digital newsletter on countless large billboards and advertisements in public transit spots, which was paradoxical, to say the least. Rather than aiming for direct newsletter sign-ups, Oatly opted to spark conversations and create a buzz around their brand.

The billboard in the subway says, "There are probably better ways to promote a newsletter about an oat drink than 5543 pop-ups. Well, too late."[5]

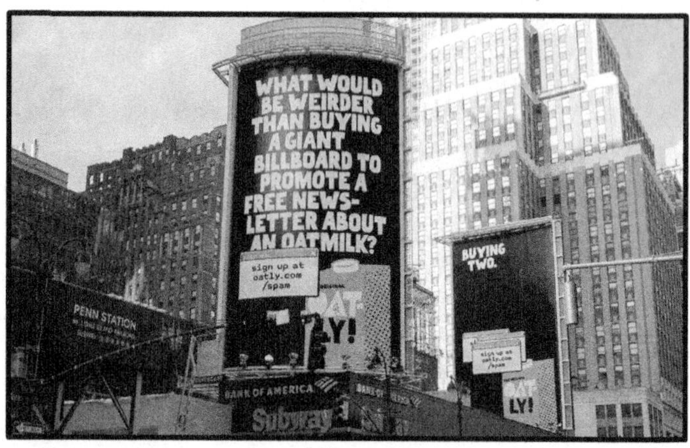

The first billboard says, "What would be weirder than buying a giant billboard to promote a free news-letter about an oatmilk? Sign up at oatly.com/spam," while the second billboard says, "Buying two."[6]

Oatly's unexpected approach sent the internet into a frenzy. Photos of Oatly's billboard campaign flooded Twitter, and marketing professionals sat up and took note. Even negative reactions on Reddit contributed to the wider conversation. So, what valuable lessons can we extract from this?

The first takeaway is to give your "bad" ideas some breathing room. Oatly's Creative Director Kevin Lynch revealed that the Spam newsletter campaign began with one person jokingly saying, "Wouldn't it be funny if..." When you stop worrying about coming up with a perfect plan immediately, and just share your unusual or seemingly ridiculous thoughts, you allow your brain to explore unique ideas. Start talking about designs by saying things like, "This might sound a bit wild, but..." Even thoughts that seem bad at first might turn out to be amazing if you just give them a chance.

The second takeaway is to present your uniqueness unapologetically. While many appreciated Oatly's daring strategy, others criticized it for its unconventional tone. Yet, Lynch held firm in his belief that a brand should act fearlessly. According to him, the real threat to brands isn't criticism; it's being ignored.

This brings us to the heart of Oatly's approach: understanding their audience and *making them care*. They knew launching a newsletter wouldn't be enough to capture attention. They needed to make it interesting and relevant to their audience. By answering the fundamental question: "How can we make our customers *care*?", they successfully turned what would have been an unmemorable launch into a viral sensation.

Brands that fail to define their ICAs and make their audience care about their offerings will struggle to draw leads into their sales funnel. In the Oatly example, they targeted young urbanists who appreciate dry humor and street art, and who are interested in alternative food culture. Most importantly, their ICAs find conventional ads from big brands off-putting and inauthentic. So, by making their quirky newsletter launch conversation-worthy, Oatly ensured that their target audience not only noticed the campaign, but also cared enough to engage with it, discuss it, and share it.

CHAPTER RESOURCES

Action Items

Let's add a few more details to your ICAs, and really get to the heart of your ideal customer. Then, examine your competitors to see how you are different. How does your offer stand apart from the sea of like products? Feel free to use ChatGPT (more in Chapter 16) to help you with any of these steps!

1. Create a detailed list of demographic details, hobbies, motivations, and pain points for each of your 2-3 ICAs. Include specific traits to make these personas vivid and relatable.
2. After outlining your ICAs, identify at least two common desires or needs among them. Clearly explain why YOUR business is uniquely positioned to cater to these shared desires/needs.
3. List all your competitors and detail their strengths and weaknesses. If you have many direct, category-based,

and need-based competitors, start with just direct competitors.

4. Brainstorm concrete ways to: 1) stand out distinctly from your competitors and 2) position your brand as the preferred choice for your ICAs.
5. Based on the common traits of your ICAs and competitor analysis, select the top 3 areas in your business that need improvement (i.e. revamp your brand voice, improve your website etc.). Keep these three areas in mind as you continue reading the book because the following chapters will provide actionable content to address those areas.

RELEVANT TOOLS

The needs and budgets of each business are unique, so here's a wide variety of the top tools to mix and match to fit your specific business. General tools to help you get started:

- **Think With Google** offers marketing research tools like **Google Trends** for insights on product demand, **Google Analytics** for user location and behavior breakdowns, **Market Finder** for market research, and **Rising Retail Categories** to identify retail trends.
- **SEMrush One2Target** is an audience research tool that provides reports on demographics, socioeconomics, behaviors, and audience overlap, helping to identify high-potential audiences and enhance marketing strategies.
- **BrandMentions** tracks social media posts with specific keywords, offering sentiment analysis—perfect for

market, ICA, and competitor research to understand trends.

- **Statista** streamlines industry data from reputable reports into user-friendly charts and insights, making it an essential tool for data-driven market and customer research.
- Tools like **Paperform** and **SurveyMonkey** allow you to create market research surveys to gain deeper insights into your audience.

If you're comfortable with AI, here are some additional AI-powered tools:

- **User Persona Generator by FounderPal** is a free AI tool that generates a detailed customer avatar in 10 seconds. Just describe your business and target audience segment.
- **GapScout's** AI-driven market research tool finds gaps, opportunities, and key themes in the market through custom review analysis and competitor research.
- **VenturusAI** analyzes the viability of your business idea and helps you identify a target audience from demographic data.
- **CrawlQ AI Audience Research** does predictive niche research based on the seed inputs you provide about your target audience.
- **Wayyy** uses AI to create surveys that help you gain deeper customer insights.

ChatGPT EXAMPLE PROMPTS

Example 1

"Review the three narratives I've crafted about my ideal customer avatars below. After reading them, I'd like you to analyze and identify their common elements. Specifically, I want you to outline the recurring themes, desires, pain points, or goals that appear across all three avatars. ICA 1: [Paste] ICA 2: [Paste] ICA 3: [Paste]"

Example Prompt 2

"You are a marketing consultant with over 20 years of experience, but the e-commerce industry is where you shine. Your goal is to help me differentiate my brand. You will ask me 5-10 questions about my company, and I will type the answers. Only ask me one question at a time. Do NOT proceed to the next question without my confirmation. Once I have answered all the questions, you will then provide an in-depth report about: 1) gaps and opportunities in the market and 2) how to differentiate my brand from existing competitors."

Example 3

"Imagine you are a marketing expert specializing in brand positioning. Create a brand positioning statement for a company named "UnityVerse" in the category of "VR social networking." The target audience for this brand is remote workers and digital nomads, who seek virtual spaces to socialize, network, and unwind after work. Use the following structure to craft a detailed response, avoiding jargon:

- How do we describe ourselves?
- How do we describe our audience?
- Why will our audience care?
- Implications for what we do
- Implications for how we feel"

3

THE RISE AND FALL OF RDIO

Traffic is Everything

In August 2010, founders Janus Friis and Niklas Zennström launched Rdio, a pioneer in the modern music streaming industry. Because smartphones were still relatively new, Rdio offered a $5 streaming plan exclusively on the web.

Rdio was created with the goal of making a product that was not only beautiful and easy to use, but also very social. It had interesting features, like letting you see what music your friends were listening to and selecting songs for you based on their playlists.

With these new ways to connect with other people, Rdio felt like a tool from the future. After two years of diligent development, the resulting product was a polished combination of smooth design and a simple grid layout for album artwork, a refreshing alternative to the chaotic spreadsheets of iTunes.

While Rdio had a very promising product, its downfall lay in its nearly absent marketing strategy. The company struggled to keep a dedicated marketing chief, and the fact that it relied on outside agencies made it hard for it to gain traction. As such, despite its excellent product and early debut in the American market, it remained largely unknown.

As it grew painfully slowly, Rdio was quickly overshadowed by Spotify, a bold and well-funded competitor that excelled at generating buzz. By 2015, Spotify had 28 million paying subscribers while Rdio faced bankruptcy.

This may seem like an extreme example, but it shows how excellent products can fail without sufficient marketing to drive awareness. Success doesn't necessarily favor the best or even the first; it often goes to the person who creates the most awareness.

Without awareness and traffic, sales opportunities *simply can't begin to develop and grow*. That's why generating traffic (the number of visitors to your website) is an essential step in any successful sales funnel. In what follows, we'll break down the most effective strategies to generate traffic, including social media advertising, content marketing, search engine optimization, influencer campaigns, and more.

HOT, WARM, AND COLD TRAFFIC

In the world of digital funnels, traffic is the key to success. But not all traffic is created equal. There's a spectrum of engagement levels, ranging from hot to cold traffic. Understanding these distinctions is essential if you want to customize your funnel strategies and deliver personalized experiences to maximize conversions and increase sales.

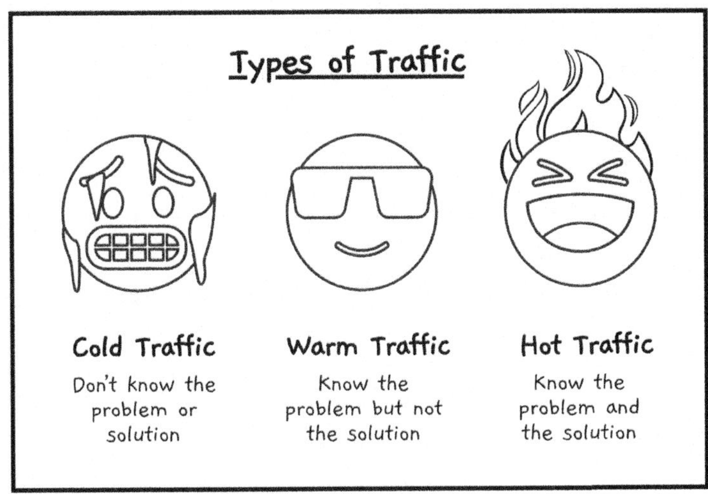
Types of Traffic
Cold Traffic
Don't know the problem or solution
Warm Traffic
Know the problem but not the solution
Hot Traffic
Know the problem and the solution

Cold Traffic

Cold traffic refers to individuals with little to no prior knowledge of your business, products, or services. They may have stumbled upon your website through a Google search or clicked on your social media post because it had an enticing hook. Cold traffic is the most challenging type of audience to convert because they are unfamiliar with your brand and may not even realize they have a problem that your offers can solve.

Warm Traffic

Warm traffic refers to individuals who may not be familiar with your brand or offerings yet but are *aware of potential solutions* to their problems. They may have stumbled upon similar products, services, or information to meet their needs through various channels, such as social media, recommendations from friends, or online research. While they haven't landed on your doorstep just yet, they are open to discovering new possibilities and are actively seeking solutions to help them meet their goals and aspirations.

So, how do you spot warm traffic? Look for signs of engagement. Maybe they joined your email list, subscribed to your blog, followed your social media accounts, or engaged with your content in some way. These interactions indicate that they have taken the first step to connect with your brand and learn more about what you have to offer.

Another helpful way to identify warm traffic is to see which individuals have already formed relationships with influencers, experts, or businesses in your industry. Find those people who are engaging with other brands in the same niche. For example, let's say you are in the fitness industry, and someone is following popular fitness influencers on social media. They have seen workout routines, healthy recipes, and lifestyle tips shared by these influencers. Although they haven't stumbled upon your specific brand yet, they are ready to explore other fitness-related content and offerings because they are interested in the overall niche.

Hot Traffic

Hot traffic is the group of individuals who are well-acquainted with your brand and offerings. They have moved beyond mere awareness and have actively engaged with your content. Maybe they have subscribed to your email list or started following you on social media platforms. They have traveled through the stages of being *unaware, problem-aware, solution-aware, and product-aware.*

When engaging with hot traffic, it's important to focus on deepening the relationship, gaining their trust, and nurturing their loyalty. Provide them with valuable and relevant content that addresses their specific pain points and challenges. Offer exclusive deals, promotions, or bonuses to reward their loyalty and make them feel appreciated.

SOCIAL MEDIA TRAFFIC

Social media has become an exceptionally powerful tool for generating traffic to your funnel and driving potential customers to engage with your brand. With billions of users actively engaging on various social media platforms, you can tap into a vast pool of potential leads.

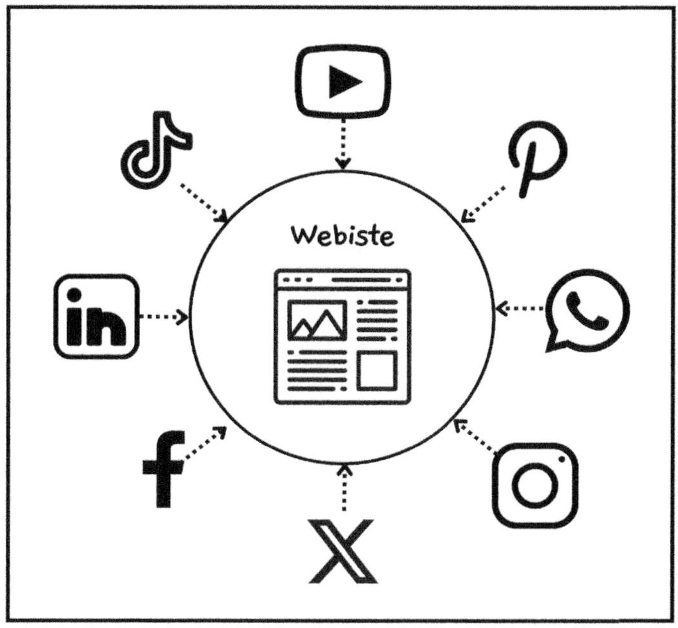

Social media traffic refers to the website visits you receive through social media platforms.

When advertising on social media, it's important to select the right platform(s) to reach your target audience. Each social media platform attracts a unique user base with different demographics, interests, and behaviors.

For example, Pinterest is popular among users seeking inspiration and visual content, making it suitable for businesses in the fashion, home decor, or food industries. TikTok, on the other hand, appeals to a younger audience and is known for its short-form videos, making it ideal for brands targeting Gen Z. YouTube, with its video-focused approach, is excellent for businesses looking to share visual or how-to content with a large pool of viewers. With its professional focus, LinkedIn is a valuable platform for B2B advertising and targeting business professionals.

If you know who your ideal customers are and where they like to hang out on social media, you can spend your advertising money where it will do the most good. Let's look at a step-by-step plan that will help you set up your social media ads so that they get the best results.:

STEP 1

Define Your Objective

Start by clearly defining the objective of your ad campaign. Are you trying to generate leads, drive sales, increase brand awareness, or promote a specific offer? Having a clear goal will help you design a better-performing ad.

STEP 2

Keep your ICA in Mind

Using the information you collected for the ideal customer avatar exercise from Chapter 2, consider how your ad can appeal to their interests, behaviors, and pain points. How will you change your social media ads depending on the ICA you're targeting?

STEP 3

Craft a Compelling Hook

Your hook, or ad headline, should be specific, grab attention, and clearly convey your message. ChatGPT can be especially helpful in this step if you struggle with writing or simply want more ideas (as mentioned, view Chapter 16 for more ChatGPT and AI content).

*__Pro tip:__ *use language that speaks to your ICAs. If you're targeting lawyers, your copy may look more formal and authoritative, but if you're targeting newly-engaged couples, your hook might be more romantic and dreamier.*

Take a look at this ineffective hook: "Take Our Online Course to Learn How to Make Passive Income"

This headline is too general. It lacks specificity and pizazz. While it mentions the goal of making passive income, it doesn't provide any compelling reasons why the audience should choose this particular course over others. It lacks a unique selling point and an emotional plea, making this headline ineffective. It fails to capture attention and doesn't differentiate itself from other similar courses, resulting in lower conversions.

In contrast, a great hook could say: "Escape the 9 to 5 Grind and Build a Life of Freedom with Our Proven Passive Income Course"

This hook is more powerful because it addresses a clear pain point—the desire to break free from the traditional 9 to 5 work routine and achieve a life of freedom. It offers a clear benefit of passive income and positions the course as a solution to help the audience achieve that goal. The use of words like "escape," "build a life of freedom," and "proven" evoke aspirational emotions and create a sense of possibility.

If you're not sure what kind of hook would work best with your ICAs, then experiment with different approaches. Test different headline variations: try using humor, storytelling, or a bold statement to grab attention. Then monitor the performance of your ads and adjust your approach based on the results using A/B testing, which we'll discuss next.

STEP 4

Create Engaging Visuals

Select/design/outsource visually appealing images or videos that relate to your ad's message and speak to your target audience. High quality, and even unexpected, visuals can capture attention and make your ad stand out in a crowded social media environment. AI text-to-art tools like Midjourney are amazing for creating on-brand images or graphics in seconds (for more AI resources, view Chapter 16)

STEP 5

Clear Call-to-Action (CTA)

Your CTA should be clear, compelling, and aligned with your campaign objective. Use action verbs that specify the desired action, such as "Shop Now," "Learn More," "Sign Up," or "Book Here." You can also experiment with less conventional ICAs that may resonate more with your ICAs, like "Find Your Match" or "Get Your Dream [insert solution]".

STEP 6

Test and Iterate

I've mentioned a few times during the previous steps to "experiment" if you're not sure which hooks or CTAs will attract your ideal customer avatars. But what does it mean to experiment? How do you test your ads?

That's where A/B testing comes in. It's essentially a method to compare two versions of a marketing element to determine which performs better. A/B testing can be used with an ad, landing page, or email. Let's take a closer look at the A/B testing process:

First, determine the specific element of your ad that you want to test. It could be the headline, ad copy, images/video, call-to-action, formatting, or even the color scheme. Focus on one variable at a time to measure its impact accurately.

Then, develop two versions of your ad, A and B, with only *one single* element that differs. Keep all other aspects consistent, such as targeting, audience, and placement. This ensures that any differences in performance can be attributed to the tested variable.

Launch both variations of your ad simultaneously and track their performance. In some cases, you can launch several ads at once (A/B/C/D and so on) to find the best combination faster. Monitor metrics such as click-through rates, conversions, engagement, and other relevant Key Performance Indicators (KPI). After you've collected enough data, analyze the performance of each variation. Identify the ad that outperforms the other in terms of your defined objective.

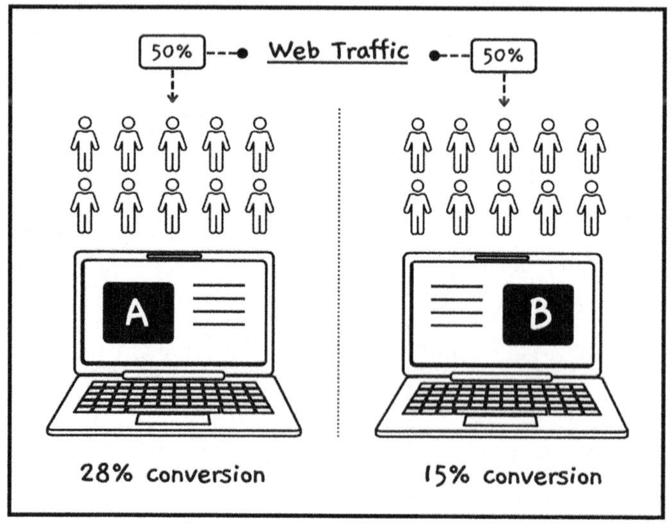

In this example, the web page is being tested on 2 variations, and the A/B test shows that a left-justified image (version A) converts better.

Based on the data, use the winning variation as the primary ad. Use what you learned to optimize your future ad campaigns and apply the successful elements to other marketing materials.

By testing all sorts of variations, you can discover what message, visuals, call-to-action, or headline performs best. This can lead to higher click-through rates, engagement, and ultimately, conversions.

CONTENT MARKETING

Content marketing is like giving away free samples of a cake you've baked. Instead of telling people how great your cake is, you can offer them a taste. That way, they can see for themselves how good it is.

In the same way, generating traffic with content marketing means giving away free information that is useful or interesting. You could offer articles, YouTube videos, podcasts, or social media posts. Again, AI tools are your best friend here (more in Chapter 16). The goal is to show your business's expertise and ability to address customers' needs. By consistently providing free and helpful information, you will create a positive impression on your audience. So, when it's time for them to make a purchase related to what you offer, they will remember the value you provided and choose your business over others.

One company that excels at content marketing is Airbnb. Instead of just showcasing a catalog of rental properties, Airbnb curates a narrative around unique trips by providing articles discussing interesting features about the destination. This approach to content marketing, which emphasizes storytelling and experiences, has played a pivotal role in its success.

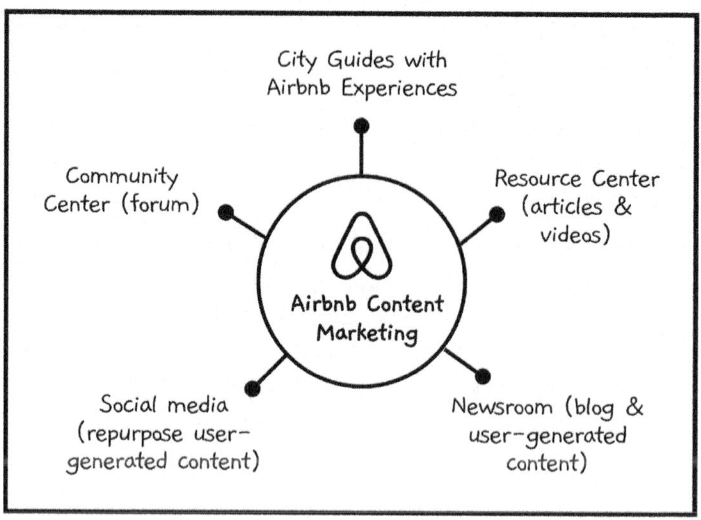

Airbnb's content marketing strategy

Airbnb's brand narrative revolves around the concept of "Belong Anywhere." The platform positions itself as a facilitator of unique experiences. Airbnb invites users to explore the world from a local's perspective, stay in unconventional places, and create memories that are distinct from typical tourist activities or hotels.

Airbnb emphasizes storytelling through its blog posts and city guides. For instance, a user looking to book a trip to Paris will find rental listings on Airbnb, as well as articles about hidden gems in the city, the best local bakeries, or quirky workshops like a baguette-making class. By providing these additional layers of free information, Airbnb is enhancing its service value.

Another cornerstone of Airbnb's content marketing strategy is its focus on user-generated content. Harnessing the power of its large user base, Airbnb encourages its hosts and guests to share their experiences, photos, and stories. They've cleverly turned their customers into brand ambassadors, creating an authentic and diverse stream of content that is highly relatable to their target audience.

The beauty of user-generated content lies in its authenticity. It is *real content* created by *real customers*, which instills a sense of trust and credibility that content created by professionals may lack. Airbnb recognized this early and quickly embraced their community's contributions as a valuable resource.

The key here is that user-generated content doesn't just live on Airbnb's website. They strategically repurpose it to share across various channels, including social media and emails. For instance, beautiful photos shared by Airbnb hosts might be compiled into a blog post showcasing the most unique accommodations or highlighted in a social media post to inspire travel wanderlust. This strategy not only maximizes the reach of their content but also creates a consistent brand experience across multiple touchpoints.

In the end, Airbnb's content marketing approach conveys the message that booking with them is not just about finding a place to sleep, but about *finding experiences that make traveling worthwhile.* Just like Airbnb, remember that content marketing should create value, foster connection, and enhance customer experiences. Here are some questions to consider as you develop your content marketing strategy:

1. What types of content will be most appealing and valuable to my audience? (i.e. blog posts, videos,

podcasts, etc.) Choose one channel to start and expand from there.

2. How can you differentiate your content from competitors? What unique value can you offer?
3. What are your content marketing goals? (i.e. increasing website traffic, growing an email/SMS list, boosting brand awareness, etc.)
4. How will you measure the success of your content marketing strategy? Which metrics will you use?
5. What resources (time, budget, personnel) do you have to create and distribute content, and how can you make the most effective use of these resources?
6. How can you ensure that your content aligns with your brand's voice and identity?
7. How can you incorporate storytelling and user experiences into your content to engage your audience on a deeper level?

SEARCH ENGINE OPTIMIZATION (SEO)

How does SEO work? Generally speaking, SEO is the process of optimizing your website with text, keywords, etc. so that search engines, like Google, understand who you are and how to rank you, making your website more visible to the people who are actually searching for you.

Here's the long answer: The purpose of SEO is to make sure Google knows *exactly* what your site is about. Each page on your website has a specific purpose, and if you want Google to find it, you have to be crystal clear about the purpose of that page. The best way to do that? Use words! When Google scans your website pages using "spiders", it analyzes the text to determine the overall topic and what the page is about. Then, it matches those search terms people type into Google with the words on your page. That is how you get indexed in Google (aka show up on a Google results page). And when your website climbs higher on that search engine result page (SERP), guess what happens? More people are going to pay you a visit and enter your funnel.

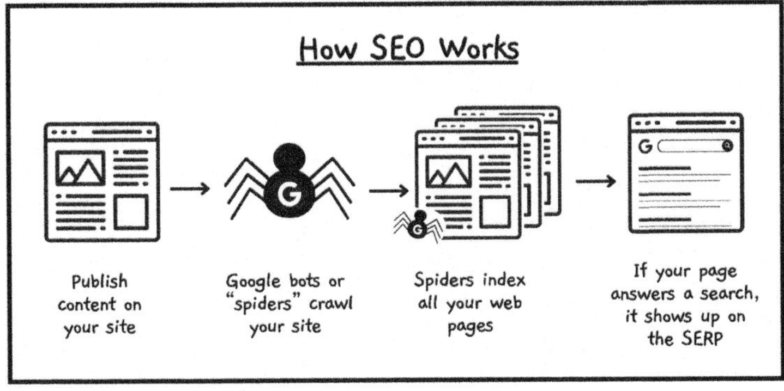
How SEO Works
Publish content on your site
Google bots or "spiders" crawl your site
Spiders index all your web pages
If your page answers a search, it shows up on the SERP

The better your website SEO is, the more your pages will show up on Google's search engine result page (SERP)

Traditionally, writing text for SEO required a LOT of time and effort. But with the rise in AI, tools like ChatGPT can offer real, time-saving opportunities. If you're not using ChatGPT yet, it's completely understandable (for an introduction to ChatGPT, view Chapter 16). It can be intimidating to figure out how to use it to get the best results. And even if you *are* using it, you may not know how useful it can be for SEO—you just need to know the right prompts. Like most things in life, a great recipe goes a long way.

So let's look at how *exactly*, and how *not*, to ask ChatGPT for SEO help that you can modify and use for your own business:

Bad prompt: "Come up with blog post ideas for a food blog."

Good prompt: "Provide me with 3 blog post ideas that a food blogger focusing on healthy recipes and plant-based diets could write for SEO purposes. These post titles should incorporate keywords such as healthy recipes, plant-based meals, vegan cooking, and nutritious eating. Additionally, ensure that the post titles are optimized for SEO, with keyword placement at the beginning and a length between 50 and 160 characters."

Bad prompt: "Write a product description for a laptop bag"

Good prompt: "Craft an engaging product description for a sleek and versatile laptop bag designed for modern professionals. This description should be around 150 words and highlight the bag's key features, such as its padded compartments for secure laptop storage, multiple pockets for organizing accessories, and a durable yet stylish design. Mention the bag's compatibility with various laptop sizes and its adjustable shoulder strap for comfortable carrying. Incorporate relevant SEO keywords like 'laptop bag,' 'professional briefcase,' and 'portable office.' Finish the description by conveying the benefits of using this bag, such as safeguarding valuable electronics and making a fashion statement in business settings."

Bad prompt: "Keywords for a web design agency"

Good prompt: "Help me generate a comprehensive list of mid-tail and long-tail SEO keywords specifically tailored for a web design agency located in San Francisco. These keywords should be optimized to target local search traffic and showcase our expertise in responsive web design, e-commerce solutions, and WordPress development."

SEARCH ENGINE MARKETING (SEM)

In a nutshell, SEM advertising allows you to place ads on various search engines, and you only pay when someone clicks on your ad. It's like having a personal marketing assistant, who ensures that your message reaches the right people at the right time. With SEA, you have the power to choose which specific keywords, locations, and even the time of day your ads will appear. It's a laser-focused approach that maximizes your chances of attracting prospects—people who are on the brink of making a purchase.

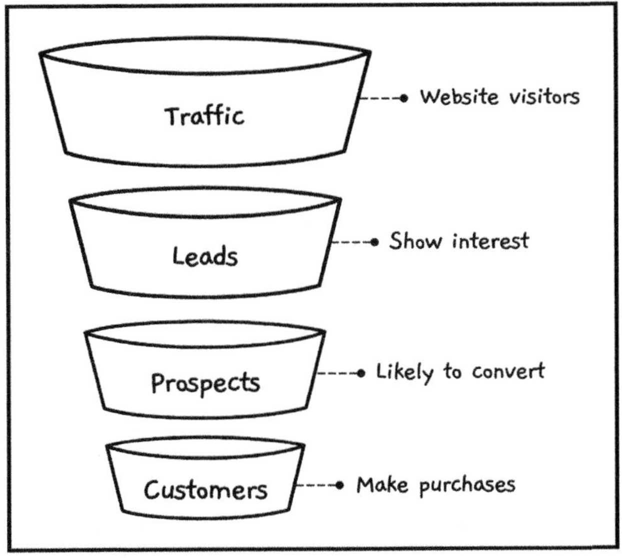

How traffic, leads, prospects, and customers are related

SEM advertising and social media advertising work differently in the way they reach users. With social media advertising, you target users based on their personal details, like their age, interests, and online behavior. But with SEM, your ads show up on search engine result pages when users search for specific keywords that match the words in your ad. These ads usually appear as text-based links, so creating compelling ad copy that grabs attention and encourages users to click is crucial. For example, let's say you want to promote your online course on making passive income.

The title of your SEM ad could say: *"I Make 6-Figure Months Working 15 Hours a Week. And So Can You."*

Under the title, you would have a meta-description that would say: "*Looking to work whenever, wherever? The Passive Income Course is **proven** to teach you everything you need to go from zero to a million. Learn more here.*"

This SEM ad would target your ICAs, (i.e. users who are actively searching for passive income ideas and strategies), so it's important to pick the optimal keywords that relate to the descriptions of your ICAs. For instance, some potential keywords for that specific ad could include: "passive income course" or "online passive income ideas."

Mastering the art of keyword research is an important step in maximizing the effectiveness of your SEM ad campaigns. By knowing which keywords your target audience is using, you can create highly targeted ads that drive quality traffic to your website.

Let's go through a step-by-step guide to successful keyword research, which can help you with both SEM ads and SEO:

Similar to your social media ads, you want to make sure your SEO and SEM ad copy is as compelling as possible to your ICA. Use words, language, and phrases that will resonate with them, so they—spoiler—*CLICK* on the ad.

Begin by brainstorming a list of seed keywords related to your products, services, or industry. These are the broad terms that come to mind when thinking about your business. Don't hold back—jot down as many seed keywords as possible.

Then use keyword research tools to expand your list of potential keywords. Popular options include Google Keyword Planner, SEMrush, Moz Keyword Explorer, and of course ChatGPT (for more SEO/SEM tools, view chapter resources). These tools provide valuable insights into search volumes, competition, and related keywords.

To make the most of these tools, look at the following keyword options while considering potential keywords for your SEM campaign.

ANALYZE KEYWORD RELEVANCE

Review how each keyword relates to your business. Consider the intent behind the keyword to decide whether it aligns with your offerings and the goals of your SEM campaigns. Focus on keywords that reflect the needs and desires of your ICAs.

ASSESS SEARCH VOLUME

Evaluate the search volume of keywords, and how often they are searched, to determine their popularity. High search rate keywords indicate that many people are searching for that particular term, which can help drive traffic to your website. However, it's important to keep in mind that high search volume keywords often have more competition, as many other advertisers are targeting those keywords as well.

Low search volume keywords may have less competition, but they may also indicate limited traffic potential. While targeting low search volume keywords can help you reach a niche audience and potentially reduce competition, limited search volume may not generate enough traffic to meet your campaign objectives.

The key lies in finding a sweet spot—the middle ground between search volume and competition. Aim for keywords with a moderate level of search volume that align with your ICAs' search behavior and have a reasonable level of competition. These keywords can help you attract relevant traffic to your website without facing overly fierce competition.

Consider Long-Tail Keywords

Long-tail keywords are specific, highly targeted keyword phrases that are typically longer and more specific than generic search terms. Long-tail keywords provide a more detailed description of what the searcher is looking for than long-tail keywords, which are broad and generic. They may include additional information such as product features, locations, or specific attributes that help refine the search.

For example, let's say you have an online store selling running shoes. A short-tail keyword might be "running shoes," which is a broad term with high search volume and high competition. However, a long-tail keyword could be "women's trail running shoes with arch support," which is more specific and targeted. This long-tail keyword indicates that the searcher is specifically looking for women's trail running shoes that provide arch support.

Short-tail keywords are often searched more often than long-tail keywords. However, long-tail keywords tend to have higher conversion rates because they attract more qualified and intent-driven traffic. People using long-tail keywords are typically in the later stages of the buying process and have a clear idea of what they want (this is warm traffic!).

ANALYZE KEYWORD COMPETITION

Assess the competitiveness of keywords to understand the level of effort required to rank for them. Some popular tools for keyword research include SEMrush, Ahrefs, Moz Keyword Explorer, Ubersuggest, and more (refer to chapter summary for more details). Look at the competition metrics, such as keyword difficulty scores or paid advertising competition, provided by keyword research tools. Consider targeting a mix of high and low-competition keywords to optimize your strategy.

EXPLORE KEYWORD VARIATIONS

Expand your keyword list by exploring variations, synonyms, and related terms. This helps you capture a wider range of search queries and ensures your ads reach a diverse audience. Most of the previously mentioned keyword research tools provide suggestions for related keywords.

Pro Tip: A/B isn't just limited to ads. It's a great way to accelerate the experimentation process for *any* area of your business, including keyword optimization.

CONSIDER LOCAL KEYWORDS

Use location-specific terms if you have a local business or want to reach people in a certain area. This helps you get relevant traffic from people in your area who are looking for goods or services.

GROUP KEYWORDS INTO THEMES

Organize your keywords into thematic groups or ad groups based on their relevance and intent. This grouping allows you to create targeted ad campaigns and improve the relevance of your ads to the user's search results.

Using the example of a digital marketing agency offering services in search engine optimization (SEO), social media marketing, and content creation, group keywords into themes related to each service. This strategy is more effective than creating one broad ad group for all the services. For example:

SEO AD GROUP

- SEO services
- Keyword research
- On-page optimization

SOCIAL MEDIA MARKETING AD GROUP

- Social media management
- YouTube advertising
- Instagram marketing

CONTENT CREATION AD GROUP

- Blog writing services
- Content strategy
- Content marketing

By organizing keywords into specific ad groups, you can create ad campaigns tailored to each service category. When you understand what the user is searching for, you can create compelling ad copy that directly grabs their attention, increasing the likelihood of attracting them.

INFLUENCER CAMPAIGNS

It's no secret that influencer marketing can do wonders for a brand, but few companies have leveraged this strategy as effectively as Gymshark. A relative newcomer in the fitness apparel market, Gymshark made a tremendous leap from a garage-based startup to a globally recognized online brand, mainly because of its brilliant use of influencer marketing.

Since its launch in 2012, Gymshark has embraced a new marketing tactic: influencers. Early on, it saw that fitness fans with large social media followings could be a good way to sell their products in a real, relatable way. In the beginning, Gymshark didn't have a massive advertising budget to compete with established giants, like Nike or Adidas. Instead, they invested time and effort into building relationships with fitness influencers who shared their brand values. They aimed to develop long-term collaborations with these influencers, building a full marketing strategy.

To achieve this, Gymshark reached out to several fitness influencers, sending them free apparel in exchange for wearing and endorsing the products on their social media platforms.

This strategy proved to be effective. The influencer campaign had an immediate effect on sales. From there, Gymshark decided to sponsor 18 influencers, who had a combined following of over 20 million people. Fast forward to 2016, Gymshark was named the fastest-growing retailer in the UK. Revenues had soared to around $50 million, up from $1.5 million in 2013.[7]

In January 2020, Gymshark took influencer marketing to another level with its "66 Days: Change Your Life" challenge. The campaign featured a range of health and fitness influencers, who challenged followers to create positive habits over 66 days. This campaign was unique because it encouraged active participation, creating a community around the brand.

So, why has Gymshark's influencer marketing strategy been so successful when compared to other gym-wear brands? Gymshark chose influencers who genuinely embodied their brand values. This authenticity resonated with their target audience, millennials and Gen Zs, who value transparency, which cultivated trust. They also focused on building long-term relationships with their influencers, making them part of the 'Gymshark family'. These strong relationships fostered loyalty to the brand and led to influencers becoming genuine brand advocates. Plus, Gymshark consistently engaged with its community, treating customers as friends—an approach that established Gymshark as not only a clothing company, but a *lifestyle choice*.

Gymshark's influencer marketing strategy has undoubtedly been a key factor in its phenomenal growth. Through authentic, long-term partnerships, they've turned loyal customers into influencers and influencers into loyal customers. They have set an example for others to follow in the rapidly evolving digital marketing landscape. Some questions to consider before working with influencers include:

1. Is your target audience active on the platform where the influencer operates?
2. How will you find influencers? Tools like InfluencerMarketing.ai can help.
3. Does the influencer's content, persona, and values align with your brand's image and messaging?
4. What is the engagement rate of the influencer? Do their followers actively engage with their content?
5. Is the influencer's content authentic and genuine? Do they have any past controversies that could negatively impact your brand's reputation?
6. What is the cost of this influencer partnership, can you afford it, and does it make sense with your overall marketing budget?
7. What are the expected deliverables from the influencer and what form will the content take (posts, stories, reviews, etc.)?
8. How will you track the effectiveness of the influencer campaign? (i.e. using trackable links to monitor how much traffic the influencer is directing to your site or landing page)

We've looked at the main ways to generate traffic to your business, but remember *you don't have to implement everything at once*. Being in the early stages of a business means you won't have endless resources or time, so focus on the tactics that make the most sense for targeting your ideal customer.

No matter which method you choose, ensure that you can answer these three key questions for your campaign:

- Where will my ideal customers find me?
- What kind of campaign will they engage with?
- What does conversion look like?

By keeping these questions in mind, you can make sure your strategy is focused and effective, setting you up for success.

COMMON TRAFFIC METRICS

Once you've implemented your traffic initiatives and are ready to measure their effectiveness, several metrics come into play.

- **Views**: The number of times your content or advertisement has been displayed to an audience.
- **Sessions**: A collection of user interactions on your website within a specific time frame. It typically starts when a user arrives on your site and ends when they leave or become inactive.
- **Impressions**: The number of times your ad or content has been shown to users, regardless of whether they interacted with it or not.
- **Visits**: Refers to the number of times users have visited your website within a specific period. A visit is counted each time a user arrives on your site, regardless of the duration or number of pages they view.

- **Users**: The count of unique individuals who have visited your website or interacted with your content within a defined period.
- **Ad click-through rate**: The percentage of users who clicked on your advertisement out of the total number of impressions it received. This metric helps evaluate the effectiveness of your ads in capturing user interest and generating clicks.

To make the most of these metrics, it's important to keep a close eye on them and analyze them alongside other relevant data—look for interesting patterns, trends, and areas for improvement.

Don't be afraid to experiment; try different strategies, like fine-tuning your targeting, tweaking your ad copy, or improving your landing pages with better keywords. By leveraging the insights from these metrics, you can maximize your traffic efforts, increase engagement, and ultimately guide users further down your sales funnel.

CHAPTER RESOURCES

Action Items

1. Identify the top 3 traffic-generation methods that align with your ICA descriptions and your business model.
2. Select one method from the 3 to start using immediately.
3. Within your chosen method, perform A/B testing on specific variations (test variations like headlines, CTA buttons, visuals, formats etc.) to determine your audience's response.

4. Apply the A/B test insights to fine-tune the content. Once it's optimized, you can invest more to promote it, knowing it will deliver the highest impact.
5. After finishing steps 3 and 4, circle back to step 2 and pick the next method to focus on. Repeat this cycle for all 3 strategies to diversify your traffic sources and maximize reach.

RELEVANT TOOLS

As a reminder, the needs and budgets of each business are unique, so this list provides a wide variety of the top tools that you can mix and match to reach your goals.

Tools to get you started:

- **Google Keyword Planner** is a free tool that provides insights into keyword search volume, competition, and cost-per-click data.
- **SEMrush, Moz Keyword Explorer** and **Ahrefs** are comprehensive SEO/SEM tools that help you analyze keyword competition, search volume, keyword difficulty scores, ranking positions, and more.
- **SpyFu** is a competitor analysis tool that uncovers your competitors' top-performing keywords for both organic and paid search.
- **LongTailPro** is a keyword research tool specializing in generating long-tail keywords, helping you identify less competitive and more targeted keyword opportunities.

AI-powered SEO/SEM tools:

- **Surfer SEO** uses AI to streamline your content creation process by taking care of keyword research, writing, and optimization.
- **SEOdity** offers a variety of AI-powered SEO features, like keyword research, competitors ranking analysis, SEO content editor, team collaboration, Google integrations, and more.
- **GrowthBar** helps you and your team plan and write long-form blog content optimized for SEO.
- **Scalenut** offers an AI-powered marketing platform that helps with SEO analysis, content marketing, social media management, and email marketing.
- **Adzooma** optimizes online advertising campaigns with AI insights, suggestions, and performance improvements.

AI-powered social media tools:

- **aiCarousels** simplifies the design and writing process of creating engaging carousel posts.
- **Creasquare**, **Ocaya, Practina** are all-in-one AI platforms for creating, writing, and scheduling social media content.
- **ClipBuddy**, **Pictory** and **Flowjin** automatically create short, shareable clips from long-form videos, so you can repurpose content.
- **InfluencerMarketing.ai** helps you find influencers, manage campaigns, and easily track performance insights.
- AI-Powered Content Marketing Tools (To help with written, visual, and video content. For a more comprehensive list of AI tools, view Chapter 16):

- **Jasper.ai** and **WriteSonic** use AI to help you create on-brand written content, ranging from blog posts to marketing and website copy.
- **Midjourney** is one of the best generative art platforms. Similar to ChatGPT, when you provide detailed prompts, it will design captivating images and graphics. If you need help writing your Midjourney prompts, MJ Prompt Tool is a great resource.
- **DALL-E 2**, similar to Midjourney, uses AI to generate images from text prompts.
- **Steve AI** and **Pictory** help you create videos for your business in seconds. They also have video templates depending on the purpose of the video.
- **VidIQ** helps you optimize video content to increase YouTube views.

ChatGPT EXAMPLE PROMPTS

Example 1

"Imagine you're running an Instagram ad campaign promoting drones to beginner drone pilots, who feel overwhelmed by the options available in the market. Your main selling point is that your drone bundles are curated by professionals, allowing beginners to spend less time figuring out what parts to buy and more time flying. Your goal is to create a list of hooks that will entice these beginner pilots to click on your ad. Each hook should be one sentence and should encourage users to take action. Here's your task: come up with 10 potential hooks that highlight the benefits of your curated FPV drone bundles and address the needs of these beginners. Remember to use copywriting and persuasion best practices to draw in users that are most likely to engage."

Example 2

"Generate 10 creative and engaging short-form video content ideas for TikTok about how to propagate indoor plants. Provide diverse and captivating ideas that resonate with plant lovers. Each idea should describe the shots in the video and include a 15-20 second friendly yet informative script."

Example 3

"Create a fully detailed, long-form, 100% unique, creative, and human-like informational article that is SEO optimized for the keyword "online payment gateways". Make sure to include the keyword 'online payment gateways' in the SEO title, meta description, and headings. The article should have a minimum of 2500 words. Include a table of contents and FAQ section at the end. Use a combination of paragraphs, lists, and tables for readability."

4

THE TRUST HORMONE

Discovery With the Value Pyramid

Trust is the lifeblood of business.

Trust is what makes people feel comfortable buying from a brand. In today's online world, earning trust can be especially challenging. One solution lies deep within our biological makeup, in our natural "trust hormone," called oxytocin. Oxytocin plays a key role in fostering social connection and reciprocal behavior. In short, when someone is kind to us, it makes us want to help them in return.

In a study published in the Public Library of Science, subjects who received free money from a stranger experienced a surge in oxytocin and were likelier to return the kindness.[8]

Similarly, in the book *Go Wild*, Harvard Medical School professor John Ratey, MD, and journalist Richard Manning unpack how this hormone regulates social behavior in the context of business. The idea is simple: increasing oxytocin levels during transactions can lead to reciprocal behavior, fueling a cycle of trust that can boost sales.[9]

So, how can you influence potential customers to release more oxytocin? One technique is to use lead magnets—free offers that attract leads and encourage them to explore the value you offer.

The model referred to as the value pyramid uses free offers that act as stepping stones, guiding customers toward discovering your paid offers.

Think of the value pyramid as a structure with different levels, each representing a certain offer or category in your business. As customers ascend the pyramid, the value of your offerings increases, along with the corresponding price. Customers smoothly transition from accessing free resources to considering your higher-value products/services.

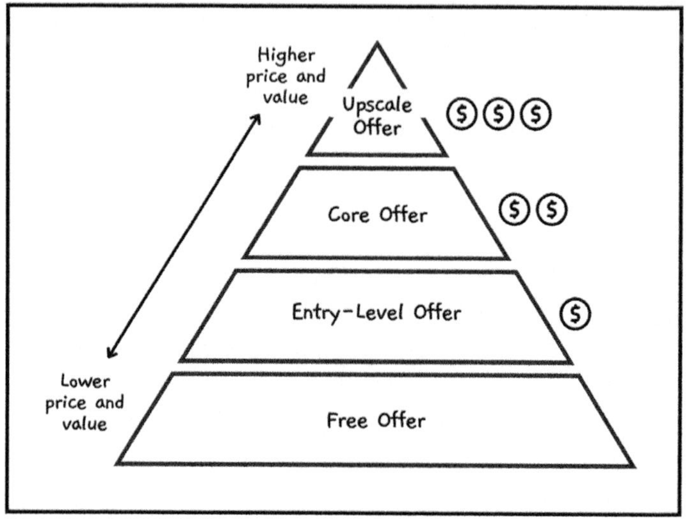

The value pyramid is designed to help customers discover your offers, and the free offer acts as the gateway for upselling.

At the pyramid's base, you offer free, high-quality content or services to trigger a sense of gratitude, creating a subconscious bond between your brand and the lead. The concept is grounded in the principle of reciprocity.

People are naturally inclined to reciprocate when they receive value, particularly when it comes without any strings attached. The principle of reciprocation, paired with the trust-building properties of oxytocin, can encourage consumers to progress up the value pyramid, transforming them from curious observers to engaged customers.

LEVEL 1

Free Offers - Create Irresistible Value

Free offers, called lead magnets, lie at the foundation of the value pyramid. These offers act as enticing bait, capturing the attention of potential customers and converting website traffic into valuable prospects. Lead magnets may be lower in value, but they serve as a powerful entry point to your funnel by establishing the initial point of trust. ChatGPT and AI tools can be valuable resources as you brainstorm and design your lead magnet (for relevant tools and example ChatGPT prompts, view chapter resources). Let's take a look at a step-by-step approach for creating free offers that captivate your audience and lead to sales:

Solve a Problem

Identify a common pain point or challenge your target audience faces and create a valuable solution. Whether it's an e-book, a video tutorial, or a downloadable guide, make sure your free offer provides actionable insights and tangible benefits directly targeted to your ICA.

Showcase Expertise

Position yourself as an authority in your industry by offering free resources that demonstrate your knowledge and expertise. Share valuable tips, industry secrets, or case studies that highlight your ability to solve problems and deliver results.

Leave Them Wanting More

While your free offer should provide value, it's essential to leave your audience *craving additional guidance.* Tease them with a glimpse of what's to come in your higher-tier offers, sparking curiosity and motivating them to ascend the pyramid.

Don't forget that your lead magnets need to be interesting and fun for your audience. Use compelling visuals, storytelling techniques, or interactive elements to make your content more enjoyable and memorable.

For instance, let's say you're in the food industry. You could design a lead magnet titled "5 Healthy, Mouth-Watering Recipes That Take 15 Minutes". Include high-quality food photography, engaging anecdotes about each recipe's origin, or a quiz to help your audience discover their ideal cooking style.

Regardless of the format (template, webinar, cheat sheet, etc.), it's important that your lead magnet is professionally designed and well-crafted. Use clear language, error-free copy, and attractive visuals to enhance the overall value of the offering. There are many you can use to create your lead magnet, like Canva, Beacon, and Attract (more details in chapter resources).

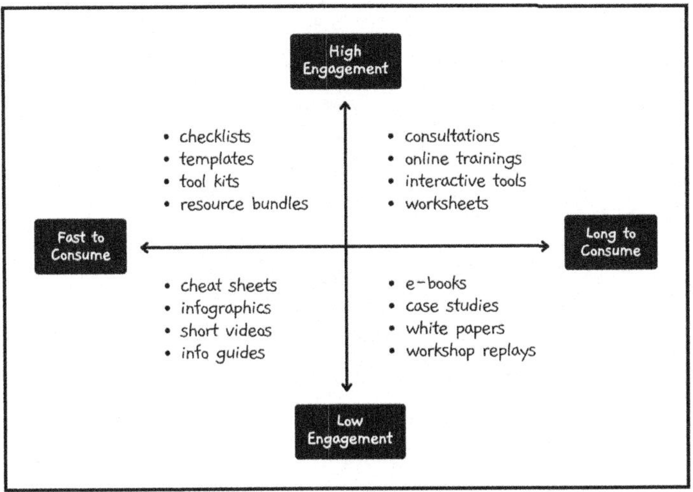

Lead Magnet Matrix

Avoid the Trust Deficit

While lead magnets can be powerful, pay attention to a few things.

1. The quality of your free offer is critical. This offer is meant to demonstrate the value of your brand and set the stage for future interactions. If your lead magnet is low quality, it may deter potential customers from exploring further paid offerings.
2. The transition to paid offerings should be seamless and logical. Each stage of the value pyramid should naturally lead to the next, demonstrating an increasing degree of value at each level. This approach can guide consumers to discover offers higher up the value pyramid without making them feel overwhelmed or manipulated.

3. Focus on authenticity and transparency. In an era where consumers are savvy and discerning, integrity is essential. Make sure your free offer is genuinely useful, not just a thinly veiled sales pitch.

LEVEL 2

Entry-Level Offers - Initiating The Transaction

As we ascend the pyramid, we reach the front-end offers, which is the first point of purchase your customers will encounter. These offers should provide a lot of value while remaining affordable. Your customers should experience enough value to develop trust in your brand. Here's how you can optimize this stage:

Offer an Irresistible Entry Product

Create an attractive, entry-level product that offers a clear benefit to your customers. This could be a mini-course, a digital product, or a low-cost subscription. Ensure the price matches the perceived value, making it an irresistible offer to jumpstart the customer journey.

Upsell and Cross-Sell

Once customers make a purchase, seize the opportunity to upsell or cross-sell complementary products or services. Offer relevant add-ons, upgrades, or bundles that improve the initial purchase and provide additional value. This strategy not only increases the customer's overall satisfaction but also boosts the average value of each sale (more on this in Chapter 7).

Provide Exceptional Customer Experience

Focus on delivering exceptional customer service at this stage. Respond promptly to inquiries, offer personalized support, and go above and beyond to exceed customers' expectations. A positive experience will increase customer loyalty and set the stage for their ascent up the value ladder, resulting increased and repeat sales.

Some examples of entry-level offerings include:

1. STARTER KITS OR BUNDLES

Create a curated package of products or services that offers a comprehensive solution to a specific problem or addresses a particular need. For example, suppose you have an e-commerce beauty brand. You can offer a skincare starter kit with a cleanser, toner, and moisturizer, providing customers with everything they need to kickstart their skincare routine. If you are not sure how to structure your kits or bundles, provide data to ChatGPT about your products, and it can help you brainstorm ideas.

2. ENTRY-LEVEL COURSES OR WORKSHOPS

Develop a short introductory course or workshop that gives useful information or teaches a specific skill. This can be delivered through video lessons, downloadable resources, or live webinars. For instance, if you run a digital marketing agency, you can offer a beginner's guide to social media marketing, covering the basics of creating effective campaigns. Tools like Teachable, Steppit or GoToWebinar can be helpful.

3. DOWNSCALED SERVICES

Offer a scaled-down version of your premium services or a one-time consultation at a lower price point. For instance, if you're a business coach, you can provide a one-hour strategy session at a reduced rate to help clients understand your coaching approach. This allows customers to experience your expertise and the quality of your services, creating interest and trust to encourage future purchases.

4. INTERACTIVE TOOLS OR ASSESSMENTS

Develop interactive tools or assessments that help customers gain insights or solve specific problems. This can be through quizzes, calculators, or self-assessment tools. For example, a financial planning company can offer an interactive retirement savings calculator to help individuals assess their financial readiness for retirement.

Remember, the key to optimizing your Entry-Level Offers is to balance value and affordability while creating a positive first impression of your brand.

LEVEL 3

Core Offers - Enhancing Value And Commitment

As customers progress in their journey, you are preparing them for the core offer. These offers cater to customers who are ready to invest more in their desired outcome and are willing to pay a higher price for the enhanced value and benefits you provide. Your core offer should deepen the customer relationship, solidifying their trust and commitment. Here's how to approach this stage:

Identify Targeted Segments

Categorize your customers into groups based on their needs, preferences, or purchasing behavior. For example, if you sell treadmill desks, your groups might include remote workers who want to upgrade their home office, fitness enthusiasts who want an active lifestyle, or busy parents who have minimal time to exercise.

Personalize the Offering

Customize your core offers to cater to these different groups. Offer consultations, programs, or exclusive access to specialized content based on group-specific characteristics. By providing more personalized offers, you demonstrate your commitment to their success and improve the customer experience.

Emphasize the ROI

Clearly communicate the return on investment (ROI) that customers can expect from your core offers. Showcase testimonials, success stories, or quantifiable results to illustrate the value they will receive. This builds trust and confidence in your offering, making the price a justifiable investment for the customer. The following are a few examples of core offers:

1. COMPREHENSIVE COURSES OR TRAINING PROGRAMS

Develop comprehensive online courses or training programs that offer in-depth knowledge and practical skills in a specific area. These programs can be delivered through a combination of video lessons, written materials, interactive exercises, and assessments. For example, if you're in the health and fitness industry, you can create a 12-week transformation program that includes workout routines, nutrition guides, and personalized coaching.

2. CONSULTING OR COACHING PACKAGES

Offer personalized consulting or coaching services that provide one-on-one guidance and support to your customers. These packages can include regular coaching sessions, personalized action plans, and ongoing email or messaging support. For example, if you're a business consultant, you can offer a core package that includes monthly strategy sessions, performance analysis, and implementation guidance.

3. ONLINE WORKSHOPS OR MASTERCLASSES

Conduct online workshops or masterclasses on specific topics or skills. These sessions can be delivered live or pre-recorded and provide interactive learning experiences, practical exercises, and expert insights. For instance, if you're a graphic designer, you can offer a core masterclass on advanced logo design techniques, where participants can learn and practice under your guidance.

4. HIGH-VALUE DIGITAL PRODUCTS

Create high-value digital products, such as e-books, templates, toolkits, or software that provide specialized knowledge, resources, or time-saving solutions. These products can offer advanced strategies, insider tips, or industry-specific templates. For example, if you're a financial consultant, you can offer a higher-end financial planning toolkit that includes comprehensive budgeting templates, investment calculators, and retirement planning guides.

LEVEL 4

Upscale Offers - The Ultimate Experience

At the top of the value pyramid are the upscale offers. These are your highest-priced offerings, providing the most comprehensive value and delivering exceptional results. At this stage, you're taking care of your ICAs, those who recognize and appreciate the value you bring and are eager to get the highest level of service from your business. Here's how to make the most of this stage:

Exclusivity and Uniqueness

Create upscale offers that are exclusive and unique to your most loyal customers. These offerings should provide exceptional value, such as VIP access, advanced training, or personalized coaching. By offering something they can’t get anywhere else, you solidify your relationship with your true fans.

Continuity and Membership Programs

Develop continuity programs or membership sites that provide value and benefits over time. Offer exclusive content, resources, and community access to create a sense of belonging and foster long-term engagement. Continuity programs ensure ongoing revenue while offering continuous value to your most dedicated customers.

Cultivate Advocacy

By giving your high-end customers a great experience, you encourage them to become brand supporters. Delight them with surprise bonuses, rewards, or special events. Their positive word-of-mouth and testimonials will attract new customers to your funnel and reinforce your brand's credibility and desirability. Some examples of upscale offers include:

1. MEMBERSHIP SITES WITH PREMIUM CONTENT

Create a membership site or a subscription-based platform where customers can get access to premium content, exclusive resources, and ongoing support. This can include in-depth tutorials, advanced training materials, live Q&A sessions, and a community forum. For instance, if you run a photography business, you can offer a membership site that provides information about advanced photography techniques, editing tutorials, and a community of fellow photographers. While there are many tools for creating membership-based services, Patreon is a popular platform that lets you create tiered membership access (more in chapter resources).

2. EXCLUSIVE PRODUCT BUNDLES OR PACKAGES

Combine your best-selling or premium products/services to create exclusive product bundles or packages. These bundles can provide added value, savings, or exclusive bonuses for customers willing to invest at a higher price point. For instance, if you're an e-commerce business selling high-tech home gadgets, you can create a core bundle that includes a smart home hub, smart lights, and a home security camera system.

3. PREMIUM ACCESS OR EARLY-BIRD OFFERS

Provide exclusive access or early-bird offers to new products, services, or updates. This gives your upscale customers a sense of exclusivity and makes them feel appreciated for their commitment. For instance, if you're a software company, you can offer upscale customers early access to new features and updates before they are released to the general public.

4. DONE-FOR-YOU SERVICES OR CUSTOM SOLUTIONS

Provide premium services or customized solutions tailored to your customer's specific needs. This can include personalized branding and design services, custom website development, or tailored marketing campaigns. For example, if you're a social media agency, you can offer an upscale-level package that includes a customized social media strategy, content creation, and campaign management.

Now, let's bring this concept to life with FitLife Academy, an online fitness and wellness business that implemented the value pyramid.

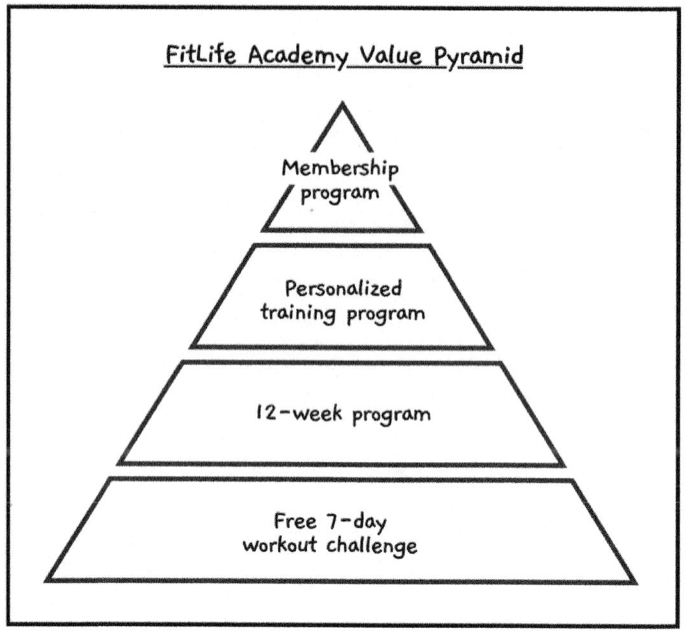

At the base of the pyramid, FitLife Academy offers a free 7-day workout challenge. This serves as an irresistible entry point, attracting fitness enthusiasts, who want to kick-start their journey to a healthier lifestyle. Customers discover FitLife Academy's offers, establishing trust and demonstrating its expertise through this free challenge.

Moving up the pyramid, FitLife Academy presents a front-end offer: a comprehensive 12-week fitness program. Reasonably priced, this program includes a structured workout plan, nutrition guidance, and ongoing support. Customers who complete the free challenge are now motivated to take the next step and invest in their fitness goals with this comprehensive program.

As customers progress in their fitness journey, they're primed to discover the core offer. FitLife Academy introduces a personalized training program, where customers receive one-on-one guidance, tailored workout plans, and nutritional counseling. This upgraded service is more expensive, but customers receive the individual attention and support they need to reach their fitness milestones.

Finally, at the top of the pyramid, FitLife Academy unveils its elite membership program. This exclusive offer provides VIP access to advanced training techniques, specialized workshops, and personalized coaching from industry experts. It's the ultimate package for those committed to achieving exceptional results and willing to invest in their health and well-being.

FitLife Academy strategically guides customers through the value pyramid to discover various offers tailored to different levels of commitment and deals that fit their budget. It all begins with the free 7-day challenge, which attracts a broad audience while encouraging those who are truly interested in fitness goals. As customers progress up the pyramid, FitLife Academy provides increasingly valuable offerings, fostering a strong connection and trust that ultimately leads to long-term customer loyalty.

As a side note, I want to emphasize that, as you begin to create your value pyramid, you don't have to create all levels of your offers at once. The value pyramid serves as a framework that can guide your approach to designing offers in the long term. Ultimately, by *vertically extending your offers*, you can serve customers at different stages of your funnel, offering them the precise level of value they desire. This approach not only generates revenue but also helps identify your ICAs, who can afford and appreciate your highest-level offer.

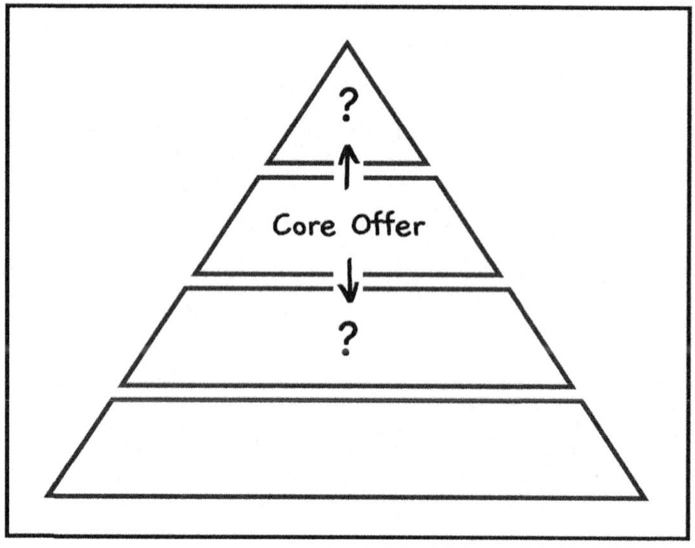

If you feel stuck while creating your value pyramid, try vertically extending your core offer: 1) create the upscale offer by adding additional features/ bonuses to your core offer 2) create the entry-level offer by stripping down or condensing your core offer.

As your sales funnel deepens and your value offerings expand, each customer progressing up the pyramid becomes more valuable to your business. The more value they receive, the more they are willing to invest in their desired outcomes. It's a win-win scenario, where your customers achieve their goals while fueling the growth and success of your business.

CHAPTER RESOURCES

Action Items

1. Sketch a value pyramid and begin by identifying your core offer.
2. If you already have entry-level and upscale offers, add them to the sketch. Otherwise, use the vertical extension approach.
3. Now that you've clarified your entry level and core offers, define the purpose of your lead magnet (i.e. will it provide a glimpse of your product/service, offer educational content, drive specific actions, or a combination?)
4. Brainstorm five distinct lead magnet types/formats that fit your criteria from step 3. You can use ChatGPT to help you in this process.
5. Pick the most promising lead magnet concept. As your business evolves, consider crafting lead magnets for different segments to categorize your leads easily.

RELEVANT TOOLS

General tools to get you started:

- **Optinmonster** is a powerful lead generation tool that helps you capture leads with features like targeted pop-ups, floating cards, slide-ins, and much more.
- **Beacon** and **Attract** are budget-friendly and intuitive tools that let you easily create lead magnets, like guides, checklists, worksheets, e-books, and more.

- **Interact** generates leads through interactive quizzes, helping grow your email list, segment leads and recommend products to boost sales. (More on quizzes in Chapter 10)
- **Convertflow** and **Upflowy** help turn website visitors into leads through interactive flows and website widgets (i.e. forms, quizzes, pop-ups, referrals etc.)
- **Canva** is a free drag-and-drop design tool that simplifies any design process—it can help with designing your lead magnet, creating ads, designing social media posts etc.
- **CapCut** and **Veed** are simple video editing tools that can help with any area of your business, from promotional videos to self-paced workshops.
- **Teachable** is an intuitive and affordable way to create paid online courses.
- **GoToWebinar** is a platform for hosting and attending online webinars and virtual events.
- **Patreon** is an ideal platform for creating membership programs with different paid tiers.
- Additional AI-powered tools:
- **MarbleFlows** is a no-code funnel builder that includes AI-generated forms to capture leads for your free or paid offers.
- **Steppit** is a free tool that uses AI to help you plan, build, and sell unlimited courses.
- **Beautiful.ai** and **Gamma** use AI to design eye-catching and engaging slide decks. They provide content, design, and speech suggestions so you can deliver memorable presentations/workshops/webinars.

- **Steve AI and Pictory** are AI-powered video editing tools that support you from creating videos from blog posts to auto-generating captions.
- Although Canva was already mentioned, if you want to take it a step further, consider using **Magic Design by Canva**. It's a free AI design tool that's like an on-brand creative assistant.

ChatGPT EXAMPLE PROMPTS

Example 1

"Generate at least 20 lead magnet ideas for people with small apartments that are both typical and out of the box. The lead magnets should be specifically designed for an online business that designs and sells furniture for small spaces, maximizing functionality without sacrificing style. Organize your ideas into a table format that includes the following columns:

- Lead Magnet Idea
- Type (e-book, workshop, checklist, free course, DIY guide and more)
- Target Audience
- Unique Selling Proposition (USP)
- What Problems It Solves

Provide a brief explanation of each lead magnet idea, as well as its type, target audience, and unique selling proposition. The USP should highlight what makes each lead magnet unique and compelling for your target audience."

Example 2

"Provide five customer groups for a coffee and tea tasting subscription box brand that delivers a variety of gourmet coffees or teas, along with tasting notes, brewing tips, and unique accessories. Each group should be defined by a deep underlying category-related need. Assign an emoji and a title to each group. Write a 50-word-minimum paragraph describing the category-related needs for each group. Then below the paragraph, include bullet points suggesting creative initiatives or product recommendations to best meet the needs of each group."

Example 3

"You are a Content and Digital Marketing Strategist. Your role is to brainstorm ideas for a social media management business, whose core offer is to provide comprehensive services for various platforms, like Instagram, Pinterest, and TikTok. Brainstorm 5 ideas for downscaling the offer to provide budget-friendly options and 5 ideas for upscaling the offer for premium services. Provide unique and creative approaches for each one. Consider factors like platform-specific packages, content creation, engagement strategies, analytics, and emerging trends. Prioritize ideas that are novel and aligned with branding principles."

5

A HUMAN TOUCH

The Key to Nurturing Prospects

Brands are more than products or services; they have distinct personalities. They tell stories, evoke emotions, and build relationships, just like humans do. This phenomenon, known as "brand humanization", is a psychological process where consumers perceive brands as possessing human traits. There are three main ways to look at brand humanization—the human-focused, self-focused, and relationship-focused perspective.[10]

From the human-focused perspective, consumers associate brands with emotions and personalities. For instance, consumers may see a brand as "friendly," "creative," or "reliable," which helps consumers build a stronger relationship with the brand.

From the self-focused perspective, consumers see a brand as an extension of themselves. The more a brand aligns with their personal beliefs, values, or image, the stronger the connection. The brand essentially becomes a part of the consumer's self-identity.

The relationship-focused perspective is when consumers relate to brands the way they would relate to people. Depending on how the brand's personality and values resonate with the consumer, this relationship can be anything from a casual acquaintance to a close partnership.

So, how does understanding consumer psychology and the broader concept of brand humanization relate to your funnel strategy? The answer is simple: humanizing your brand creates stronger customer relationships, which translates to more funnel conversions. Relational dynamics ultimately impact a consumer's level of attachment, loyalty, and commitment toward a brand.

SCENARIO 1

Identify Buyers

While the main focus of this chapter is on nurturing prospects using consumer psychology and brand humanization, there's one crucial step to take before diving into that process.

As soon as you've qualified your leads, you should identify the actual buyers in the crowd. Once someone provides their name and email address and hits your lead magnet's "submit" button, redirect them to a sales page featuring your entry-level offer. Here's the catch—this offer should be incredibly affordable. Why? So you can immediately identify the real buyers in the crowd. Regardless of how inexpensive the offer is, you want to understand who is ready to take out their credit card for something you're selling.

The idea is that, if someone is *willing to buy* (regardless of the price), it indicates their receptiveness to your offers and their potential for repeat purchases. So if you know who is willing to make that initial purchase, you can invest more into marketing to them.

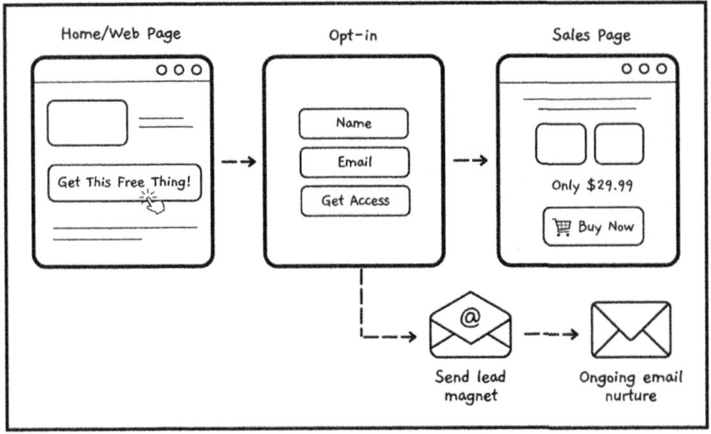

Keep in mind, you need consent to add someone to your newsletter. You can add a simple checkbox on the lead

If a lead doesn't make an immediate purchase after being redirected to your sales page, there's a second scenario to consider. In this case, you'll need to nurture the lead through targeted communication methods including email, text, and social media.

SCENARIO 2

Nurture Prospects

One way to add that human touch to your brand is to personalize it. More than 70% of consumers consider personalization a basic expectation.[11] In fact, in digital marketing, personalization is transitioning from being a bonus to a prerequisite.

The era of generic email blasts is coming to an end. We live in a disruptive, post-advertising era where people actively seek connections with brands, and then willingly engage and support them. Nurturing those connections isn't about pitching or selling. It's about serving. Next, we'll look at several customer-centric tactics that create value, nurturing prospects to continue down your sales funnel.

DYNAMIC CUSTOMIZATION

Modern email marketing has strong tools like dynamic content and real-time customization to help you create personalized, interesting emails. With dynamic content, email elements like text, images, and calls-to-action change based on the person's data. This makes sure that each prospect receives an email tailored to their specific interests, preferences, and behavior. By drawing on data from their browsing history, location, and other relevant information, you can deliver content that increases engagement levels. Tools like Mailchimp, Campaign Monitor, GetResponse, Klaviyo, and more (for details, view chapter summary) can help you create interactive email content based on the information of your ICA.

For example, Brooklinen, the bedding brand, uses dynamic content to give personalized recommendations based on how people browse its website. Notice how their email copy cleverly makes you feel like the products were chosen *just for you.*

We've Got Something We Know You'll Like

We noticed that you've been eyeing our products. Now that we know each other better, we put together some picks just for you.

Super-plush robe
Shop Now

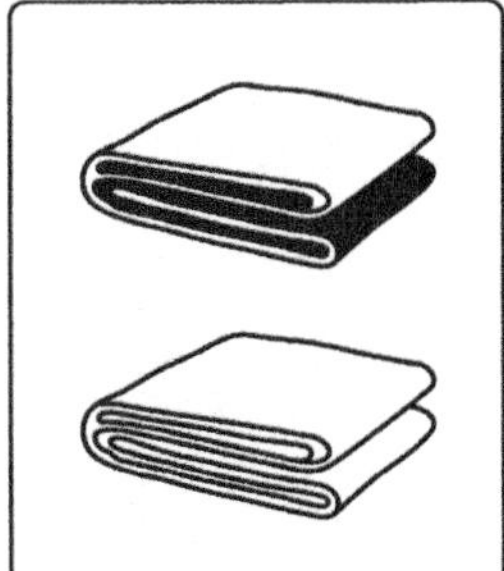

Down-comforters
Shop Now

Brooklinen's Dynamic Content Email

PREDICTIVE SEND TIME OPTIMIZATION

Predictive send-time optimization is another powerful feature in email marketing that uses AI to determine the best time to send emails to prospects. Brands used to send emails based on predetermined schedules or general best practices, such as sending emails during business hours on weekdays, but emails often got lost in crowded inboxes or were overlooked with this approach because they weren't relevant to the recipient's personal preferences.

With predictive send-time optimization, AI algorithms find patterns and trends in user behavior, including the times when recipients are most active and likely to open emails. By sending emails using these insights, you can significantly increase the chances of customers noticing and engaging with your emails. Some AI-driven tools that have predictive send-time optimization features include Brevo, OptimalSend by Mailchimp, GetResponse, and more (for more details, view chapter summary).

INTERACTIVE MEDIA

Adding interactivity and rich media to your email nurturing campaigns can be a game-changer. Carousels, image rollovers, and polls allow recipients to interact with your content directly within their inboxes. This hands-on approach can create a stronger bond with your audience as they actively participate in the email experience.

Examples of interactive email media

Another strategy is to incorporate video content or other multimedia elements, such as GIFs and animations, in your email and texts. Visuals are a powerful way to captivate your audience, especially for product-centric brands, because you can show the item from different angles, demonstrate how to use it, create "before/after" animations and much more. Videos, in particular, are highly effective in showing information quickly and intuitively.

Integrating gamification elements can also take your email nurturing to new heights. Quizzes, contests, or interactive puzzles create a fun, interactive experience for prospects, encouraging them to engage with your content on a deeper level.

Regardless of which interactive mediums you choose, personalization is key in this era of nurturing. Using interactivity and rich media allows you to give each person an experience that is just right for them.

MOBILE-FIRST APPROACH

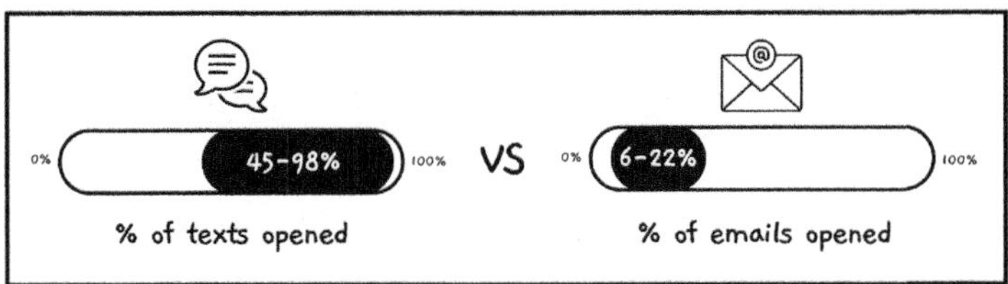

Almost everyone has their smartphone within arm's reach at any moment. It's our go-to device for browsing, scrolling, and keeping in touch with friends and family. Wouldn't it be great if your business could connect with prospects where they hang out most of the time?

By meeting people where they are—on their smartphones—you can tap into a powerful and cost-effective channel. That's where text marketing comes in. It's a low-friction and engaging way to build relationships with prospective and current customers.

We all prefer convenient, instant communication at our fingertips. That's why texting is the perfect channel. Not only is texting fast and intuitive, but messages are short and easy to read. Most importantly, the open rate of texts hovers between 45% and 98%, while for emails it's only between 6% and 22%.[12]

So, by combining email marketing and text messaging (i.e. iMessage, WhatsApp, Instagram DM and Messenger from Meta) in your mobile nurture strategy, you increase the chances of converting your audience. When including text as one of your communication channels, consider using a text marketing tool like ManyChat, SendPulse, Twilio, Brevo, SimpleTexting and more (for more details, view chapter summary).

TEXT BOTS

Most traditional marketing channels, like TV, direct mail, email, print, and radio, are one-way communication. Companies talk to you. On the other hand, text bots (similar to chatbots but for messaging apps), change this dynamic by communicating *with* you.

Prospects receive messages that can be easily customized based on their interactions, creating a two-way communication experience—which is how it should be. The best part is that automating text bot responses makes it incredibly scalable.

Before we look at how to create workflows for your text bot, let's discuss how they work. In general, text bots automatically send content to prospects/customers based on their actions. The two most common types of actions include clicking call-to-action buttons or typing specific keywords. Some text bot tools that offer those capabilities include ManyChat, Chatfuel, Botsify, Landbot, Customers.ai, and more (for more details, view chapter summary).

Unlike email autoresponders, text bots offer logic branching and greater personalization. Like a conversation, the text bot delivers different outputs depending on the person's answers to prompts and questions. Instead of sending the same message to everyone, text bots provide menu options that increase engagement and create personalized interactions. For example:

When a text bot provides a menu of choices, like in this travel assistant example, people can pick the information they are *actually interested in receiving*. Giving people this type of control is another reason text marketing has such high engagement rates.

Now that we've covered what text bots are and what they can do, let's take a step further and see how they're automated. With text bot tools, you can automate messages with workflows based on what the prospect chose. For example, ManyChat is a text bot workflow with three types of steps: Content, Action, and Go-To.

- **Content** steps allow you to send different types of messages, like text, videos, and galleries.
- **Actions** let you trigger specific actions, like tagging users, subscribing them to a specific sequence, notifying an admin, or starting a conversation.
- **Go-To** steps let you send your subscribers to a particular workflow from your bot content with just one click.

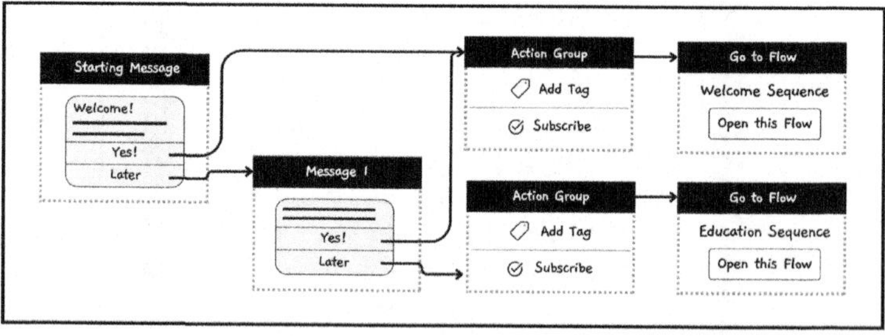

Here is an example of a ManyChat text bot workflow. The sequence of the steps is represented by lines that connect Content (messages), Action and Go-To steps.

This is just one example. Most text bots (and chat bots) operate on a similar logic structure using workflows to automate answers.

TEXT MARKETING/BOT BEST PRACTICES

When it comes to text marketing and text bots, it's easy to get carried away. Before creating your text nurture campaign, let's go over some best practices.

1. Keep it short and sweet

Once people give you permission to text them, don't abuse their trust. Be concise and engaging. Offer attractive deals or useful information to provide value. Receiving low-quality texts might make future customers unsubscribe, and you'll lose contacts.

2. Add multimedia

Although you're keeping messages short, they don't have to be boring. Earlier in the chapter, we looked at different ways to add multimedia to your communication, including your texts. Use pictures, videos, GIFs and emojis to make your messages more interesting.

3. Personalize messages

If you know something about your contacts, use that info to make your messages personal. Use their names, send special offers, or mention products they viewed. Personalized messages catch attention and stand out from generic ones.

4. Let them opt-out

Always give subscribers the option to stop receiving your texts. Include instructions like "text STOP to cancel" in your responses and text sequences (many platforms make this mandatory). Make it easy for them to stop receiving messages if that is what they want.

Pro Tip: Make a special text club that offers text-only content and deals. Coupons, discounts, and sneak peeks at new products can attract people, especially if they feel like they're part of an exclusive group.

THE FUTURE IS SOFT SELLING

Sure, one of the main goals of your sales funnel is to sell, but just because you want to sell doesn't mean your audience wants you to sell to them. High-pressure "hard" sales techniques often drive customers away instead of attracting them to your brand and offers. That's where "soft" or "consultative" selling comes into play.

Unlike the hard sell, soft selling humanizes your brand. While it may seem counterintuitive to focus on things other than generating sales, soft selling focuses on nurturing trust. When you understand and empathize with your audience's pain points, you can show how your products and services solve those problems. *That* is the heart of the soft sell: listening, not pitching.

Soft selling may take a longer or less direct path to convert leads into sales, but it lays the groundwork for long-term customer relationships and future sales. The key characteristics of soft selling include:

- Focusing on their needs, not just what you're trying to sell.
- Using questions and research to guide your content, nurture trust, and build relationships.
- Talking less and listening more (using the consultative approach, which we will explore next).

When it comes to building meaningful relationships with customers, the slow-and-steady approach wins. So before creating any nurture-related content, ask yourself this simple question: "Am I stealing time and attention, or am I providing value?" For example, let's look at this nurture email from the reusable bag brand, Baggu.

This email from Baggu is an excellent nurture email for a few reasons:

1. CLEAR AND VALUABLE

By sharing simple tips, it is offering genuine value to recipients, showing them how to extend the life of their bags and get more use out of them. This helps to build trust and credibility with their audience.

2. VISUAL APPEAL

The visual, infographic-style makes the email more engaging and easier to understand. The simple icons and headers quickly communicate the care instructions without overwhelming the readers with excessive text. This visual approach captures attention and encourages readers to explore the content further.

3. RELEVANT CONTENT

The email also addresses a specific need—how to care for Baggu products. By providing relevant content, Baggu shows that they understand their customers' concerns and are dedicated to helping them make the most of their purchases.

Baggu builds trust in the company and its products by giving useful information in an interesting way. This can be a selling point for people who want bags that are easy to take care of, which could lead them to buy. Now, let's look at two types of soft-selling approaches through text.

THE BRAND-FIRST APPROACH

The outdoor gear brand, Cotopaxi, used a unique approach to engage their text subscribers during Memorial Day. Instead of the usual sales and promotions, they focused on their brand identity and values. Cotopaxi focused on resonating with its audience's adventurous spirit by sharing a carefully curated playlist for road trips and outdoor activities during the long weekend.

This creative strategy goes beyond selling products; it fosters a genuine connection. By appealing to their prospects on a personal level, Cotopaxi demonstrates that they care about their audience's interests and lifestyles. This personalized approach lays the foundation for long-term loyalty, making prospects more likely to choose Cotopaxi for their future outdoor gear needs.

THE CONVERSATIONAL APPROACH

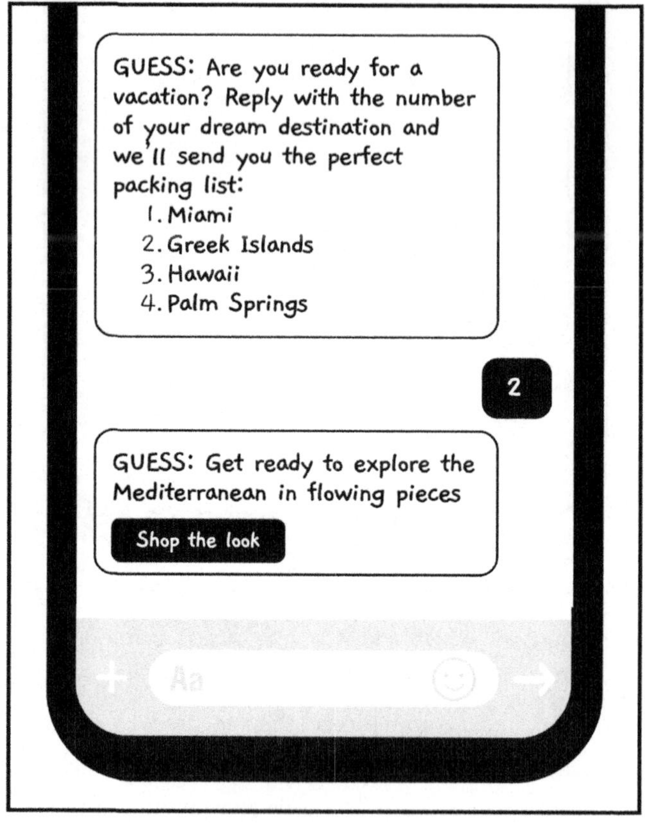

Using a conversational text approach, clothing brand, GUESS, transformed its nurture strategy into an interactive experience. They used a quiz-like format to gather information about the subscriber's dream travel destination and generated personalized product recommendations based on their answers. An important aspect of this approach is that it's non-intrusive. If a prospect showed no interest or chose not to respond, they wouldn't receive product recommendations, avoiding any sense of hard selling.

Creating a conversational text message can also make prospects feel like they are having a one-on-one interaction with the brand. This human touch is a great way to foster a deeper connection and build trust. GUESS's conversational approach moves beyond a transactional relationship and focuses on building a genuine relationship with its audience.

OMNICHANNEL NURTURING

While email and text are powerful tools to connect potential customers, using more channels can maximize the impact of your content. A "channel" simply refers to the way your brand communicates with your audience. By combining email/text marketing with other platforms, you can provide a consistent and seamless experience. Before we explore how to do that, let's take a look at three different channel approaches for nurturing prospects.

Single Channel Nurturing

This approach involves using only one channel, like email, to communicate with potential customers. While it can be effective to some extent, it can limit your ability to reach prospects who prefer other communication methods.

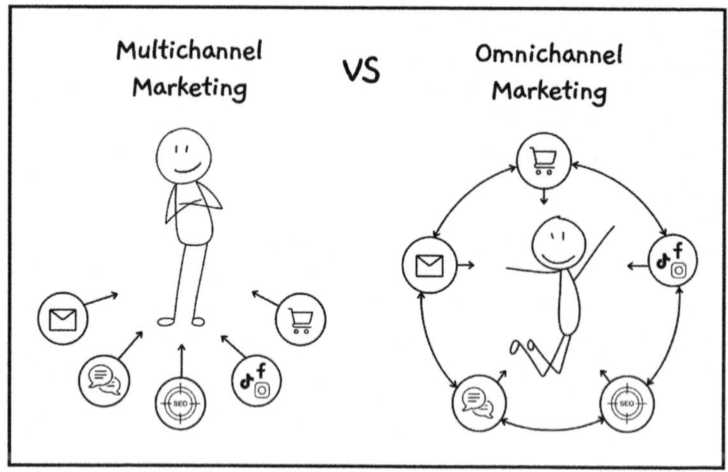

MULTICHANNEL NURTURING

Multichannel nurturing means using more than one channel to market and communicate with prospects. In this approach, the different channels are not integrated with each other. Each channel offers a separate, independent communication opportunity, but they don't work together seamlessly.

Omnichannel Nurturing

In omnichannel nurturing, you also use multiple communication channels, but the key difference is that these channels are integrated to create a smooth and seamless experience for the customer. This approach allows customers to switch between different channels with consistent messaging and personalization. It leads to a more cohesive and effective nurturing process. Let's put this difference in context using social media as an example.

In a multichannel approach, the goal is to increase followers, comments, likes, and shares on your social media pages and posts. These metrics indicate that more people are engaging with your brand on social media.

In contrast, an omnichannel strategy places less emphasis on quantity-based metrics. It focuses on ensuring that prospects can easily transition from your social media page to your website.

Now, let's talk about the importance of social media in nurturing prospects. Unlike email and text, social media doesn't provide direct access to consumers, but it still plays an important role in the nurture stage. When someone shows interest in your offers (i.e. by downloading a lead magnet), they may choose to follow you on social media. That's why it is important to create nurturing content on social media that builds trust. It could gently nudge them to purchase through links in your bio, tagged products, or social media shop.

One of the best ways to nurture on social media is to teach. It's no secret that social platforms want to keep users on their apps, and people typically use social media to be entertained, informed, and connected. Entertaining your audience may not always be relevant for your brand, but teaching is universally applicable. Regardless of your industry or audience, providing valuable, informative content can be an effective way to engage potential customers.

For example, you can create helpful content using short videos or carousel posts with bite-sized pieces of information. For example, Figma, a design and prototype tool, does this exceptionally well on its Instagram page. They share a variety of educational content, including how-to tutorials like "How to create a folded gradient in Figma," valuable resources like "UX Career Checklist," and practical tips like "Advice to Junior Designers." Their goal is to promote their product by providing broader UX/UI resources for their audience.

Now that we understand omnichannel nurturing and what good nurture content looks like, let's see what an omnichannel nurturing journey might look like:

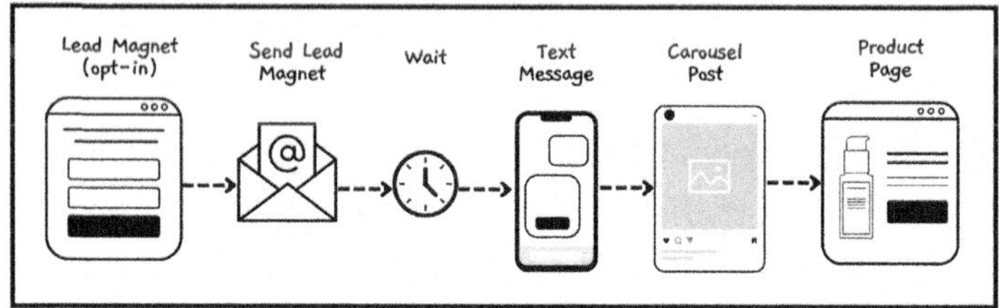

1. The prospect downloads your lead magnet and provides their email and phone number.
2. You send the lead magnet to their email address.
3. You follow up with an SMS containing a snippet of educational content and encourage them to read the full content by clicking a link.
4. The link redirects them to a value-packed carousel post on Instagram.
5. If they are ready to make a purchase, they can access your website through the link in your Instagram bio.

When done well, this seamless transition between channels allows prospects to immerse themselves in your brand experience and eventually make a purchase.

CHAPTER RESOURCES

Action Items

1. Set up "Scenario 1" after visitors opt-in to your lead magnet, directing them to a sales/shop/recommended products page to immediately identify buyers.
2. Prepare "Scenario 2" for non-buyers. Determine which communication channels to use based on your ICAs and pick one to start with.
3. Brainstorm at least 5-10 ways that you can add value to your audience through this communication channel (Chat GPT can help). Remember, nurturing is about *serving before selling*
4. Draft a concise, engaging, and visually appealing nurture sequence with 3-5 messages. Note: many of the email tools listed in the following section provide email/text templates, but you can also use ChatGPT or other AI copywriting tools to help!

RELEVANT TOOLS

General tools to get you started. Please note, this is not a comprehensive list of marketing automation tools:

Tool	Email Marketing	SMS Marketing	Text Bots	Whatsapp Marketing	Instagram DM	Messenger by Meta
Mailchimp and MailerLite	✓					
GetResponse and Campaign Monitor	✓	✓				
Klaviyo	✓	✓	✓			
Brevo and Twilio	✓	✓		✓		
Builderall and SendPulse	✓	✓	✓	✓	✓	✓
ManyChat		✓	✓	✓	✓	✓
Clicksend		✓	✓			
SimpleTexting		✓				

While these tools are missing certain categories, you can easily integrate them using affordable software, like Make (which integrates with all of the tools in this table). For example, you could integrate Mailchimp with SimpleTexting or Klaviyo with ManyChat.

Additional AI-powered tools

- **SmartLead** is an AI-powered email marketing tool that helps you personalize emails, create follow-up sequences and auto-rotating accounts.
- **tinyEmail** is an AI email marketing platform that helps you create personalized emails, generate optimized copy, and easily segment your audience.
- **AIAssist** is a ChatGPT-powered tool that automatically answers customer emails and inquiries within seconds.
- **Writecream** uses AI to help you generate marketing copy, audio, and images in seconds.

- **Maverick** and **Gan.ai** are AI-powered tools that craft personalized video messages to nurture customer relationships through channels like email and SMS.
- **Moda** is an AI Shopify extension that automatically segments your audience, optimizes email/SMS campaigns, and provides real-time insights across workflows.

ChatGPT EXAMPLE PROMPTS

Example 1

"Imagine you're a copywriting expert who's been hired by an online store where people can make their very own perfumes by picking fragrances. Your task is to develop an SMS nurture sequence with 5 text messages for potential customers who downloaded a lead magnet about '5 DIY Fragrance Recipes to Try at Home'.

The brand voice should be friendly and approachable. Focus on educating the audience and adding value to them (this can be through tips, common mistakes, etc.). Remember, the recipient of this sequence is a potential customer. For every text message, include a phrase like 'Reply to learn about it!' but change the phrase each time. The last message in the sequence should offer a discount (if they reply)."

Example 2

"Provide a detailed plan for an omnichannel digital nurture strategy tailored for an urban cycling gear e-commerce store. This strategy should involve the following communication channels: SMS, Email, and ChatBots. Offer actionable insights for how to communicate with the target audience (urban commuters) using each channel. Then show how these channels integrate by providing at least three distinct workflows."

Example 3

"Write a concise soft-selling email for an online career coaching business. The focus of the email is to add value to the audience by giving them information about common virtual interview mistakes. Do not hard-sell. The readers of the email are familiar with the brand, so there is no need to introduce the company. Make the email concise and easily readable. Include rich media in the email to make it more engaging. The tone should be conversational, relatable and motivational."

6

CHEESECAKE FACTORY SYNDROME

Simplify the Sales Process

The summer before I started college, I visited my cousins. One evening, we decided to eat at The Cheesecake Factory. The moment I opened the menu, I had a mini existential crisis. It was a massive leather-bound book that could double as a dumbbell. With 250 items to choose from, I couldn't help but wonder how many options were actually worth it…220 of them probably weren't very good.

We see websites like this all the time—too many menu items, countless pages, paralyzing lists of services, competing calls-to-action, and paragraphs upon paragraphs of text. Cheesecake Factory menu syndrome, officially known as Hick's Law, is a conversion killer. Hick's Law says that the more choices an individual has, the longer it will take to reach a decision.

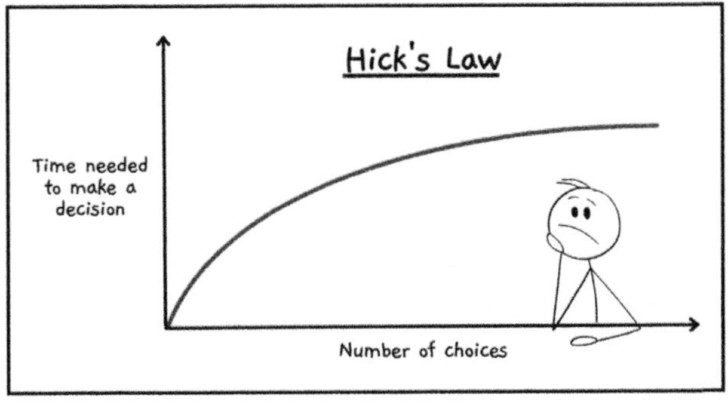

Sheena Iyengar, a Columbia University professor, conducted a fascinating study on the principles of Hick's Law.[13] She and her team set up a booth in a supermarket, offering various jam samples. Every few hours, they alternated between offering a wide assortment of 24 jams and a more limited selection of only 6.

While you might think more choices would lead to higher sales, most participants in the first group became confused and overwhelmed. Only 3% of customers from the booth with 24 flavors bought jam. In contrast, an impressive 30% purchased jam from the booth with only six flavors. Fewer options converted far higher.

The takeaway is that **confusion is the enemy of conversion**. Let's look at how to apply Hick's Law to create a high-converting customer journey on your website.

TACTIC 1

Optimize Your Menu

The easier it is for customers to find the right products, the likelier they are to buy. But it doesn't end there. Once customers have found what they're looking for, it's just as important to assist them in discovering more products that may interest them. To achieve this, you need strategic navigation design, specifically in the main site menu or navbar.

It is essential to find the sweet spot between too little and too much information in the main site menu. With too little information, users may struggle to find the items they're looking for, leading to frustration and ultimately bouncing off the website.

On the other hand, overwhelming users with too much information can trigger decision fatigue, causing them to abandon their search.

To strike the right balance, you can try "Goldilocks'ing" your menu. This method includes making the navigation easier and adding key conversion points to help users take the action they want to take. The key is to provide just enough information and options to facilitate a seamless browsing experience without overwhelming them.

One aspect of optimizing the main site menu is to include clear and distinct product categories. Most e-commerce stores implement this practice, but it's surprising to note that around 18% of them use a single dropdown item, such as "Services" or "Shop," for all their categories.[14] This approach hurts conversion rates by reducing transparency and, in some cases, requiring users to perform a "double hover" – first hovering over the main navigation item, then hovering over the categories within the dropdown. This additional step can create friction and make the user experience more complicated.

Milo has clear and simple categories in its menu, like "Dutch Oven," "Skillet," and "Sets." No confusion there.

If you have dozens of categories, group them to decrease friction. By incorporating specific product categories directly in the main site menu, users can easily navigate and explore the items they are interested in seeing. This approach reduces friction and minimizes the cognitive load on users, leading to improved conversion rates.

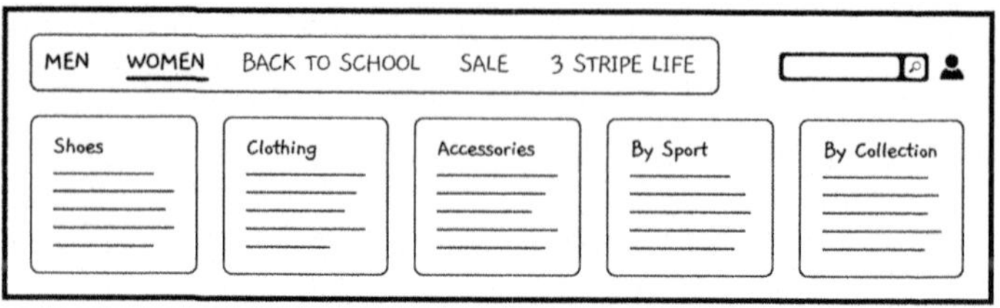

The navbar for Adidas has a dropdown "mega" menu with easy-to-skim groupings.

TACTIC 2

Scroll Vs. Click

Scrolling is an *instinctual* action for most users, driven by the desire to explore and consume more content without much cognitive effort. On the flip side, clicking requires a user to make a *decision*, which is a cognitive commitment.

If a website relies heavily on click-based navigation, asking users to make decisions on what to explore next could lead to decision fatigue. Users might stop the process entirely if they perceive it as too complex or time-consuming.

To combat decision fatigue, the scroll-based design works exceptionally well, offering an effortless journey of discovery.

The user can consume information at their own pace, reducing the number of decisions they need to make and providing a more relaxed, enjoyable experience.

Make sure the scrollable content is well-structured, engaging, and relevant. Long, monotonous pages can lead to user disinterest and high bounce rates. Content should include compelling visuals, headlines, and interactive elements to maintain engagement and guide the user naturally toward the desired action. If you're not sure which version of your homepage is better, use Google Optimize to A/B test your website. You can also use heat maps and scroll maps to identify where on your website visitors click and where they bounce (for relevant tools, view chapter resources).

ABOVE THE FOLD

What is the most important part of your home page? It is the first part or the "above the fold" (ATF) area of your website that people see before scrolling down. In seconds, they try to figure out what your business does and if you're the right fit for them.

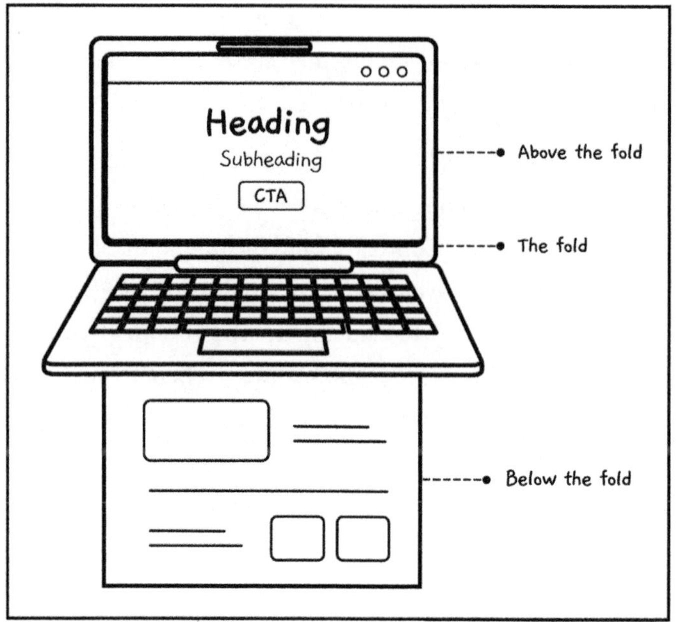

When visitors first see your ATF section, it has to be easy to understand and grab their attention. If it doesn't, they're likely to leave your site or "bounce."

Usually, there are two main reasons people bounce. The first reason is weak messaging. People can't figure out what your product does, they find it dull, or they don't see how it's useful for them.

The second reason is bad design. If your site's design looks unprofessional, outdated, or simply isn't pleasing to the eye, visitors might not want to stay or explore your site any further. Let's look at how this heading can be improved starting with a bad example, and then we'll break down how to make it better.

- *Bad example:* Your all-in-one digital branding solution.
- *Better:* Design stunning websites, logos, and graphics. For Free.

The first heading is less effective than the second because it sounds like corporate speak. Phrases like "all-in-one solution" are often overused in business contexts and can come across as vague and impersonal to the average reader. This type of language might make sense to those within the industry, but to the general public, it doesn't tell what the product or service *actually does.*

On the other hand, "Design stunning websites, logos, and graphics. For Free." is a much better choice. This heading is clear and straightforward. It tells the reader exactly what they can expect from the service. Rather than using business language or complex phrases, it communicates in words that are easy to understand and paints a vivid picture of the value it provides: designing stunning digital assets without any cost. The use of the phrase "For Free" creates a strong value proposition. It instantly communicates to the visitor that they can gain significant value without any financial commitment, making the service even more appealing.

The improved heading also gives the reader a specific idea of the service's features. It mentions websites, logos, and graphics—tangible things people can easily understand. These specific words make the service more attractive and help to set clear expectations for the user. Let's look at another example:

- *Before:* Your Next Career: Master Blockchain Development
- *After:* Become a Blockchain Developer in 3 Months

Here, in the first headline, the description is vague. The reader can see the ultimate goal, but the lack of a timeline decreases the value of the offer. In the second headline, the startup could be offering an educational course equivalent to a master's degree in digital blockchain development at an expedited rate. This is perfect for those who want to break into the development field without losing years learning necessary skills.

Your brand's unique value proposition should be front and center in your heading. This is what grabs people's attention and keeps them engaged as they scroll down. Implementing these changes can significantly impact your conversion rates, increasing them by 10-30%.

CRAFT YOUR SUBHEADING

So far, we've focused on creating an engaging heading. Now, it's time to complement it with a subheading that provides more information about your product's unique qualities. The subheading serves two main purposes:

- Elaborate on how our product works.
- List features that support the heading's bold claim.

Let's take a look at an example from Flodesk.com:

- *Heading:* Design beautiful emails. Sell online.
- *Subheading:* Beginners and experts use Flodesk to send emails people love to get, create high-converting checkout pages, and grow their business—all in one place

In this example, the heading tells us what the platform does (creating attractive emails for online selling), while the subheading explains how it achieves this by offering features like checkout pages and providing an all-in-one email marketing solution.

Action Items

- Revise your subheading to provide an explanation of how your heading claim is accomplished.
- Highlight the top 2-3 features of your product.

Pro tip: Your subheading should be 1-2 sentences—lengthy paragraphs kill interest.

CALL TO ACTION

Your call-to-action buttons should add to the excitement and curiosity generated by the heading. When the CTAs align with the story you started, they make it easy for visitors to move to the next stage. Clicking on these buttons feels intuitive because they propel the visitor further into the narrative and provide a clear path to take action.

Let's look at an example from Post Mates, a food delivery service.

- *Heading:* You want it. We get it.
- *Subheading:* Food, drinks, groceries, and more available for delivery and pickup.
- *CTA:* Find food

Post Mates has a strong call to action because it fits well with the story introduced in the heading. The heading understands the user's desires, and the subheading explains the available options like food, drinks, groceries, and more for delivery and pickup.

The call to action button, "Find food," is a natural next step that allows users to continue their journey seamlessly. It's easy for users to click on the button because it aligns with their needs and helps them move forward in the process. This cohesive message and clear call to action make it compelling for users to take action and find what they're looking for.

Now let's look at a second example from Spotify.

- *Heading:* It's play time.
- *Subheading:* Say hello to the most entertaining Spotify ever. Play free or subscribe to Spotify Premium.
- *CTA:* Play Free - Go Premium

In the case of Spotify, their double call to action makes sense because it caters to different types of users. The "Play Free" button appeals to those who want to enjoy music without cost, while the "Go Premium" button targets users willing to pay for additional benefits. This double call to action allows Spotify to convert users at different stages of their music streaming journey.

SALES PAGE PSYCHOLOGY

After the Call to Action, we go to the sales page, which should be carefully crafted for the psychology of decision-making. When it comes to buying decisions, we all face an internal tug-of-war between our logic and our emotions. Understanding this internal struggle is key to persuading someone to buy from you. It's like you have two different voices in your head when making decisions: the quick-fix voice and the careful voice.

The quick-fix voice just wants to solve the problem at hand and doesn't worry about what's coming later. The careful voice wants to avoid problems in the future. These two voices don't always agree. For example, a careful voice may warn you about your health if you keep eating fast food. The quick-fix voice just wants to end your hunger right there on the spot.

If you can find a way to make both voices happy, you have found the sweet spot for getting people to buy what you're offering. If you can't do that, try to appeal to the quick-fix voice, not the careful one.

Logic Doesn't Convince Us to Buy

Using an EEG monitor, we can see what's happening in our brains when we look at ads. A study in the *Journal of Neuroscience, Psychology, and Economics* checked brain activity in people while they looked at two types of ads: ones that use facts and numbers to convince them to make a purchase and ones that use powerful images to make people feel a certain way.[15]

When people looked at ads that used facts and numbers, the parts of their brains that help with making decisions were really active. These parts, like the amygdala and the hippocampus, help us weigh the pros and cons and crunch numbers to stop us from buying things on a whim. Ads that used powerful images and little text didn't activate these decision-making parts of their brains.

If your brain is trying to figure out if you should buy something, you'll probably find reasons not to buy it. By providing logical facts and numbers, we stimulate the careful voice in our brains to say "no." On the other hand, the language of emotions encourages us to decide if we *want* to buy something. The decision-making parts of our brain aren't as active. The quick-fix part of our brain is ready to say yes, regardless of the consequences.

We often buy things based on feelings and then use logic to back up our choices. Both our minds and our hearts ask two questions when we decide to buy something: "Is this relevant to me?" and "Is this worth it?"

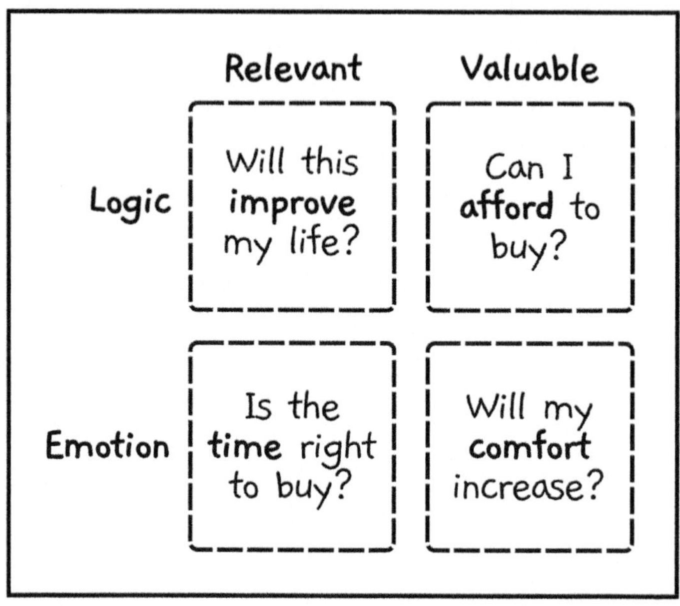

The Buyer's Decision Quadrant

There are four main things people consider when buying something: Status, money, time, and happiness. Every time we buy something, we believe it will improve at least one of these things. If something can improve all four, it's an easy sale. If you want to convince someone to buy something, you need to show them how it will improve at least one thing for their mind (like status or money) and one thing for their heart (like time or happiness). If you can't do that, people will easily say no.

Having logical reasons on your sales page is good, but if you only talk about saving them money and improving their status, you won't sell much. The best sales pages highlight in the headings how your product can save time and increase happiness and then give logical reasons underneath.

We Often Trust Our Feelings

Our brains handle feelings and logic in different ways. Sometimes, even when something doesn't make sense, we go with our "gut feeling". Our instincts tell us when something that doesn't seem logical is still the right choice.

For example, in a card game study, players picked from four decks of cards.[16] Some cards gave rewards and some gave penalties. The players wanted to get more rewards than penalties. What they didn't know was that some decks were set to give more rewards, and some were set to give more penalties. After 10 cards, many players felt anxious when reaching for the bad decks. Their feelings were telling them not to make bad choices, even though their logical minds were still figuring things out. After about 80 cards, most players figured out which decks were better and picked their last 20 cards from those decks.

Harvard professor Gerald Zaltman also conducted a study demonstrating that 95% of buying decisions are made subconsciously.[17] Our brains are like supercomputers, and our thinking mind is a very small part of it. That's why we often rely on our feelings to guide us to the right decision. The moment we subconsciously decide to buy something is different from the moment we logically justify our purchase. That's why we need to differentiate between the "Call-to-Action" and the "Buying Decision".

- Call-to-Action: Prompts us to make a purchase
- Buying Decision: Inner decision to make a purchase

The "Call-to-Action" speaks to our logical side. It gives us a clear, step-by-step plan to swap something we have with something someone else has. The "Buying Decision" happens inside us. It doesn't happen on a website, in a contract, or during the checkout process. The "Buying Decision" happens when our heart tells our brain it's okay to go ahead.

Sometimes, our heart can even make our brain do something that doesn't really make sense. On your sales page, if you only give logical reasons, without making people feel strong emotions, it's not likely to make them buy something. For example, one study discovered that headlines with negative words, like "never" or "worst", get people's attention 30% better.[18]

The logical side and the emotional side of the brain are different, and we need to treat them differently. As Jeffrey Gitomer said, "People hate to be sold, but they love to buy." You can't just sell something with a logical call to action. You also need to reach people's 'Buying Decision', which comes from the emotional side of our brain.

To craft a message that persuades, you need to appeal to emotion and then appeal to logic. In Aristotle's work *Rhetoric*, he identified three elements of persuasion:

- Ethos - your credibility, based on your character, experiences, and education
- Logos - the logic of your argument, backed up with evidence
- Pathos - the emotional bond you create with your audience

When Harvard professor, Carmine Gallo, analyzed 150 hours of TED talks, he found that the most engaging presentations included 65% pathos, 25% logos, and only 10% ethos.[19] This highlights the fact that emotions carry more persuasive power than logic. So, as you draft your sales pages, promotional newsletters, and content marketing, make sure you amp up the emotional resonance.

For every piece of logical evidence—each statistic, reason, or justification for making a purchase—try to include 2-3 emotions. If you can sway the heart more than the mind, you'll be more successful in persuading people to buy your product.

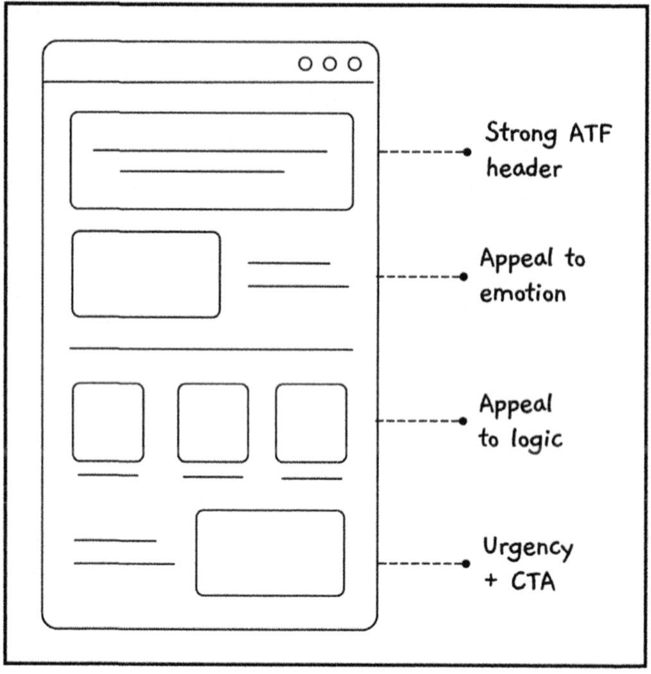

Psychology of a Sales Page

USING THE DECOY EFFECT TO SELL MORE

You may have seen it at your local restaurant chain, movie theater, or favorite coffee spot. It's called the Decoy Effect, also known as the attraction effect, and it happens when your choice between two options changes drastically with the introduction of a third option: the decoy.

The decoy is a price strategy that businesses use to make us switch from one option to a pricier one that benefits us more. By adding a decoy, businesses can guide our choices without us even realizing it. Now, let's unpack what makes a good decoy and how you can apply it to your sales page.

We have seen that more options make decision-making more difficult. An overload of choices can overwhelm us and spike our anxiety about making the "wrong" choice, leading to difficulty in making any decision at all.

When making a decision, we consider many factors. The more uncertain we are about which factors are most important, the harder it is to choose.[20] That's why we usually focus on just a couple of criteria, such as price and quantity, to determine the best value for our money.

Interestingly, we generally are more averse to lower quality than we are to higher prices.[21] That's where the decoy comes into play! It takes advantage of this human tendency, nudging us towards an option that is both higher quality and higher priced, making us feel like we're making a rational and informed decision. Most times, we don't even realize the impact decoys have on our choices. Whatever we choose, we believe we've made the choice independently.

The power of the Decoy Effect lies in its invisibility. It gently nudges us toward how we see the "important" aspects of our choices, without using big rewards or threats. There's evidence that, when making decisions, our main goal isn't to pick the correct option but rather to justify a choice we've already made.[22] Decoys provide an easy justification, making us feel more comfortable with our choice.

Let's take a classic example. The *Economist* magazine offered readers three subscription options: $59 for a digital subscription, $125 for a print-only subscription, and $125 for both print and digital access. Can you spot the decoy? The print-only option offers less value for money. When MIT professor Dan Ariel tested this model on 100 of his students, the presence of the decoy significantly influenced their choice towards the target option, i.e., print & digital access.

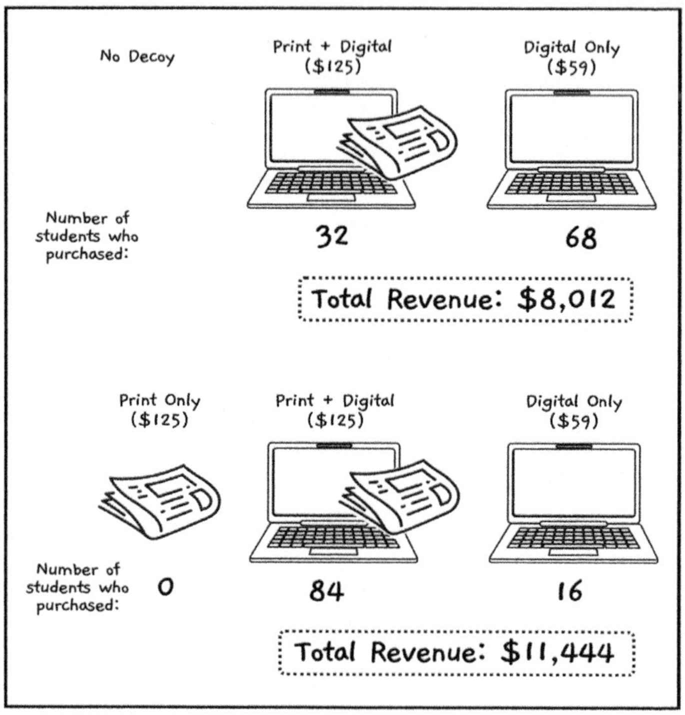

By introducing a print-only subscription as a decoy, the interest in the target choice (print + digital) skyrocketed from 32 to 84 students, increasing total revenue by over 40%.

Now, how can you use the Decoy Effect in your business? Here's a three-step guide.

1. CHOOSE THE PRODUCT YOU WANT TO PROMOTE

The decoy could be a product or service that has more benefits, is priced higher, or has a higher profit margin. But remember, a decoy isn't a cure-all. Customers must already like the target. If your product isn't good or there's no product-market fit, introducing an inferior version might not be enough.

2. INTRODUCE A SUBTLE DECOY

The price of the decoy should be close to the target product but less valuable. The goal is to make the more expensive target seem like a better deal. Remember to keep the decoy subtle. If your pricing is too extreme, customers might catch on. To make the decoy price still favorable (relative to the target), but overall less appealing, you can introduce a new, irrelevant feature.

3. INCLUDE A THIRD OPTION

When consumers are presented with two options, they tend to weigh the pros and cons of each pretty easily. However, the introduction of a third option can disrupt this binary decision-making process. It effectively creates a distraction and forces the consumer to reassess their preferences.

This third option, often crafted to be less attractive than the target, acts as a decoy. While it might not seem like a compelling choice in itself, its real value lies in making the target option seem to be the best choice. It's usually priced close to the target but offers less value, so it enhances the perceived value of the target option.

Pro tip: Design this third option carefully. It needs to be attractive enough to be considered a legitimate choice, yet not so attractive that it becomes the preferred option. If the third option outshines the target, it no longer serves as a decoy but becomes the competition.

UNCERTAINTY

The Sales Process Killer

According to Jonah Berger, a professor at Wharton, not knowing what will happen is one of the top five barriers that stop people from changing their minds.[23] When customers feel unsure, they may stop shopping and leave your site without making a purchase. Even being uncertain about small changes, like getting new shoes or signing up for something, can make us hesitate.

And it gets worse. If we're unsure about a product or service, we see it as less valuable.[24] This drop in value is known as the "uncertainty tax". So, to encourage customers to choose something new, your offer can't just be a bit better. It has to be a lot better.

But don't worry, there's still hope. When you want customers to do something new, like consider buying your offer, you should address their main concerns before they get in the way. To put it simply, your offer might have a lot of benefits, but if there's even one question or worry that the customer can't answer, they might not take your offer. On the other hand, if your business spots and addresses all of the customer's questions and worries, just one good reason to buy can be enough.

Typical worries include questions such as "Will it solve my problem?" or "What if it doesn't work for me?" Not knowing the answers to these questions and others can stop any sales process in its tracks. That's why the most successful companies, like Netflix, Paypal, and Zara, work hard to remove any uncertainty at each step of the sales process. If you're struggling to understand why a customer might not want to sign up for a free offer, look at this detailed breakdown of how Netflix removes any worries that could stop potential customers from signing up for its free trial.

Netflix Free Trial Page

As you can see, they address any worries a customer might have (like whether they can cancel at any time and whether they'll be charged without knowing), answering these questions at the front of their sign-up process. Other ways to decrease uncertainty are to include security badges on your website and checkout, including SSL certificates, payment badges, antivirus software logos, a money-back guarantee, and customer reviews. Since feeling unsure is a common problem, it is important to understand your customers' main worries and how to deal with them before thinking about ways to encourage them to buy from you.

ACTION ITEMS

1. Simplify your menu by having no more than 6 buttons in the navigation bar; if you have too many links/products, create a mega-menu with grouped categories to make it easy to navigate.
2. Try creating at least 3 variations of your ATF section and get feedback from friends, family, UX testing services (listed under relevant tools) or AI A/B testing tools, like ABtesting.ai.
3. Tweak your home page layout so it's scroll-friendly. Decide what *main action* you want visitors to take from your home page (i.e. view your portfolio, shop a specific product category etc.). This CTA should be above the fold, in the heart of the home page, and (optionally) repeated in the footer. Heat maps can help you optimize your CTAs and remove/replace ineffective ones.

4. When you feel confident about your homepage, pick at least one element on your sales or product pages to improve. Consider techniques like sales page psychology, decoy pricing, guarantees etc.

RELEVANT TOOLS

General tools to get you started:

- **Google Optimize** helps you A/B test your website by creating variations of web pages to analyze user interactions to find the most effective elements.
- **Hotjar** provides heat maps that show you where users scroll, click, and interact so you can remove friction. It also has features like A/B test variants and session recordings.
- **Useberry, UsabilityHub**, **UXtweaks**, and **Loop11** offer user experience testing services to improve your website usability and brand experience (prices of these tools are in ascending order).
- **Builderall** is an all-in-one marketing and funnel building platform with a suite of over 40 tools, including a website builder, social proof widgets, chatbots, click maps and more.
- **TrustPulse** and **Fomo** are social proof and trust badge tools for your website.

Additional AI-powered tools:

- **ABtesting.ai** simplifies A/B testing with AI-generated suggestions for headlines, copy, and call-to-actions for your website.

- **Hexometer** is an AI website monitoring tool that proactively identifies issues across availability, performance, user experience, SEO, security and more.
- **WebWhiz** lets you train ChatGPT on your website data and create an AI chatbot capable of instantly answering customers' questions.
- **Jasper.ai**, **Copy.ai** and **Copymatic** are AI copywriting tools that can help you write your website copy in a fraction of the time.
- **e-Commerce Prompts** provides ready-to-use ChatGPT prompts for setting up e-commerce stores and marketing campaigns quickly.
- **Manifest.ai** is a ChatGPT-powered shopping assistant for Shopify stores that helps visitors find products that meet their needs.

ChatGPT EXAMPLE PROMPTS

Example 1

"Draft the layout of a website wireframe for a premium yoga equipment store. Avoid excessive click-based navigation. Instead, the website home page structure should be scrollable, engaging, and relevant. Organize the homepage structure in a way that optimizes conversions and creates a smooth customer journey.

The store has 3 main categories:

- Yoga mats
- Yoga props and accessories
- Yoga studio supplies"

Example 2

"Brainstorm 10 website footer CTAs for a virtual interior design agency. Write in the active voice and start with an action verb. The CTAs should consist of around 3 words each. The brand voice should be friendly and creative."

Example 3

"Write the sales page copy for my online course "Freedom on Wheels", which teaches people how to renovate a van from scratch to make it livable. The target audience is people who want a mobile home/office that lets them work from breathtaking locations. Make sure the sales page (which should fit in one of the 3 psychological categories below) includes a course breakdown, instructor bio, testimonials, and FAQs. The high-level sales page structure should appeal to the following psychology: 1) the beginning appeals to the emotions of my target audience, 2) the middle appeals to their logic, and 3) the end creates a sense of urgency with a clear CTA."

7

THE PAIN OF PAYING

Design Frictionless Purchases

Paying hurts. Physically.

A team of researchers led by Brian Knutson and Roger Lowenstein uncovered a fascinating link between the act of paying for a product and physical discomfort.[25] Their study revealed that, when individuals face high prices, a region in the brain known as the insula becomes increasingly active before making a purchasing decision. This area is typically associated with negative emotions and sensations of physical pain. Another study reinforced this discovery, demonstrating that the brain's pain centers were activated when participants encountered prices, especially if those prices were considered too expensive.[26] Consumer psychologists refer to the emotional discomfort people experience during the act of paying as "The Pain of Paying."[27]

Paying for something means losing money, and since people are generally averse to losses, this triggers a negative response, leading to more cautious purchasing behavior. Recognizing this response can provide valuable insights for converting prospects at the bottom of the sales funnel. Let's explore some practical strategies that can help reduce this "pain of paying."

1. Pay in Advance

Experts have observed that the act of spending the first dollar hurts the most, while each dollar after that inflicts less pain. To illustrate this, think about the last time you ate at an "all you can eat" restaurant. You pay a fixed price upfront, which lets you eat as much as you want.

Although you felt the sting of the payment upfront, you then freely filled your plates and enjoyed your meals without considering additional costs. On the other hand, imagine a scenario where each item on the menu has its own price, and you have to keep track in your head of how much your total meal will cost. In the second scenario, the perception of cost is greater, which intensifies the pain of paying.

Academic research by Loewenstein and Prelec supports this phenomenon. Their landmark study found that, when you've paid for something upfront, the act of consumption feels almost free.[28] The discomfort linked to the payment is offset by the anticipation of the benefits the purchase will provide. They called this "prospective accounting," which means that thinking about the future benefits helps reduce the discomfort of paying upfront.

This concept is highly applicable across industries; consider an online learning platform that offers an all-inclusive subscription. After making an initial payment, you gain access to an array of courses without worrying about the cost of each individual course. This eliminates the constant calculation and concern about accumulating fees every time you want to learn something new.

Imagine you're interested in learning a new subject on a learning platform with an individual pricing scheme. You could become discouraged by the separate prices for each course when you consider the cumulative cost. Now that's painful.

2. Sell in Bundles

Bundling, the tactic of selling multiple products as a single package, is another effective strategy to lessen the pain of paying. It operates on the principle we discussed earlier: the first dollar spent is the most painful.

For instance, when customers buy a bundle of three products, they only experience that discomfort one time. If they purchased each product individually, they'd have to go through that discomfort three times (for bundle building tools, view chapter resources).

For example, think about Vineet Kumar, an assistant professor at Harvard Business School. He found this principle to be true in his studies of the handheld video game market.[29] Between 2001 and 2005, when Nintendo essentially monopolized the market, Kumar and his team investigated the sales patterns of Nintendo's Game Boy Advance and Game Boy Advance SP consoles and their games.

They found that Nintendo substantially increased product sales when they bundled a video game console and a game. However, this increase in sales only happened when customers also had the option to purchase each item separately—a strategy known as "mixed bundling."

This approach led to a significant boost in sales, with console sales increasing by around 100,000 units and game cartridge sales exceeding a million units when offered as part of a bundle.

However, when Nintendo only offered "pure bundling" without the option to buy each piece separately, their performance suffered significantly compared to when no bundles or mixed bundles were offered. Kumar's research highlights the importance of giving customers *freedom of choice,* ultimately enhancing their engagement with the product.

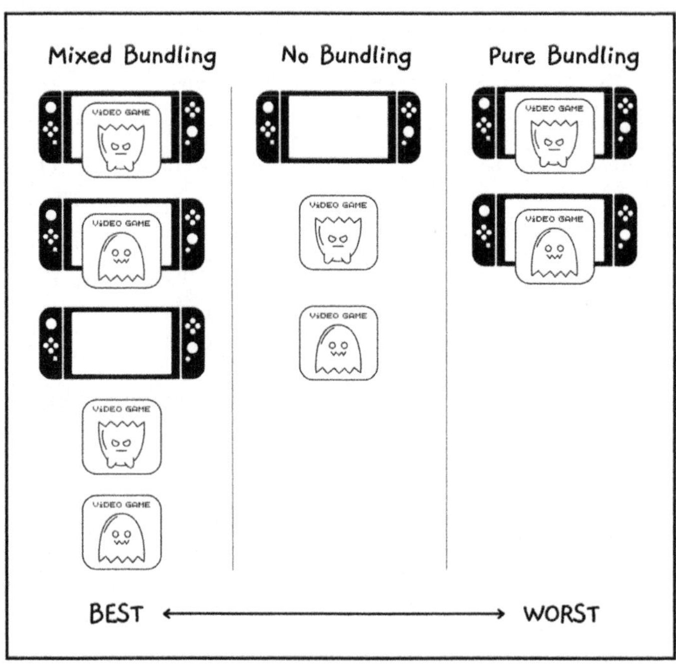

Vineet Kumar's Nintendo study. The results found that mixed bundling performed the best, no bundling performed in the middle, and pure bundling performed the worst.

3. The Power of Free

The word "free" has a magical appeal because it removes any negative associations with spending money. The word "free" still holds power even when it only applies to a portion of a product or service. Consider the following example: You're shopping online for a new hoodie and you come across these three offers:

- The hoodie costs $50 + $10 for shipping.
- The hoodie costs $60 + free shipping.
- The hoodie is free + $60 shipping.

Which of these options do you think appeals most to the customer? On a purely rational level, all options are equally valuable since the total costs are identical. But in our reality—a world driven by perception and emotion—the situation is quite different.

The first option, with no "free" element, is arguably the least appealing. According to behavioral economist Dan Ariely, the second option, a $60 hoodie with free shipping, will most likely entice customers.

You can also use the power of "free" to increase the average order value. This is where Amazon excels. As you might know, Amazon sets a minimum order of $25 to qualify for free shipping. Amazon hopes that, if you had originally planned to purchase a product for $15.99, you might buy two in order to reach the free shipping threshold. When Amazon first launched this strategy, sales skyrocketed everywhere...except France. The key difference was that the French version of Amazon had mistakenly charged a 20-cent shipping fee.[30] The small shipping cost completely removed French customers' desire to add more products to their carts. But as soon as Amazon fixed the issue, French customers acted like everyone else and bought more items to get free shipping. In many cases, adding a free shipping threshold can incite over 50% of people on your site to spend more.[31]

OPTIMIZE THE CHECKOUT PROCESS

No matter how fantastic your website is, if shoppers become frustrated or their needs are not met during the checkout process, converting them into paying customers can become an impossible task.

According to research institute Baymard, shoppers abandon their carts on e-commerce websites at an average rate of 69.82%.[32] This means that only about three out of every 10 shoppers who add items to their cart complete their purchase. Why is it important to optimize the checkout process?

The default checkout process provided by your website platform may not be the most user-friendly and efficient for your customers. By optimizing the checkout process, online retailers can reduce the number of abandoned carts, as almost 20% of shoppers abandon their purchase when they find the checkout process too complicated.[33]

Optimizing the checkout process with tools like SamCart or Thrivecart can also boost the average order value. Techniques like cross-selling and upselling, which we'll discuss later in this chapter, encourage customers to make additional purchases. The following tactics will help you streamline your checkout process.

TACTIC 1

Allow Guest Checkout

When online businesses ask first-time customers to create an account, it can cause one-third of them to abandon their cart.[34] By allowing customers to checkout as guests, you can eliminate this issue and make it easier for customers to complete their purchases without creating an account. This leads to a smoother and more efficient checkout experience, increasing the likelihood of converting visitors into paying customers.

Guest checkout also caters to customers who prefer a more straightforward and anonymous shopping experience. Some shoppers may have concerns about privacy, but whenever possible, you want to try to capture their email or phone number so you can market to them in the future. By providing the option to checkout as a guest, your brand shows flexibility and respect for customer preferences.

TACTIC 2

One-Click Checkout

Introducing a 1-click checkout option adds another layer of convenience to the purchasing process. By implementing this feature, customers only have to enter their information once, like their email, shipping address, and payment details. Some popular 1-click checkout systems include Shop Pay, Bolt, PayPal Express Checkout, Google Pay, and Amazon. Shoppers can save time and effort with this streamlined process, and their information will be securely stored for future purchases.

Time-saving is just one benefit of 1-click checkout. By automatically populating the necessary details, this feature reduces the chances of customers reconsidering their purchase and abandoning their carts. With their information readily available, they can complete their transaction without the hassle of re-entering their information each time.

TACTIC 3

Provide Multiple Payment Options

Providing customers with different payment options is another important aspect of online shopping. Customers want choices. Roughly 9% will not complete their purchase if their preferred payment method is unavailable.[35] To avoid losing potential customers, you should offer a variety of payment methods at checkout.

Consider including popular options like debit or credit cards, shopping apps such as Shop Pay and PayPal, digital wallets like Samsung Pay, Apple Pay, or Google Pay, and "buy now, pay later" solutions. By offering different payment methods, you cater to various customer preferences and increase the chances of completing successful transactions, sometimes by as much as 20%.

TACTIC 4

Have an Abandoned-Cart Email Sequence

When shoppers leave items in their cart without completing the purchase, you have an opportunity to re-engage them. One effective strategy is to send them reminder emails with a link back to their cart. This helps to recapture their interest and encourages them to finish their purchase. You've likely seen these emails, and although they might feel like spam, they actually do work.

An abandoned cart sequence is usually a series of 3 to 5 emails (you can also adapt this for text). It's important to plan the timing and content of these emails carefully to maximize their impact. Here's an example of what the timing sequence for the emails could look like:

- Email 1: Sent within 1 to 24 hours after the cart abandonment.
- Email 2: Sent 2 days after the cart abandonment.
- Email 3: Sent 4 days after the cart abandonment.
- Email 4: Sent 7 to 10 days after the cart abandonment.

Now, let's take a closer look at the content of these emails and how they can be structured to win back customers and encourage them to complete their purchases.

#1 EMAIL CAPTURE AT CHECKOUT

To follow up with potential customers, you need to collect their contact information. The simplest way to do this is by requesting their email when a shopper adds a product to their cart—keeping it frictionless. This step is important because, if you don't ask for contact information early, you won't recover the maximum number of abandoned carts. During the checkout process, they can provide additional details, like their address and payment information.

#2 THE "DON'T FORGET" EMAIL

These initial emails serve as friendly reminders in an abandoned cart email series. They are typically sent within an hour after a customer leaves without completing their purchase, reminding them about the items they left behind in the cart. The subject lines for these types of emails often take the following approach:

- Don't leave us hanging!
- Did you forget something?
- Don't worry, we've got you.
- Whoops! You left something in your cart.
- Where did you go?

These examples grab attention in an email and serve as gentle reminders that encourage the shopper to take action by making them think, "Oh yeah, I need to complete my order."

Now, let's take a look at an example of the email body, which should also include appealing visuals of the products from the shopper's cart:

- *Heading:* Still deciding?
- *Subheading:* Take a look at [insert product] before it's gone.
- *CTA:* Shop now

Another example:

- *Heading:* Don't miss out!
- *Subheading:* Your cart is reserved for 24 hours.
- *CTA:* View my cart

You can use keywords like:

- Forget/forget
- Whoops/oops
- Leave/left
- Still
- Interested
- Complete
- Saved

#3 THE "INCENTIVIZED OFFER" EMAIL

One key reason people hesitate to complete their checkout is the presence of hidden costs, like shipping fees. Although we often buy items to be shipped, we tend to dislike paying for shipping. You can leverage this knowledge to your advantage by offering free shipping in your emails. The subject lines for these types of emails often include phrases like:

- Welcome + Free Shipping.
- Free Shipping Just for You!
- Free 2-Day Shipping—Today Only.
- Free Shipping Sitewide Ends Sunday.
- Don't let free shipping go to waste.
- Free Shipping, Free Returns.

As you can see from the list above, there are various ways to highlight the free shipping incentive. This flexibility allows your brand personality to shine through, even in the subject line. In summary, the two words you must remember for this subject line are "Free + Shipping."

Now, let's explore an example of the email body:

- *Heading:* Remember that thing you wanted? We saved it for you!
- *Subheading:* Free shipping for orders over $50
- *CTA:* Go to cart

Another example:

- *Heading:* Shipping on us!
- *Subheading:* Enter code [insert code] at checkout for free shipping.
- *CTA:* Complete your checkout

#4 THE "FOMO ALERT" EMAIL

The fear of missing out (FOMO) is a powerful sales tactic because it plays on our dislike of the feeling of not getting something we want. It's important not to manipulate customers excessively, but using this psychological aspect in your abandoned cart sequence can be effective. Consider incorporating the following subject lines:

- Final call: Last chance to save BIG.
- Last hours to save $150!
- Time is running out to save 20%
- Final Hours, Last Chance to Save!

Now, let's explore some examples of the email body:

- *Heading:* Don't miss out on your favorites.
- *Subheading:* Just a heads up: our most popular items sell out fast.
- *CTA:* View your cart.
- Another example:
- *Heading:* Still interested?

- *Subheading:* Your cart is about to expire.
- *CTA:* Complete checkout.

As you can see, phrases like "last chance" and "final" are frequently used in these types of emails. Other ideas to consider include:

- X days/hours left.
- The item in your cart is selling out.
- Selling fast/out.
- Cart is expiring.

#5 THE "LIMITED DISCOUNT" EMAIL

Everyone loves a good discount. When you're nearing the end of a sale and want to seal the deal, offering a discount can be the deciding factor. Let's take a look at how different brands craft subject lines for their discount emails:

- Don't miss out! Save 40% before it's gone.
- Half-off sale! Get 50% off [insert product].
- Bonus gift: Last chance to save on [insert product].
- Today only: Save on your order.
- Limited-time offer | Save up to $60.
- It's on! Enjoy 15% off storewide.

Notice a common theme? The word "save" takes center stage. Now, let's look at some examples of the email content:

- *Heading:* Treat yourself to a special discount.
- *Subheading:* Take 15% off your entire order.
- *CTA:* Start saving today!

Another example:

- *Heading:* Hey, we saved something for you.
- *Subheading:* Enjoy 15% off your purchase.
- *CTA:* Save 15% now!

Other phrases and words that tend to be effective include:

- Get a discount of $XX.
- Enjoy XX% off.
- Last chance to save.
- Final day to save.
- Half-off sale.
- Special sale.

Usually, including the actual discount amount (either as a percentage or dollar value) in the subject line can be very powerful. Many brands also create a sense of urgency by emphasizing that it's a limited-time offer or the final opportunity to save. By combining the mention of savings with a touch of FOMO (fear of missing out), you can craft the last email so it captivates your audience.

CROSS-SELLING AND UPSELLING

It's generally 3-5 times easier to sell to an existing customer than to a new one.[36] This is because your current customers have already overcome the biggest hurdle in doing business: trust. They've already built confidence in your brand and your offers. If you keep offering them attractive products and consistently deliver high value, they will keep buying from you.

Yet, making this happen can be tricky. Two strategies that come in handy are cross-selling and upselling. When correctly implemented, these methods can help you to sell more products to your customers. Cross-selling and upselling are like two sides of a coin. In both cases, you are trying to sell another product to someone who has already made the decision to buy from you.

In the case of cross-selling, you're suggesting a product that complements the customer's original purchase. Upselling, on the other hand, involves encouraging the customer to make a more expensive purchase by offering an upgrade or premium option.

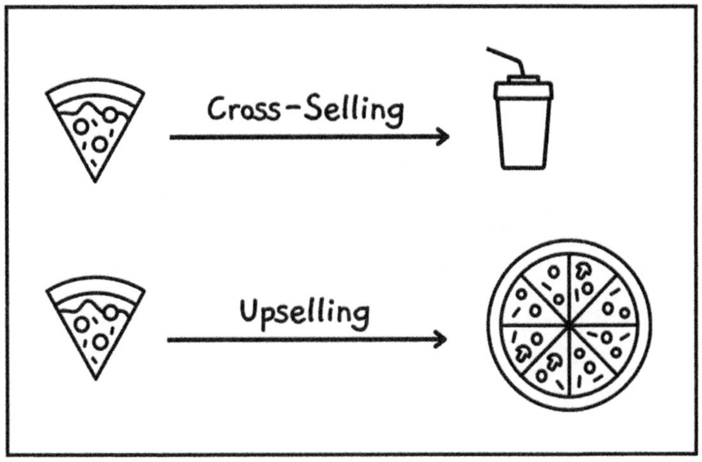

Cross-selling suggests a product that complements the original purchase (i.e. soda complements your slice of pizza). Upselling is upgrading the original order (i.e. convincing you to get the pizza pie instead of only a slice)

Cross-selling, upselling, and product recommendation methods are responsible for increasing sales by 20-30%.[37] But why?

Imagine you've just moved into a new apartment, and you've found the perfect sofa for your living room on a furniture website. You're ready to make the purchase when you see an additional offer. For just $50 more, you can get a matching coffee table. Since you're already committed to furnishing your new place, you decide to go for it, add the coffee table to your cart, and complete the purchase. Congratulations, you've been upsold! It was an easy sell because you were already planning to buy the sofa, and the coffee table seemed like a small addition to complete your living room setup.

Now, let's consider another scenario. You receive an email from a furniture company offering a complete living room set with a sofa and coffee table. But your apartment is already furnished, and adding more furniture is not a priority right now. So, you decide to skip the offer and close the email.

See the difference? The first offer was more attractive because of the timing. When it comes to upselling and cross-selling, timing is *everything*. These strategies work because people often buy multiple things at once. When someone is in the mindset to buy, they're usually willing to buy more than one product or service to solve multiple problems at once.

Cross-Selling

Amazon has mastered the art of cross-selling, and we should all take a page out of their book. If you've ever noticed product suggestions under tags like "Customers who bought this item also bought" or "Frequently purchased together," you've been targeted for a cross-sale by Amazon.

Let's say you bought a camera. Amazon immediately offers you a memory card. Or, if you've picked out a laptop, Amazon suggests a mouse and an external keyboard. These suggestions aren't to replace your original choice; they're helpful extras designed to make *your* life easier. Amazon is recommending the items you need, so you don't have to search for them. So as Amazon helps you, you are, in return, helping Amazon make extra sales.

Cross-selling is especially effective when the price of the additional product or service is significantly cheaper, ideally less than 20% of the initial item's price. This takes advantage of a psychological principle known as price anchoring.[38] Once we've agreed to pay $200 for an item (our anchor), an extra $20 to improve our initial product feels like a bargain.

Consider this scenario: you've decided to purchase a $219 barbecue grill. A $7 grill brush—just 3.3% of your original purchase—appears extremely affordable and helpful for a better grilling experience.

However, sometimes, cross-selling can go wrong. The most successful cross-sells are *benefits*, not *requirements*. For instance, Apple's new iPhones no longer include a charger or headphones. Headphones, like Apple's AirPods, are a great upsell because they're not essential to using your phone. However, without a charger, you can't use an iPhone. The absence of a charger has created a *forced cross-sell opportunity,* which isn't a best practice because it hurts the customer experience.

On the iPhone checkout page, you won't see a pop-up for an unrelated product, like the latest Apple Watch or MacBook. These products have nothing to do with the original purchase, and they likely exceed the customer's planned budget, highlighting the importance of careful price anchoring.

Upselling

Upselling is used to persuade customers to buy a more expensive item, upgrading their initial selection to a product that offers higher value. While cross-selling identifies additional products related to the original purchase, upselling strategies focus on replacing the initial item with one that has a higher price and higher value.

Tesla's customer experience is built on upselling strategies. When shopping for a Tesla vehicle, customers have the option to "customize your product," which serves as a gentle upsell tactic. This customization process involves a series of upsells, as every addition or upgrade increases the vehicle's final price.

Let's dive deeper into Tesla's strategy. When a customer selects a base model, Tesla gives them a number of ways to upgrade the car, like interior materials, wheel style, number of seats, or advanced self-driving features. Each upgrade not only elevates the car's functionality and luxury but also significantly raises its cost. Tesla effectively tailors the car-buying process, subtly encouraging customers to spend more for personalized upgrades.

Upselling can often fall short if it's not personalized to the customer. A common mistake is when websites resort to generic pitches like, "Hey, would you like to try this superior version?" They might support these claims with impressive stats, demonstrations, and testimonials, but if they fail to address the customer's individual needs and preferences, the upsell attempt will likely fail.

WHEN TO CROSS-SELL AND UPSELL

Upsell and cross-sell strategies can be used at every step of the customer journey (for upselling/cross-selling tools, view chapter resources), but it's important to understand when to upsell or cross-sell. Timing is crucial.

#1 Before The Purchase

Upselling can start the minute a customer visits your website. On the pages showcasing cheaper offers (remember the entry-level offers in your value pyramid), consider offering upgraded versions.

Alongside or below the main product/service, display complementary items for cross-selling. You can encourage customers to consider these additional items with non-aggressive phrases like:

- Bundle with [complementary product] and save $10
- Frequently bought together
- Complete the look with our recommended accessories
- Customers who viewed this item also bought

Cross-sell by offering a discount.

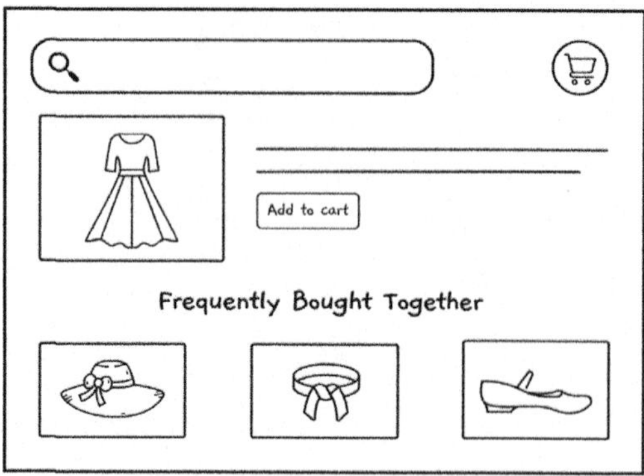

Cross-sell with recommended products.

Pre-sale upselling involves offering an "upgraded" version of the product on the product page or sales page. To encourage customers to consider these upgrades, you can use phrases such as:

- Upgrade your experience with our premium version
- Enhance your order with our deluxe package
- Take it to the next level with our advanced features
- Maximize your value with our bundled offerings
- Customize your order with these personalized upgrades

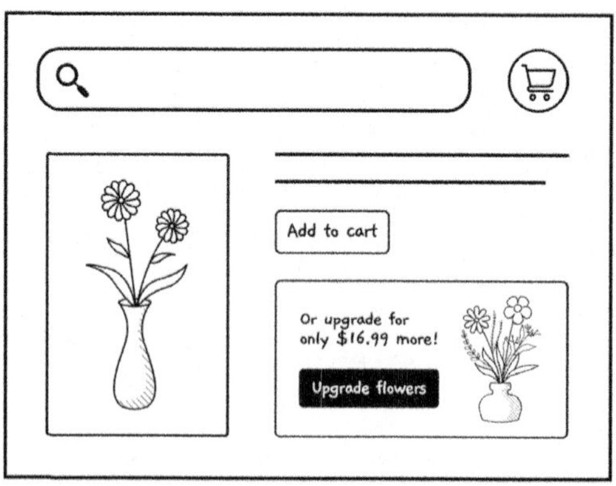

Example of an upsell before checkout.

#2 During the Purchase

The checkout phase offers an excellent opportunity for both cross-selling and upselling. When a customer is in their cart or on the checkout page, they're in a *buying mindset*. This is a prime time to introduce offers that enhance their purchase. Offers could include bulk-buy discounts, customization options, quicker shipping methods, gift-wrapping services, or extended warranties.

Your checkout process could include only three steps, keeping it streamlined and easily navigable to discourage cart abandonment. As the customer proceeds through the checkout, present a special, one-time offer (OTO) to entice them to add another product to their cart. Here's how a 3-step checkout process might look:

1. Billing Information: The customer enters their payment details.
2. Customize Order: This is where the upsell or cross-sell happens. The customer is shown a special offer or an upgraded version of their chosen product.
3. Order Complete: The customer finalizes their order, which now includes any additional items they chose in step 2.

Here's an example of a cross-sell page during the checkout process.

You could upsell by inviting the customer to upgrade their order once an item has been added to their cart. This could be done via a pop-up or a separate upsell page.

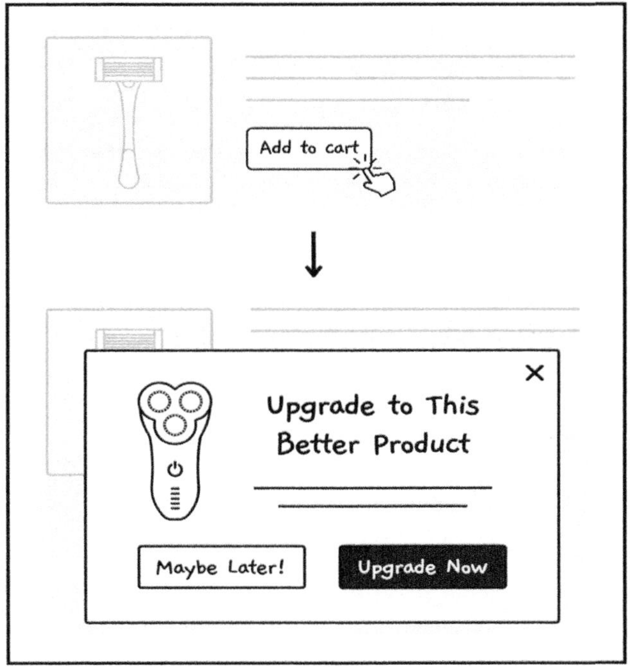

Here is an example of upselling after the initial product was added to the cart. You can also offer a limited-time discount on the upgraded product to incentivize the purchase.

#3 After The Purchase

Upselling doesn't end after the initial purchase is complete. There are still opportunities to increase the order value by offering enhancements to the customer's order after delivery. This approach works exceptionally well for digital products or software, where adding extra features or capabilities is straightforward. For instance, a customer who's just purchased a software subscription might appreciate the chance to add advanced functionality or extra storage for a small, additional cost.

For physical products, you can engage in post-purchase upselling by offering value-added services that go beyond the product. An extended warranty, for example, can provide the customer with peace of mind, knowing they are protecting their purchase beyond the standard warranty period.

Another option is to offer customers premium support services that give them access to customer service representatives, faster response times, or even on-site assistance, all of which can enhance the customer's experience with your product. By introducing these options after the purchase, you ensure the customer sees the value in their initial purchase before considering the additional offer, increasing the chance they'll take the upsell.

Thank you page option 1: offering a coupon code to incentivize the next purchase and/or add an offer wall with relevant products to cross-sell.

Thank you page option 2: cross-sell with a limited-time offer to increase the sense of urgency.

OPTIMIZE YOUR THANK YOU PAGE

Many online businesses use the Thank You page as a way to notify the customer or potential client to check their email for a purchase confirmation or download link. However, this page is the perfect spot to include a call-to-action, promote related products, and guide the visitor to other content that can lead them further down your funnel.

When a potential client takes action on your website, the last thing they'll see before they leave your site is the Thank You page. This is the moment in the customer journey when the potential client is arguably the most prepared to take further action.

Here are 4 best practices when designing your Thank You page.

1. Always be selling with an offer wall

The Thank You page on your site is an ideal place to include more calls to action. The customer is already primed to buy if they've made it to your thank you page, so it would make sense to add an offer wall, where you can cross-sell products or upsell the product for a bulk discount.

For example, if the customer just purchased a line of skincare products, you could offer an automatic renewal option that ships the same products to the customer each month without them having to place a new order.

2. Promote your original content

This doesn't apply to every brand, but if you publish original content online via a blog or similar platform, the Thank You page is a great place to promote that. Add links, a teaser, a list of topics etc. to introduce your free content and keep them interested. The longer you can keep your customers engaged on your site, the better.

3. Provide a social share option

Mentions and interactions on social media help build brand awareness and can attract more prospects to your e-commerce website. Any time you can motivate a customer to share their purchase on social media, you're getting free promotion and social proof for your brand.

4. Build your email list

If the customer is interested enough in what your business has to offer, you should be providing them with a way to get more information from you. You'd be surprised by how effective a newsletter sign-up CTA on your Thank You page can be.

As the possible last interaction with your customer on your website, a well-designed Thank You page can contribute significantly to your sales funnel's success. By continually selling, promoting original content, enabling social sharing, and expanding your email list, you can leverage this often-underused page to enhance the customer experience and drive growth.

CHAPTER RESOURCES

Action Items

1. Choose to implement one method of reducing the pain of paying, like paying in advance, bundling products, or setting a free shipping threshold.
2. Tweak the checkout experience by including multiple payment options and offering a guest checkout feature. Depending on your business model, add a 1-click checkout option through your website platform or use an external integration (view details under relevant tools) to streamline the experience.

3. Determine products/offers that provide cross-selling and upselling opportunities for customers and implement them on your website (view relevant tools for more details).
4. Craft an abandoned cart sequence, starting with at least one well-crafted email or text. You can expand this sequence over time. Most email marketing platforms provide abandoned cart templates that you can use.
5. Choose what main action you want a customer to take from your Thank You page (i.e. connect on social media, purchase again with a coupon code etc.). Make the CTA clear and prominent so customers take action.

RELEVANT TOOL

General tools to get you started:

- **Stripe**, **Bolt** and **Shopify's Shop Pay** are just a few examples of tools that provide seamless 1-click checkout experiences for customers.
- **GetResponse** is a marketing suite that generates product recommendations, one-click upsell pages, abandoned cart emails and more (you'll need the Ecommerce Marketing plan).
- **SamCart** optimizes the checkout process with features like order bumps, 1-click checkout, express checkout, embedded checkout, pop-up checkout and more.
- **ThriveCart** offers advanced e-commerce features including customizable checkout pages, one-click upsells, order bumps, affiliate management, and integration with membership platforms.

- **Builderall** is an all-in-one marketing and funnel building platform with a suite of over 40 tools including upsells/downsells, optimized checkout, chatbots, click maps and more.
- **ConvertFlow** is a funnel builder that lets you create cart upsells, crossells, expiring offers, post-purchase funnels and more.
- **Recharge** is a Shopify app for membership and subscription services. It offers a range of features, from customizable bundles to adding one-time items to subscription orders.
- **Revy** and **Bundle Builder** are Shopify apps that help you increase average order values through customized bundles, cross-sells, upsells and more.

Additional AI-powered tools:

- **Yuspify** uses AI to analyze customer behavior and automatically offers personalized product recommendations that are tailored to each individual.
- **Aidaptive** is a Shopify app that uses AI to predict visitor preferences, customize web experiences based on real-time behavior, and adjust product placements accordingly.
- **Insight7** is an AI-powered customer insights tool that extracts patterns from data, prioritizes action items, and visualizes insights for faster decision-making.
- **Blend AI Studio**, **PhotoShoot.ai**, and **Pebblely** all help you to generate professional product photos quickly in just a few clicks.

ChatGPT EXAMPLE PROMPTS

Example 1

"You run an online store specializing in smart sleep products, catering to customers who seek enhanced sleep experiences. Your store features a range of cutting-edge products, including smart pillows, smart blankets, sleep trackers, smart sleep masks, and smart alarm clocks. Develop three unique bundle options that combine various products to target different customer needs and preferences. Craft enticing descriptions for each bundle, outlining the included products' benefits and how they work together to provide an elevated sleep experience."

Example 2

"You are an e-commerce consultant who specializes in optimizing websites to increase stores' average order value. Your goal is to help me brainstorm cross-selling strategies for an online gourmet pet food business. The core offer is gourmet cat and dog meals made with fresh, high-quality ingredients. Potential cross-selling products include mix-ins and toppers, portion control bowls, interactive feeding toys, measuring scoops, and a meal delivery subscription plan. Now brainstorm 5 different and unique approaches for a digital cross-selling strategy."

Example 3

"Using the data provided in the uploaded Excel sheet, analyze the product price, average shipping cost, and average order value from my e-commerce store. Your task is to determine the ideal amount for a "Free Shipping" threshold." (To upload Excel files, use the *ChatGPT File Uploader Extended* Chrome extension. For more ChatGPT extensions, view Chapter 16).

8

THE RED BULL EFFECT

The Power of Customer Loyalty

The slogan "Red Bull Gives You Wings" has guided Red Bull's customer experience since its establishment in 1987. Its remarkable customer experience is driven by adrenaline-boosting content through platforms like Reality Sports TV and engaging social media campaigns. They mastered the art of marketing that goes beyond being just an energy drink company by creating an approach that puts the customer first.

As Red Bull expanded, it embraced a customer-focused mindset in everything it did. From sponsoring football clubs and running skydiving camps, to having their own Formula One team, Red Bull fostered a global community centered on the thrill-seeking lifestyle they promote. Because of this, 81% of their customers, especially those in the Gen Z age group, are loyal to the Red Bull brand.[39]

But what makes Red Bull fans so loyal? Because the brand knows its customers inside and out. Red Bull has established emotional connections with their audience through exhilarating content. Red Bull keeps fans coming back for more by listening to what they want.

The Red Bull case serves as a testament to the crucial role of loyalty in the sales funnel. Loyalty drives customers to move up the value pyramid, allowing businesses to sell to them continuously and nurture long-term relationships. Just like Red Bull has cultivated an unwavering fan base, you can leverage loyalty to create a steady stream of repeat purchases and higher-value transactions.

TYPES OF CUSTOMER LOYALTY

Customer loyalty can be categorized into two main groups: behavioral loyalty (based on actions) and emotional loyalty (based on feelings). To get the best results, a winning strategy should foster a certain degree of behavioral loyalty, but should prioritize developing the emotional bonds that customers form with your brand.

Behavioral loyalty involves consistent behavior towards a specific brand. This behavior can include repeat purchases of certain products or frequent visits to a particular store. Most loyalty programs are designed to turn those behaviors into a habit.

Emotional loyalty goes beyond behavior and focuses on the emotional bonds customers develop with a business. These connections can keep customers spending money with a brand, even when no immediate financial incentives are present. Emotional loyalty is built on trust, satisfaction, and a genuine connection.

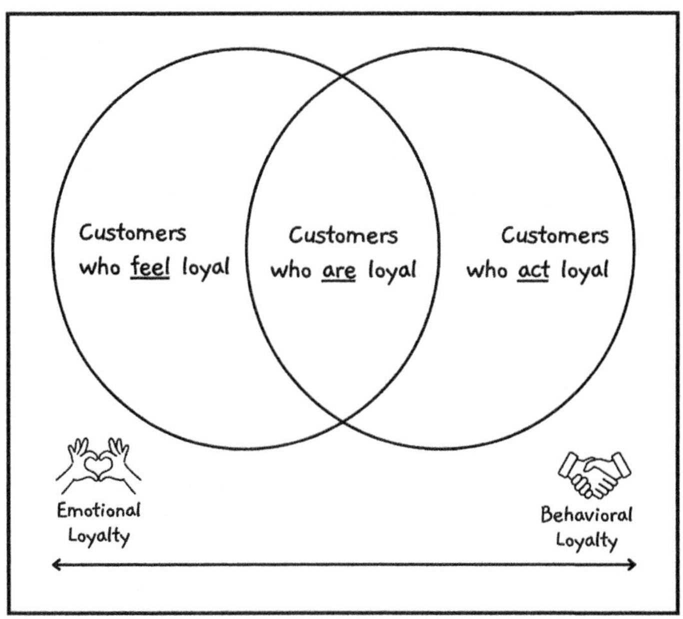

Emotional vs. Behavioral Loyalty

Why Emotional Loyalty is The Key to a Thriving Sales Funnel

The key to business growth lies in developing emotional loyalty rather than solely relying on customer habits. Consider the previous chapter that dealt with the psychology of purchase. Without an emotional connection, customers may not feel strongly enough to stick with a brand and could easily switch to competitors.

Emotionally loyal customers don't come back just because it's convenient or because you offer better deals. They come back because they genuinely care about your brand. According to consumer loyalty experts, "brand commitment is an emotional or psychological attachment to a brand within a product class, and appears to result from felt concern or ego involvement with the product or purchase decision."[40]

Emotional loyalty gives us a deeper understanding of why customers behave the way they do and how they feel about your brand. It goes beyond simple rewards and points, creating a strong bond that makes customers feel valued and respected. From a psychological perspective, feeling recognized and appreciated is essential for building successful relationships, which leads to increased commitment and dedication.

HOW TO FOSTER EMOTIONAL LOYALTY

1. Trust

Businesses can actively build trust throughout the entire customer journey by communicating clearly, providing quality products, offering helpful customer service, and implementing a loyalty program with meaningful benefits.

A prime example of a brand implementing this approach is the outdoor gear brand, Patagonia. Unlike traditional loyalty programs that focus on driving more purchases, Patagonia prioritizes ethics and trust. Its loyalty program, Worn Wear, motivates customers to repair and reuse clothing rather than buy new items. Customers earn points for trading in used gear that they can redeem for future discounts. As a result, Patagonia fosters trust by offering customers beneficial incentives while acting on their environmentally-conscious values.

2. Connection

A well-thought-out loyalty program fosters a deep emotional connection between customers and the brand. When customers have a strong emotional attachment to a brand, they are less likely to be swayed by competitors who may offer better deals or promotions.

Mastercard's Pay With Rewards program is a great illustration of this concept. The program allows cardholders to use their reward points to pay for purchases at participating merchants. With Pay With Rewards, members can use their points for a night out, covering expenses such as cab rides and dining at partner restaurants. Experience-based benefits are a big part of the loyalty program because they help people feel closer to the brand. This program ensures that every interaction with Mastercard becomes a *rewarding experience*, strengthening the emotional bond between the customer and the brand.

3. Affinity

Connection reflects the level of liking or appreciation that members have towards a particular brand. Building affinity requires the creation of exclusive experiences tailored to the customer's lifestyle.

For instance, Sephora has successfully cultivated a strong sense of connection with its customers through its Beauty Insider loyalty program. Sephora offers exclusive perks and rewards to its members, such as early access to new product launches, personalized recommendations, and invitations to special beauty events. By providing these unique experiences and benefits,

Sephora deepens the connection between its customers and the brand, fostering a sense of affinity and loyalty.

4. Acknowledgment

Acknowledgment plays a key role in nurturing emotional loyalty within your loyalty program. While offering perks and rewards for purchases is important, it is equally essential to acknowledge and reward every action your members have taken.

Take Hilton Honors, for instance. As new members join the program, they are welcomed with a generous bonus of 1,500 points, kick-starting their journey towards their first reward. This gesture makes members feel seen and valued and creates a sense of progress toward their goal, boosting their motivation to engage in the program. By consistently recognizing their actions, and giving points for a variety of purchases, Hilton Honors strengthens the emotional connection and loyalty of its members.

5. Lasting Impressions

Creating a lasting and memorable customer experience is vital to fostering emotional loyalty. It requires going beyond a transactional approach and recognizing the broader emotional journey that your product or service supports.

Airline loyalty programs are a great example of how brands can address the positive and negative emotions associated with their offerings. These programs prioritize customer experience and satisfaction by offering core benefits that aim to reduce the stress related to travel. Features such as priority boarding and access to private airline lounges create a sense of exclusivity and comfort, leaving a positive and lasting impression on loyalty program members. By catering to the emotional needs of customers and enhancing their overall travel experience, airlines can build a strong foundation of emotional loyalty.

LOYALTY PSYCHOLOGY

When we understand how consumers shop, what they think, and what they believe, we can increase the likelihood of creating a strong emotional connection with them. This connection encourages customers to keep coming back and making repeat purchases.

By using the following 4 theories of consumer psychology, you can develop a loyalty program that is exciting and valuable for everyone involved.

Means-End Chain Theory

Jonathan Gutman, a teacher at the University of Southern California, developed the means-end chain theory.[41] According to this model, customers consider their purchases as steps that help them reach their goals. The result is a value chain that connects the practical benefits of a product to the emotional outcomes that align with people's personal values.

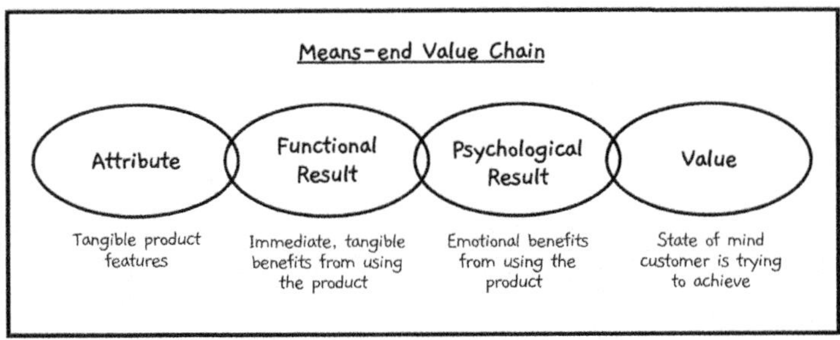

This theory shows that many shoppers value things more if they are hard to get. This idea is called the Scarcity Effect. So, rewards or special offers that are only for certain people, like members of a loyalty program, are usually highly valued.

For instance, The Body Shop gives its loyalty program members special product bundles, called Lucky Bundles, with irresistible discounts. This encourages non-members to join the program. The value chain begins with a product attribute, such as the Lucky Bundle containing multiple products in a set. The functional result of this is that the Lucky Bundle offers a wider variety of products for customers to try. The psychosocial, or emotional, result of having a wider variety is that "I feel excited and exclusive when I get it." Finally, this exclusive feeling might appeal to the personal satisfaction and the thrill of getting special deals.

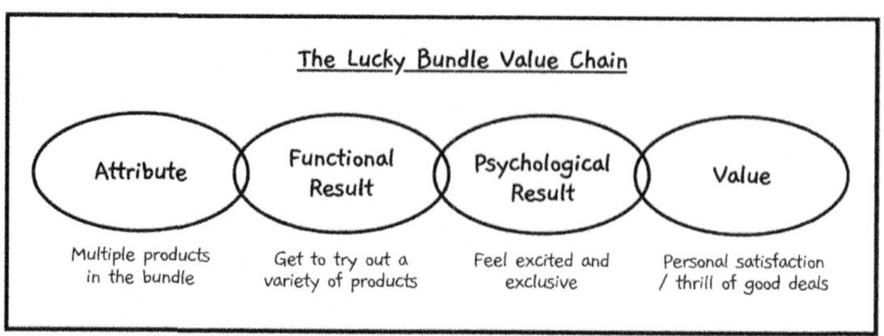

Cognitive Dissonance Theory

In simple terms, Leon Festinger's cognitive dissonance theory says that when expectations do not match reality, people tend to feel strong negative emotions like regret.[42] Festinger suggested that we all want our daily thoughts and experiences to be consistent.

So, the lesson is that being consistent in what we say and do can help reduce negative emotions in our customers, making them more loyal. For loyalty programs, this means giving people rewards and services that really matter to them and delivering them *reliably,* consistently and on time. If this doesn't happen, customers will feel disappointed and may stop using the service.

Take IKEA's loyalty program, IKEA Family, as an example. They offer several benefits to their members. They get big discounts and free coffee during shopping trips, as well as access to many home design services. If any purchases get damaged while being transported or put together, members have four weeks to return them. This perk lowers the possibility of customer regret because they see IKEA as a reliable store.

The Goal-Gradient Effect

First introduced by psychologist Clark Hull, the goal-gradient effect says that when people get close to reaching a goal, they work faster to get there.[43] This means, when a target is within reach, people are more motivated to push towards it.

Customers often do more when they're close to the next reward or level in a program. This is one of the most important things to consider when creating reward programs. If you give bigger rewards as customers get closer to their goal, they'll be more excited and involved. This strategy is sometimes called "tier sprints" or "point sprints." Point springs are often used in programs run by airlines and hotels, where customers try to get to the next level for better rewards.

Starbucks, for instance, has a smart way to get customers excited and more engaged. They show customers a visual progress tracker that lets them see how much they've already done—like how many cups of coffee they've bought and how many points they've earned.

But Starbucks doesn't stop there. They also tell customers how much more they need to do to reach the next goal or reward, like a free drink. This is known as Goal Gradient communication. These two strategies, when used together, make customers want to keep going and reach the next level. They create a kind of race where customers are encouraged to buy more and more to reach the finish line.

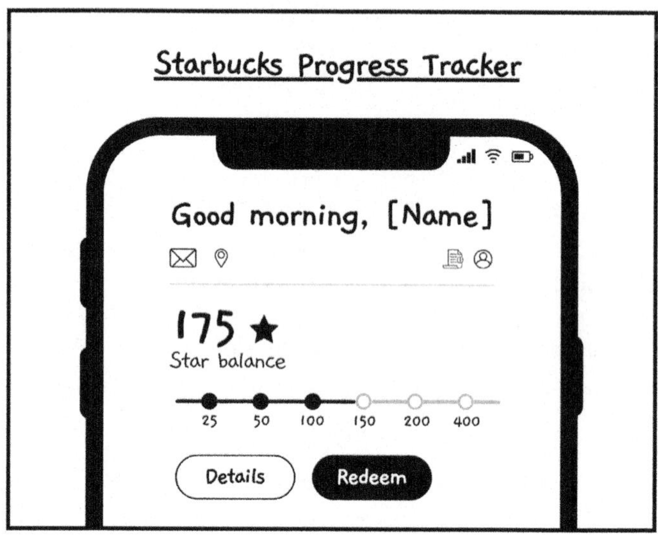

Endowed Progress Effect

The endowed progress effect highlights the idea that, when people feel like they're initially making progress toward a goal, they're more likely to continue working toward it.[44] Studying this concept, researchers found that even artificial advancement can boost someone's motivation to stay involved.

Both loyalty cards require 7 purchases for free ice cream...
FREE
FREE
10-stamp card with 2 artificially completed stamps
8-stamp card with no artificially completed stamps
This one is proven to be more motivating

The illusion of progress is motivating.

The key insight here is that offering points upfront or starting at a specific membership level upon joining can enhance member engagement. In a study involving car wash punch cards, providing the first two punches at the beginning led to a 15% increase in fully redeemed cards.

To illustrate, consider the strategy used by Sonesta Travel Pass. When new members join, they're immediately given a welcome bonus of 1,000 points. This jump-start gives them a taste of earning rewards and sets them on the path toward their first redeemable reward, which increases their engagement with the program.

THREE WAYS TO CULTIVATE EMOTIONAL LOYALTY

#1 Surprise and Delight

The surprise and delight approach is a popular marketing strategy that enhances customer interactions by offering unexpected rewards. This approach capitalizes on the fact that people tend to remember surprising events more than ordinary ones. With this approach, some businesses use gamification to actively engage customers and seamlessly integrate rewards into the overall customer experience.

For example, Subway launched a gamified brand awareness campaign in Australia and New Zealand called "Sink a Sub." The campaign introduced a game app inspired by the classic Battleships game, where players aimed to "sink" virtual subway sandwiches instead of ships. As participants played the game, they were rewarded with prizes, ranging from free drink upgrades to the chance of winning $10,000 in cash.

#2 Reward Customer Trust

Rewarding customers for their trust is an important step in generating emotional loyalty. To do it well, you need to know the right time to send your message to each member. Once again, timing is everything. For example, you can celebrate customers' milestones by rewarding them on their one-year anniversary with your brand or sending a bonus for their 100th purchase. You can also use your brand's anniversary as a milestone to celebrate with your loyal customers.

For example, Thrive Market, an online health food retailer, celebrated its 5th anniversary by rewarding its loyal customers. During Thrive Market's anniversary month, it offered exclusive discounts, free gifts, and special promotions to its loyal members as a way to express gratitude for their continued support. This initiative strengthened the emotional bond between Thrive Market and its customers.

#3 Create a Strong Community

Developing a loyalty program with different levels and rewards is similar to building a community. By fostering this sense of community, customers will feel more connected and involved with your brand. For example, you can do this by using a name and design that matches your brand's identity to describe the program.

For example, The North Face's XPLR Pass fosters a strong community of outdoor enthusiasts. Members get early access to new products, and they get invited to special events and community building "Trail Days." The program keeps members engaged through outdoor challenges, virtual expeditions, and personalized recommendations. Top-performing members can even win unique outdoor experiences and gain priority access to limited-edition gear. These activities help build a close-knit community of adventure seekers.

HOW TO DESIGN YOUR LOYALTY FRAMEWORK

Now that we've discussed how loyalty programs help businesses grow, let's explore the key factors to consider when designing one. This step-by-step framework will give you the key elements necessary to build a strong loyalty program.

STEP 1

Pick Your Loyalty Program

Most loyalty program tools (more details in chapter resources) offer diverse formats, including:

- **Point-based**: Members earn points by making purchases and can later use those points to get rewards.
- **Tier-based**: Members are assigned different levels based on how much they spend, and each level comes with its own set of benefits.
- **Cashback**: When members spend a certain amount, they receive a percentage of their money back as either cash or a coupon they can use for future purchases.
- **Paid**: Also known as a subscription program, members pay a regular fee to access exclusive program benefits.
- **Hybrid**: This type combines different elements, such as points, tiers, and cashback to provide a variety of rewards and benefits.
- **Group**: A program where a parent company offers a shared loyalty program that can be used across multiple brands within the group.
- **Coalition**: A partnership between unrelated brands where they collaborate to create a joint loyalty program.

Action Items:

1. Consider your products or services: Think about what you sell and how customers use it. Pick a loyalty program that matches what you offer and provides value to customers.
2. Assess your resources: Look at what you have available in terms of money and technology. Make sure you can

handle the loyalty program format you have chosen without any problems.

3. Check out the competition: See what other businesses are doing with their loyalty programs. Find ways to stand out and be different from them.
4. Plan your budget: Identify how much you can spend on the loyalty program. Consider costs like technology, rewards, and ongoing management.

STEP 2

Balance Reward Value

Next, you should consider the value of the rewards you will offer to customers. There are four categories based on their worth to the end user:

- **High value**: These rewards are reserved for a select few customers. For example, an exclusive invitation to a virtual event with a renowned industry expert or a personalized consultation session.
- **Medium value**: These rewards fall in the middle range. An example could be a birthday gift package containing special products or bundles.
- **Low value**: These rewards may be small in value but still meaningful. They can include discounts on specific items or vouchers that can be used across different channels.
- **Free rewards**: These rewards don't require payment and can provide customers with a sense of belonging to a group. For instance, e-badges or digital badges that customers can earn and display.

By balancing your reward offerings across these categories, you can provide a range of options that cater to different customer preferences and enhance their overall experience.

Action Items:

1. Generate a list of potential reward options for each value category (high, medium, low, free) based on your understanding of your ICAs. Consider their preferences, behaviors, and demographics.
2. Remove any reward options that don't align with your brand identity. For example, if you have an eco-friendly e-commerce store, on-brand rewards could include discounts for biodegradable products or exclusive access to sustainability-focused events.

STEP 3

Define Reward Accessibility

Now you need to set limits or boundaries for your rewards program. Your reward program is another basis for customer trust and loyalty. Not being able to fulfill the promises you've made in the reward program offer can seriously disintegrate trust and ultimately affect customer progress through the funnel. Think about what you can realistically offer to your customers based on what you have available.

Consider how many products you have, how much it costs to ship them, and how much you can handle. By setting clear limits, you make sure your rewards program is affordable and manageable for your business. Some limitations to consider for your program include the following:

- **Time constraints**: Adding a time limit to your rewards creates a sense of urgency and encourages customers to redeem them sooner. By setting an expiration date, you can increase the likelihood of customers taking action and using their rewards quickly.
- **Quantity constraints**: When you have a limited quantity of rewards available, it creates a sense of exclusivity and drives customers to compete for them.
- **Tier constraints**: Implementing rewards based on different tiers or levels of loyalty motivates customers to strive for higher tiers. By offering exclusive rewards or benefits to customers who reach certain levels, you create a sense of achievement and progression within your loyalty program.

Action Items:

1. Define your constraints: Set limitations for your loyalty program by establishing time, quantity, and tier restrictions to create a sense of urgency, scarcity, and exclusivity, which drives engagement.
2. Monitor and adjust: Continuously track customer engagement, redemption rates, and feedback to identify areas for improvement. Make adjustments to your constraints as needed to optimize the program's effectiveness.
3. Seek customer feedback: Collect feedback from your loyalty program participants to understand their perceptions of the constraints. Use this feedback to

refine your loyalty program constraints and improve the overall customer experience.

CHAPTER RESOURCES

Action Items

1. Pick your reward program format by considering your offers, customer preferences, competitors, and budget.
2. Brainstorm a list of feasible loyalty rewards for each value category (high, medium, low, free) and then pick the ones that most appeal to your ICA.
3. Define loyalty program constraints (i.e. time, quantity, or tier limits).
4. Collect participant feedback to understand pain points and frictions. This feedback will help you refine the loyalty program and improve the overall experience.

RELEVANT TOOLS

General tools to get you started:

- **Yotpo**, **LoyaltyLion**, **Smile.io** and **Marsello** provide loyalty solutions that help you create different loyalty programs and other initiatives like gift cards. They support various e-commerce platforms, like Shopify, Shopify Plus, BigCommerce, WooCommerce and more.
- **ReferralCandy** drives growth with referral programs, where loyal customers are incentivized with rewards for successful referrals.
- **VYPER** helps you launch digital contests, giveaways & reward programs to foster brand loyalty.

- **SurveySparrow**, **Survicate** and **Emojics** (emoji-based) are customer feedback platforms that let you create and distribute surveys to gather feedback from customers.
- Most email/text marketing platforms (like **Mailchimp, Klaviyo, GetResponse, SendPulse, ManyChat** etc.) let you send personalized emails to your loyalty program members. You can use it to communicate exclusive offers, rewards, and updates to your customers.

Additional AI-powered tools

- **RealFeedback** is a ChatGPT-driven chatbot that engages users conversationally to collect valuable insights to help you improve the customer experience and boost loyalty.
- **Monterey** and **BetterFeedback** use AI to streamline data analysis and user feedback so you can address customer pain points, laying the groundwork for brand loyalty.

This is a particular area where, surprisingly, there are very few AI tools for small businesses. However, it's worth mentioning Antavo and Capillary Intelligent Loyalty, although at the time of publishing this book, these tools were still priced mainly for larger enterprises.

ChatGPT EXAMPLE PROMPTS

Example 1

"Imagine you run an online store that sells sustainable, non-toxic cleaning products. The target audience is parents who prioritize a safe and healthy environment for their children, seeking products that minimize exposure to harmful chemicals. Based on the business and target audience, determine the top 3 loyalty program structures that will most likely perform the best. Some loyalty program structures to consider include points-based, tier-based, cashback, a subscription program, hybrid, group, coalition etc. Make sure to explain why your top 3 choices are optimal for this particular target audience."

Example 2

"My company specializes in virtual craft workshops and DIY project kits. Generate a list of 15 community-building initiatives for customers who have purchased from my business. Focus on strategies that encourage interaction, collaboration, and a supportive atmosphere among the customer base."

Example 3

"Brainstorm 5 different strategies for using the Endowed Progress Effect to encourage repeat purchases for an online travel gear store. How can the store incorporate this psychological phenomenon to create a more engaging shopping experience and increase customer retention? The ideas should be specific, innovative, and travel-related."

Part II

PRO FUNNELS

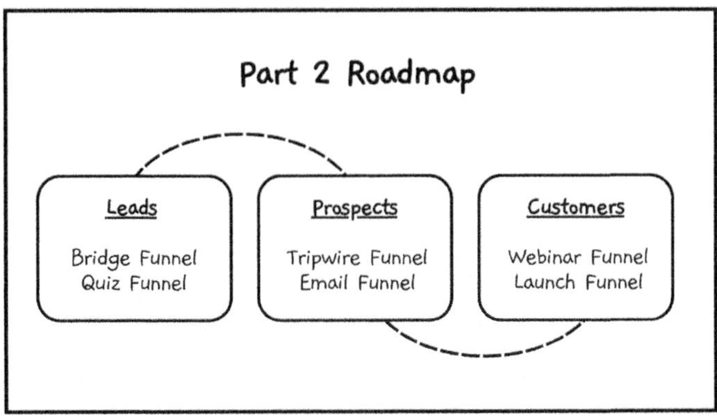

In Part II, we'll expand our horizons, looking beyond the sales funnel to explore six additional Power Funnels. Each of these six pro funnels has the potential to boost your marketing strategy, but not all of them will work with your particular business or offers. Still, this book gives you a full arsenal of strategies and the flexibility to choose which strategies work best for you. Feel free to skip ahead and read the chapters you think will be most helpful. If you're not sure where to start, here is a brief overview of the purpose and benefits of each pro funnel.

A **Bridge Funnel** can be a great fit for your business if you're looking to engage with cold traffic. This funnel acts as a bridge that creates a positive first impression with visitors who are unfamiliar with your brand and offerings. This initial touchpoint, referred to as the "pre-frame", influences their brand perception, and by pre-framing cold traffic, you can convert them more easily. Given that cold traffic is more difficult to convert than warm traffic, consider building your bridge funnel after you're confident in the traffic generation strategies you implemented from Chapter 3.

A **Quiz Funnel** is an engaging way to gather valuable insights about the needs or preferences of your website visitors, helping you to identify and streamline your ICAs. By guiding visitors through a series of interactive questions, quiz funnels help potential customers discover products or services that are tailored *specifically for them.* This funnel is most effective if: 1) your business has an extensive (and possibly overwhelming) range of products or 2) your business caters to people who know little about the field and will want product suggestions.

A **Tripwire Funnel** is a strategic approach for turning prospects into customers. You can convert people who might initially hesitate to purchase by enticing them with an irresistible low-cost offer. This funnel is especially useful if your business has many high-priced offers or if you cater to price-sensitive customers. A tripwire funnel is a powerful tool for acquiring customers, drawing in a wider audience that gradually becomes more interested in your brand.

An **Email Funnel** is an ongoing strategy to engage customers who are familiar with and interested in your brand. This funnel works best if you have a hot/loyal audience and want to foster deeper connections with them. The main goal of an Email Funnel is to strengthen relationships, but you can also use it to transition your audience into other funnels, guiding them up your value pyramid (more on creating a sequence of funnels in Chapter 15).

A **Webinar Funnel** is an accessible, convenient way to engage with potential customers. This funnel is used to deliver content that helps participants understand why your offer can help them reach their goals. A Webinar Funnel is particularly useful if your business sells complex or high-priced offerings. This is because you can provide detailed explanations, demonstrations, and interactive content that get participants excited about the solutions you provide.

A **Launch Funnel** builds momentum for your new product or service. This funnel generates anticipation among your existing audience as you design a series of pre- and post-launch content. Whether you're currently developing a new offer or are ready to introduce it, the Launch Funnel uses psychological triggers to increase conversions.

Think of the sales funnel and these pro funnels as closely related stages of the customer journey. These pro funnels complement your sales funnel, adding depth and variety to your strategy. While they are entirely optional, as you scale your business, you may find them incredibly useful in streamlining your processes and boosting conversions.

The six Power Funnels we will cover in this section are not all-purpose tools; they have specific strengths, depending on the customer journey stage. For customers in the early stages, who are still familiarizing themselves with your brand, Bridge and Quiz Funnels can be highly effective. When dealing with prospects, Tripwire and Email Funnels can provide that final nudge. Last, for upselling to your existing customers, Webinar and Launch Funnels are great choices. Keep in mind, these categorizations aren't hard and fast rules; experiment to find what works best for you.

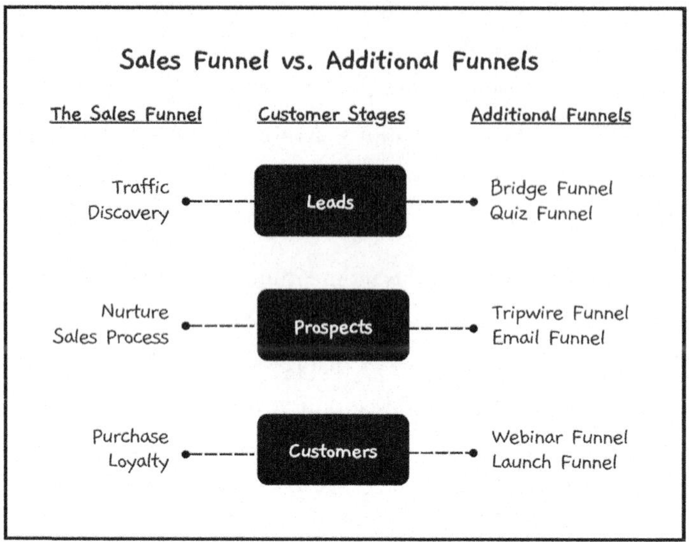

Once we've examined all the Power Funnels, we'll take a step further to explore the concept of Funnel Sequences. Funnel sequencing is the process of putting together multiple funnels in a logical order, using the momentum from one funnel to drive people to the next. The goal is to make upselling as easy as possible, allowing you to guide customers naturally toward higher-value offers.

Finally, we'll look at how you can use AI to streamline Power Funnels. Manual management is always an option, but AI helps reduce repetitive tasks and optimizes conversions. It's about working smarter, not harder, allowing you to focus on what matters most in your business.

By the end of Part 2, you'll have all the tools you'll need to build dynamic, responsive Power Funnels tailored to your unique business needs.

9

WARM OR COLD

Bridge Funnels

Setting the stage matters. A lot.

There's no better example than a study conducted at an MIT economics course.[45] The students were told their regular professor was out of town; instead, they would have a substitute teacher they had never met.

The college representative explained, "We're interested in seeing how different classes respond to different teachers. So today, we've got a new instructor for you." At the end of the session, the students would have to give feedback on this substitute.

To help them understand who this substitute was, students were given one of two short descriptions of him that listed countless economic achievements. But, they didn't know that the two descriptions had a minor difference.

Half the class received a description with the last sentence stating: "People who know him consider him to be a very warm person, industrious, critical, practical, and determined." The other half received an almost identical description with just two words changed at the end of the bio: "People who know him consider him to be a rather cold person, industrious, critical, practical, and determined."

The two versions were different when describing the substitute's personality— "very warm" or "rather cold." The substitute then taught the class, and at the end, students were asked to evaluate him.

Most students who got the "warm" description loved the substitute. They saw him as friendly, funny, and kind. On the other hand, the group with the "cold" description didn't like the instructor, even though they experienced the same class. They viewed him as self-absorbed, formal, and irritable.

This shows that *one single word* can change our entire opinion of someone, possibly affecting the relationship before it has even started. Even the smallest bit of information we get about a person or a business, often referred to as a "pre-frame," has the power to shape our judgments.

That's why it's essential to create a positive pre-frame for new customers. It can build trust and goodwill. On the other hand, a negative pre-frame can push customers away, making them think poorly of your business.

That's where a bridge funnel comes in. It helps you prepare cold traffic for what you really want to sell: your offer. It acts as a bridge, taking them from not knowing about your product or service to having a positive first impression of it. This smooth transition increases the chances of turning them into happy customers who are eager to buy from you.

The key element of any bridge funnel is your bridge page. This page essentially "bridges the gap" between where your cold traffic is coming from and your offer page (this can be a tripwire, sales page, product page, etc.)

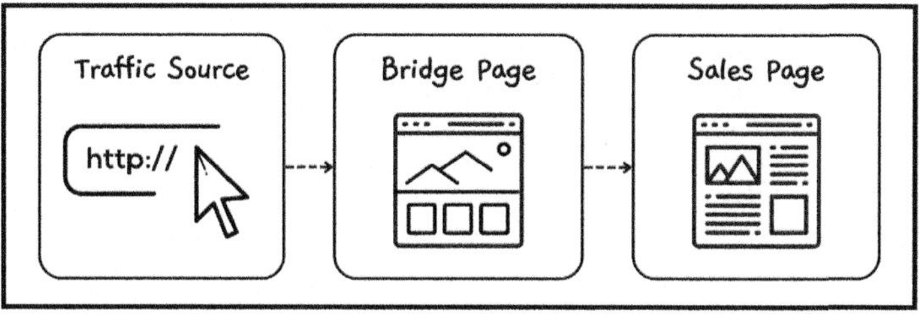

BRIDGE PAGE VS. LANDING PAGE

If cold traffic is being directed to a bridge page, isn't that just a landing page? Yes and no. A bridge page is one *type* of landing page, but not all landing pages are bridge pages. The crucial difference lies in their overall purpose.

Landing pages have one primary goal: lead generation. For lead generation, the landing page aims to collect information from visitors, typically their email addresses, for future email marketing campaigns.

A bridge page serves a different purpose: to warm up cold traffic and get them ready for a potential purchase. In short, bridge pages help people *buy into* a product before actually buying the product.

ELEMENTS OF A GOOD BRIDGE PAGE

Your bridge page will change depending on your audience and product, but there are common elements that work effectively regardless of your niche. A great bridge page should include the following elements:

- **A strong heading**: The heading is the first thing people see, so it should be short, catchy, and in line with your brand's tone.
- **Speak to your ICAs**: Understand your audience's preferences, pain points, or goals. Tailor your bridge page to communicate your message to *your ICAs.*
- **Why you're different**: Highlight what sets your product or service apart from the competition. Show your audience why they should choose you over others.
- **Serve before selling**: Remember, the goal of a bridge page is to educate visitors about your brand and your offerings and show how your product solves their problems. Avoid being overly pushy—your visitors should not feel pressured into making a purchase. Focus on providing valuable information and building a relationship with them.
- **Clear call to action**: Lead your visitors to *one* simple call to action. This could be a "Try It Now" or "Get Started" for a subscription service. Alternatively, your CTA could be "Explore Options" or "Shop Now" to direct them to your product page.

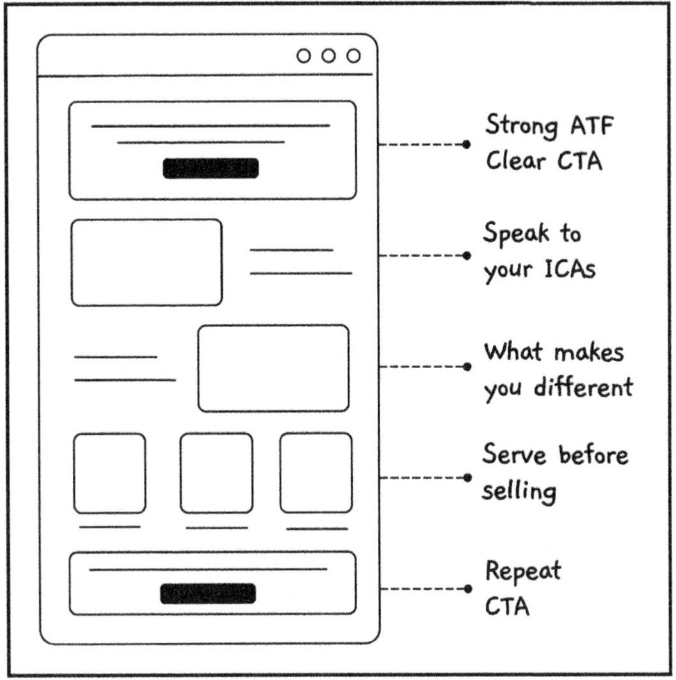

Bridge Page Anatomy

HELLO FRESH BRIDGE FUNNEL

Now that we're familiar with the components of a bridge funnel, let's see it in action with HelloFresh, a meal kit service.

If you enter "meal box," "food box," or "meal kit" in Google's search bar, you'll notice HelloFresh's sponsored link displayed at the top. Once you click on the link, HelloFresh will consider you as cold traffic, since you didn't directly search for their brand name, suggesting that you may not be familiar with them.

Because you are considered cold traffic, the link will take you to a bridge page rather than their home page. Right away, above the fold, you see:

- *The heading*: "HelloFresh Is The Go-To Meal Solution For Every Occasion"
- *The subheading*: "Fresh, pre-portioned ingredients and delicious recipes delivered to your door.
- *CTA:* "Explore Plans"

The heading immediately captures the visitor's attention by presenting HelloFresh as the ultimate meal solution for any situation. It creates a sense of reliability and convenience, suggesting that HelloFresh can cater to various needs, making it an attractive option for all types of occasions or diets. The subheading emphasizes "freshness" and convenience, which further pre-frames HelloFresh in an attractive way.

The CTA is also clear and inviting. As opposed to a more aggressive statement, like "Buy Now," HelloFresh gently prompts visitors to "explore". This phrase doesn't put pressure on the visitor to make a purchase.

When you scroll down, the bridge page contains 4 sections that pre-frame their service as the optimal meal kit choice.

PART 1

Pain Points (Speak to your ICAs)

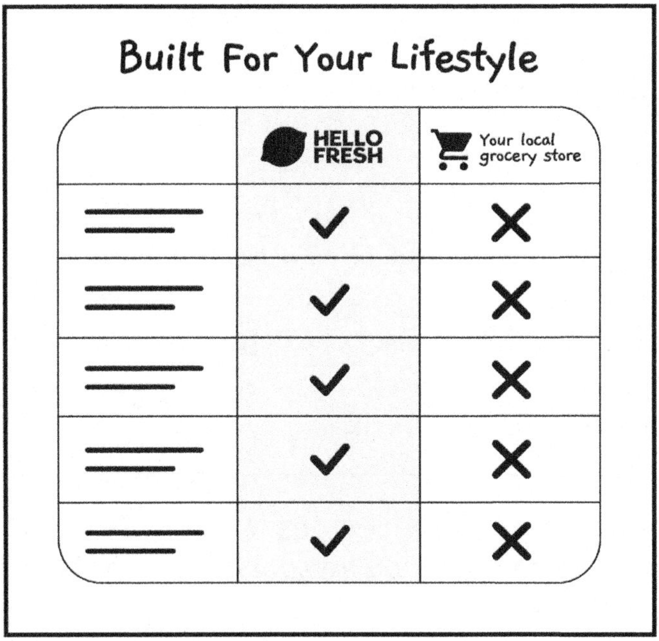

Built For Your Lifestyle

	HELLO FRESH	Your local grocery store
	✓	✗
	✓	✗
	✓	✗
	✓	✗
	✓	✗

In this section, HelloFresh presents a comparison chart to show visitors what makes HelloFresh different. This is important because it provides valuable context to visitors who are unfamiliar with the brand and are unsure how it's different from regular grocery shopping.

PART 2

Why Hello Fresh (Differentiator)

The following part of the page is straightforwardly labeled "Why HelloFresh?" Beneath the heading, three categories highlight the key aspects: time-saving, variety of options, and convenience. Instead of lengthy explanations, HelloFresh keeps its differentiators concise and accessible, using eye-catching visuals to engage visitors and encourage them to continue scrolling.

PART 3

What They Offer (Serve Before Selling)

HelloFresh recognizes that cold traffic might not be ready to make a purchase. Instead of immediately showing meal plan options, they cleverly display examples of recipes that could be in your meal kit. This spikes curiosity and gets you enthusiastic about the potential meals you could cook. Remember, you need to *serve* cold traffic before you sell to them.

Rather than simply saying they have various delicious recipes, HelloFresh shows you their selection of recipes. This encourages you to interact with their content and become curious about the service.

PART 4

Final Call to Action

- *Heading:* "Get everything you need to cook delicious meals delivered to your door!"
- *Repeat CTA:* "Explore Plans"

This final section of HelloFresh's bridge page is highly effective because it presents a compelling heading that reinforces the value proposition. The heading succinctly conveys the key benefit of HelloFresh's service – convenience and access to all the essentials for preparing tasty dishes delivered directly to the customer's doorstep.

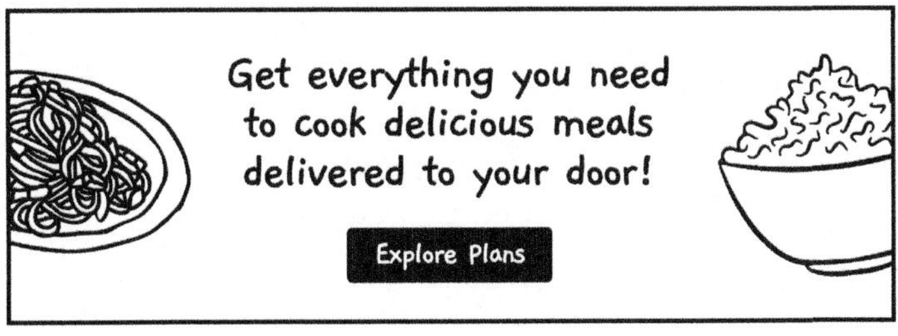

By repeating the CTA of "Explore Plans," HelloFresh encourages the visitor to take the next step and explore their meal plan options. Having a clear and prominent CTA at the end of your bridge page is essential because it guides the potential customer to the desired action. In this case, the action is exploring HelloFresh's plans. Without a final CTA, visitors may not know what to do next, leading to a missed opportunity for HelloFresh to convert cold traffic into warm leads or customers.

CHAPTER RESOURCES

Action Items

1. Create at least two versions of your bridge page heading. Test the headings using A/B testing to gauge how each version affects engagement.
2. Identify whether your ICAs prefer videos or text content, mobile or desktop experience, and other preferences. Tailor your bridge page content to match these preferences to optimize their user experience.
3. Identify three key ways your product or service stands out from competitors. Incorporate these value propositions on your bridge page in an easily digestible format, such as bullet points or graphics.
4. Craft a clear and concise CTA that aligns with the purpose of your bridge page. A/B test different CTAs to determine which one resonates best with your audience.
5. Develop content that offers a sneak peek into your product or service's benefits. For example, if you're selling an online course, share a short video or a downloadable sample module. This interactive approach helps visitors experience the value you're offering before committing.

RELEVANT TOOLS

General tools to get you started:

- **Google Optimize** helps you A/B test your website by creating variations of web pages to analyze user interactions to find the most effective elements.

- **Hotjar** provides heat maps, scroll maps, click maps, session recordings and more so you can improve the user experience on your bridge page.
- **Builderall** is an all-in-one marketing and funnel building platform with a suite of over 40 tools, like a website builder, A/B testing, click maps, cross-channel analytics and more.
- **ConvertFlow** is a funnel builder that lets you create landing pages, personalized CTAs, conversion paths, and A/B split testing for your bridge page.
- **Canva** is not a dedicated web page builder, but it helps you design elements like visuals, images, and graphics for your bridge page.
- **Google Keyword Planner**, **SEMrush**, **Moz Keyword Explorer** and **Ahrefs** are SEO/SEM tools that can help your bridge page rank higher on search results pages.
- **Google Ads** lets you pay to sponsor your bridge page at the top of Google search results for specific search terms.

Additional AI-powered tools:

- **VisualEyes** is an AI-driven user testing tool that simulates eye-tracking studies and preference tests to help you create more effective web pages.
- **Insight7** is an AI-powered customer insights tool that extracts patterns from data, prioritizes action items, and visualizes insights for faster decision-making.
- **ABtesting.ai** simplifies A/B testing with AI-generated suggestions for headlines, copy, and call-to-actions for your website.

- **Hexometer** is an AI website monitoring tool that proactively identifies issues across availability, performance, user experience, SEO, security and more.
- **SurferSEO** and **SEOdity** use AI to optimize your website for higher ranking on search engine result pages.
- **Jasper.ai**, **Copy.ai** and **Copymatic** are AI copywriting tools that can help you write your website copy in a fraction of the time.

ChatGPT EXAMPLE PROMPTS

Example 1

"You are working on a landing page for a remote team-building business. The company specializes in virtual reality and gamification to improve collaboration, communication, and problem-solving skills. The company's value propositions are:

1. We increase team engagement through VR, fun challenges, games, and workshops.
2. Our activities are meticulously designed and proven to improve team problem-solving and communication skills.
3. We quantify your team's skill development using data insights.

Your first task is to write a concise 50-word SEO-optimized and witty description for each value proposition. Your second task is to create corresponding Midjourney prompts for each value proposition, resulting in a cohesive set of 2D graphic illustrations. The brand color hex codes are #16214d, #44c7f4, and #f1632a."

Example 2

"You are developing a landing page for a DIY indoor hydroponic kits e-commerce brand. The kits help customers set up their own indoor hydroponic gardens, so they can grow a range of herbs, vegetables, and even small fruits without soil. At the bottom of the page, include a section that offers a sneak peek into the kit contents. For example, a meal kit service might showcase popular recipes from their kits that users can browse through, or an online course might provide a snippet of the first module. Your task is to brainstorm at least 3 different ideas for how users can interact with the hydroponic brand."

Example 3

"Draft 5 CTA buttons to put on a landing page for a personalized children's storybook business. The brand lets parents customize storybooks with their child's name and details, creating a personalized reading experience. The main goal of this page is to nudge parents to start designing their custom storybook. Use simple vocabulary."

10

THE ECLECTIC BEARDSMAN

Quiz Funnels

During my first year in college when I lived away from my family, I wanted to surprise my dad with a special gift for Father's Day. I knew he had been experimenting with growing a beard, so I figured a beard grooming product would be the perfect gift.

Being female, I had *zero clue* where to begin. Then I stumbled onto an online quiz by Beardbrand that promised to tell me what kind of beardsman I was. It sounded intriguing, so I decided to try it (on behalf of my dad, of course).

The quiz was surprisingly easy to navigate, even for a beard novice like me. It asked questions like "What activity do you enjoy the most?" and "What style of facial hair appeals to you?" There was even a question about preferred car models, which I found amusing.

After I answered all the questions, the quiz revealed that my dad was "The Eclectic Beardsman." I had no idea what that meant, but the quiz results page didn't leave me hanging—it provided product recommendations tailored to his unique "beardsman style." Excited about the results, I promptly ordered the recommended products and had them shipped to my dad just in time for Father's Day.

The Beardbrand quiz results

Years later, I realized I had been skillfully guided through a quiz funnel by Beardbrand. As I remember it, I must admit it was an unexpectedly enjoyable experience. Not only did I find the perfect gift for my dad, but the experience showed me the power of quizzes in guiding decision-making and providing personalized recommendations.

Let's take a closer look at quiz funnels, starting with what they *actually are*. As we saw with Beardbrand, a quiz funnel is a deliberate and planned journey created to guide potential clients toward becoming customers. Quiz funnels are especially useful if you think your customers might be overwhelmed by too many options or might be new to the product category.

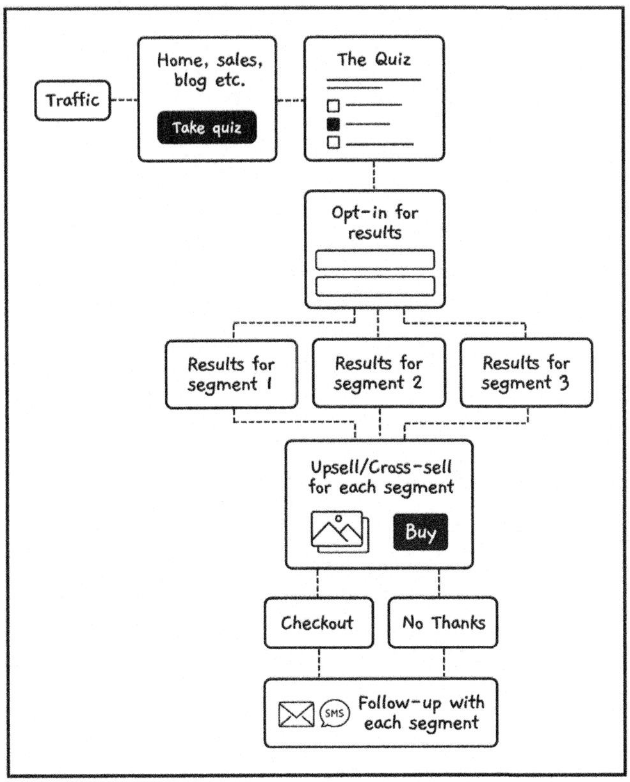

Website Quiz Funnel Workflow

While quiz funnels are great for websites, you can also create a quiz on Instagram DM or text messages with tools like ManyChat. This can be a great alternative if your audience is more active on social media or if you want to add a quiz to your text nurture strategy.

Let's look at the steps to create a quiz funnel.

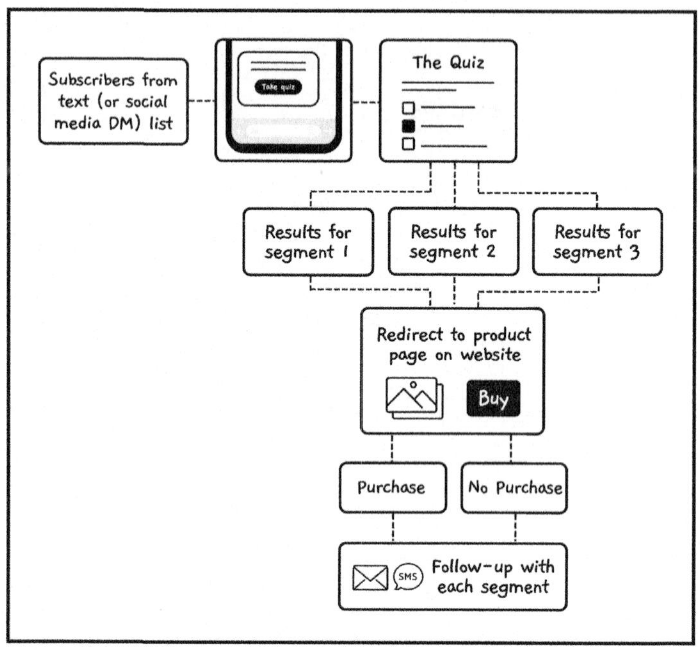

Text / IG DM / Messenger Chatbot Quiz

STEPS TO CREATE A QUIZ FUNNEL

#1 Choose the Quiz Location

Quizzes can be used at different customer journey stages to create a more engaging and personalized experience. For example, you can use an online quiz to attract new leads and build a segmented email list. In this case, the quiz acts as a magnet, enticing people to provide their contact information in exchange for valuable quiz results or insights.

If you already have an email list, you can create a separate quiz specifically for creating groups as previously discussed. By distributing this quiz to your subscribers, you can categorize them based on their preferences, behaviors, or other relevant factors. This segmentation lets you send targeted content and product recommendations, enhancing their overall experience.

Quizzes also shine when recommending specific products to warm leads. These quizzes come into play towards the end of the customer journey, when they are ready to buy. By asking relevant questions and understanding their preferences, you can provide personalized product recommendations that align with customer needs, increasing the chances of conversion. Depending on the end goal of your quiz, you can put it in different locations.

Landing Page: Place a quiz prominently on your landing page to attract visitors and encourage them to engage with your brand at the very beginning of their journey. This is an effective location for a quiz because it grabs their attention when curiosity is still high.

Website Header or Navigation Bar: Add a quiz link or button in your website's header or navigation bar, making it easily accessible to visitors on any page. This ensures that your quiz is visible and encourages engagement throughout the customer journey. Quizzes in the header or nav bar can be used for list-building or product recommendations.

Pop-up or Slide-in Form: Use a pop-up or slide-in form that appears when a visitor lands on your website or performs a specific action. This works well for lead acquisition quizzes as it catches your audience's attention and encourages them to participate in the quiz.

Blog Posts: Embed quizzes within relevant blog posts to engage readers and encourage them to take the quiz while they're interested in the topic. This can be an effective way to segment your email list or recommend specific products based on their quiz results.

Email Campaigns: Include a link to your quiz in your email newsletters or dedicated email campaigns. This allows you to reach your existing subscribers and encourage them to participate in the quiz for segmentation purposes or to receive personalized product recommendations.

#2 Choose a Relevant Topic

It's important to choose the right topic for your quiz to capture the interest and engagement of your target audience. Start by examining your ICAs and considering their pain points, desires, and aspirations. Use this information to select a topic that addresses their specific interests and challenges.

For example, if your online fitness business targets individuals looking to improve their health and fitness, create a quiz to determine the most suitable workout routine or identify the best nutritional plan based on their goals.

#3 Choose The Outcomes

Once you've chosen your quiz topic, before you start writing quiz questions, define the outcomes for your quiz takers.

Just like you need to know your destination before leaving the airport, creating the outcomes first serves as a map for your quiz questions. This approach ensures that your questions stay focused and prevents the need for extensive rewrites.

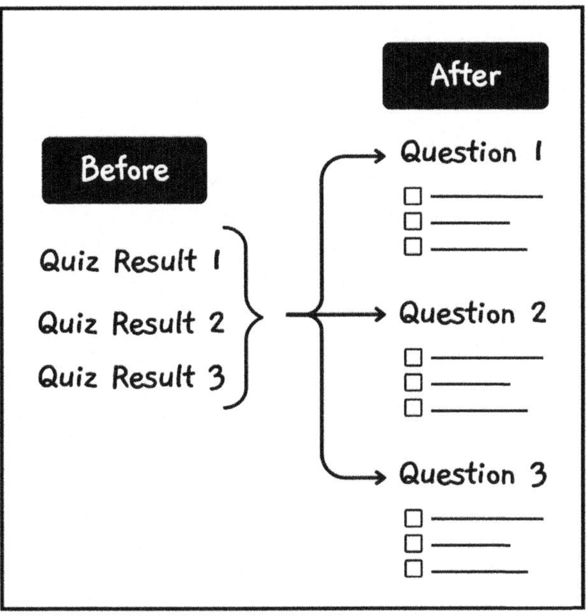

Your outcomes play a crucial role in shaping the questions you create for quiz takers. Each question provides specific information that leads them to a particular result or outcome. Here are the goals of your outcomes:

Diagnose the problem: Imagine you are a doctor with expertise in the specific problem your quiz taker is facing. You want to take their answers (their symptoms), combine them with your expertise, and provide an accurate diagnosis.

Present potential solutions to the problem: This is the most exciting part. Once the quiz-taker knows what the problem is, they want to know how to solve it. They're looking for solutions. For example, hair care brand OUAI offers a hair consult quiz on their site. Depending on the "diagnosis" of your hair type, they might offer different hair masks, oils, or treatments. By presenting impartial information about these options, the company is building trust.

Give your preferred choice: When presenting your recommendation, it's essential to provide a logical and convincing argument, so your prospect understands why your recommendation is the best path for them. Incorporate their answers into your argument This is why it is crucial to create your outcomes first. Instead of a generic sales pitch, your suggestion becomes hyper-personalized to their situation. Sure, your recommendation *happens* to be a product that you sell, but it also genuinely addresses their problems or goals.

#4 Choose Relevant (and Interesting) Questions

Engaging questions keep people interested in your quiz. If the quiz feels like a survey, potential customers are likely to abandon it before sharing their contact details, which is not what you want.

To avoid loss of interest, ask relevant questions that help you understand the quiz-takers while keeping them engaged. The tone of the questions should fit your brand personality (funny, friendly, etc.), making the quiz feel more like a conversation than a chore. At a minimum, you should aim to learn the following:

- Their goals
- The challenges they face
- The outcomes or solutions they expect.

To gather this information, you can ask different types of questions, such as:

- **Demographic questions** help to determine if the person falls within your target market and how to weigh their answers.
- **Personality questions** provide insights into the psychographic profile of your audience.
- **Problem questions** help you understand the specific problem they are experiencing and their perspective on it.
- **Outcome-focused questions** let you gauge their aspirations and their desires, allowing you to provide a relevant solution.

These questions form the foundation of your quiz. Ideally, aim for around 7 questions, but no more than 10. This is enough to gather useful information and segment respondents without overwhelming them.

QUIZ FUNNEL BEST PRACTICES

Easy to Hard

Start with easy, approachable questions to avoid scaring people away from your quiz. Think of it like getting to know someone new. You wouldn't immediately jump into deeply vulnerable or complex topics when you meet someone new. In the same way, you want to ease into the quiz. Start with simpler questions and gradually progress.

The goal is to create a comfortable, enjoyable experience for participants. Tricky or clever questions can confuse them and lead to inaccurate data. Remember, the quiz should only take a couple of minutes, so keep it concise and user-friendly.

Let Your Brand Shine

Use words that your ICAs know and understand to make your quiz stand out. Avoid using trendy references because they could make your quiz seem outdated quickly, leading some subscribers to lose interest. Instead, highlight the main themes and values that define your brand. If your audience sees your brand as a reflection of themselves, you have the opportunity to reinforce the qualities that attracted them to you in the first place. Let's look at an example of how you could use a fun brand voice in a quiz for a marketing consultancy:

Title of Quiz: "What's Your Marketing Cocktail?"

Description of Quiz: Discover the hidden ingredients in your cocktail shaker and what makes you stand out from the competition... And receive our exclusive marketing tactics to guarantee that your dream clients choose you from the menu. Every. Single. Time.

Quiz question examples:

- How long have you been running your business?

- Which of the following marketing strategies do you use?
- Which cocktail best describes your brand?

If you opt for more creative questions like the last one, make sure the multiple-choice answers you provide show distinct brand identities with explanations of your ICA descriptions. For example, instead of listing generic cocktails that don't clearly connect to different brand personalities, you could say: *Spicy Margarita - your brand embodies an adventurous spirit and leaves a lasting impression with your bold flavor and vibrant personality.*

Segmented Follow-Up

The end of the quiz is where the magic happens. While not everyone will buy the product recommendations on the results page, you can expect lead conversion rates of around 25% and a flood of new subscribers to your email/text list. Use the information to your advantage by personalizing it based on their quiz outcome and whether they've made the initial purchase.

Let's say you have four outcomes for your quiz. That means you'll have four distinct email follow-up sequences, each tailored to match the outcome and adjusted based on whether the person has purchased an offer from your results page. Here are a few points to consider for the follow-up sequence:

- Instill the buying beliefs necessary for conversion.
- Educate your prospects about your products or services.
- Include dedicated sales emails to make compelling offers.
- Focus on the core product pitch for a few days before transitioning to other topics or promotions.

TYPES OF QUIZZES

Lifestyle Quizzes

Many online brands don't realize how important it is to create *engaging* lead-generation quizzes. They are missing out on the advantages of lead generation, email lists, and relationship building.

However, some brands have mastered the art of making quizzes interesting and captivating. They pique your curiosity with a phrase like, "Discover your ultimate travel destination" This immediately sparks your interest and entices you to take their quiz to discover your perfect travel spot.

In a Buzzfeed-style quiz, a travel brand could present an interactive quiz titled "Find Your Perfect Getaway." The quiz should go beyond basic travel preferences to ask about the person's interests, such as their preferred activities, climate preferences, and desired level of adventure. Towards the end of the quiz, the quiz taker will be eager to see their results and share their email address in exchange for the answer. Keep the process straightforward.

Here's the exciting part. After revealing the results, you can take things a step further by recommending offers related to the results of the quiz. For example, the travel brand example could show personalized travel packages or experiences that perfectly match the quiz-taker's unique travel preferences, all on the same page.

A lifestyle quiz is a prime example of how to go beyond promoting your own services. In the example we used, the quiz helps the person explore *their own travel personality* and discover new destinations that align with their interests.

In general, a lifestyle quiz should:

- Gain valuable email addresses and/or phone numbers
- Learn about their prospects' interests and preferences
- Nurture their segmented leads through email marketing
- Provide highly personalized product recommendations.

Product Discovery Quizzes

Even though online shops try their best to make shopping easy, it can be hard to buy some things online. Some items need to be touched or seen and felt in person. Things like clothing, furniture, or perfumes are examples of products that are difficult to fully understand without seeing or trying them in real life.

Glasses fall squarely in that category. Warby Parker, an eyewear company, starts by welcoming new visitors with an interactive quiz on its website. The quiz helps you find the perfect pair of frames by asking about your face shape, color preferences, materials, and whether you already wear glasses.

Here's where it gets interesting. Warby Parker sets the stage for cross-selling by asking if you're interested in sunglasses recommendations as well. If you say "yes," they provide suggestions from a wider range of categories, potentially increasing the value of your purchase.

At the end of the quiz, Warby Parker gives you the option to enter your email to save your results for later. However, unlike many other brands, they don't make it mandatory. They respect your choice. While the quiz is loading, Warby Parker explains how their 5-day free trial works, adding another layer of value to their offerings.

When you receive your quiz results, Warby Parker doesn't pressure you into making an immediate purchase. Instead, they encourage you to try out five frames at home before making a final decision. This shows their confidence in the quality and style of their products.

Even if you didn't provide your email address at the end of the quiz, Warby Parker knows they can entice you with their "try at home" option, which requires an even bigger commitment. This allows them to gather valuable information about you and your preferences. In general, a product discovery quiz should:

- Uncover hidden needs.
- Identify ideal product fit.
- Facilitate personalized product recommendations.
- Enhance decision-making

Exclusive Offer Quiz

Let's look at how a brand can use an exclusive offer quiz to engage and convert leads. Imagine you visit a web design studio's website, and they welcome you with an enticing offer like "Get 20% off a website template" by clicking the "Start Quiz" button.

As you proceed with the quiz, they ask you a series of interactive questions to learn about your website goals, design preferences, and desired functionalities. This information helps them tailor their recommendations and provide personalized solutions for your website.

At the end of the quiz, they invite you to provide your email address to receive the exclusive 20% discount on a website template that suits your needs. By integrating this special offer within their quiz, the web design studio effectively captures valuable email addresses, gains insights into their prospects' website requirements, and establishes a foundation for targeted email marketing. In general, an exclusive offer quiz should include the following:

- Communicate the exclusive offer or incentive that participants will receive.
- Relevant and Interactive Questions
- Customized Results
- Email/Phone Number Capture

CHAPTER RESOURCES

Action Items

1. Evaluate your customer journey and pick the ideal location for your quiz – landing page, header, pop-up, blog, or emails.
2. Consider the needs and goals of your ICAs. Pick a quiz theme that directly addresses their specific challenges and interests.
3. Set up possible quiz outcomes that guide the type of questions you will ask in the quiz. These outcomes should lead to precise diagnosis, potential solutions, and product/service recommendations.
4. Develop 7 to 10 questions that gather crucial insights while maintaining a conversational, brand-based tone.

Consider demographic, personality, problem, and outcome-based questions.

5. The quiz results page should provide customized product/service recommendations. If the person doesn't buy, create a segmented follow-up campaign via email or text.

RELEVANT TOOLS

General tools to get you started:

- **Interact, Outgrow** and **LeadQuizzes** are three of the most popular quiz-building tools, but there are many options to consider.
- **Builderall** is an all-in-one marketing and funnel platform with a suite of over 40 tools, including a website quiz builder.
- **ConvertFlow** and **Upflowy** are funnel tools that offer website quiz-building options.
- **ManyChat** is a great tool for creating engaging quizzes on other channels, like SMS, WhatsApp, Instagram DM etc.
- The **Shopify App Store** also has a variety of quiz-building options that integrate with your Shopify store, including **Prehook**, **Shop Quiz** and **Presidio**.
- Currently, there is a limited availability of AI-powered quiz tools.
- Octane AI is an AI-powered Shopify quiz app that provides personalized product recommendations to customers.

ChatGPT EXAMPLE PROMPTS

Example 1

Help me brainstorm three distinct quiz themes for my e-commerce brand that specializes in selling a range of products tailored for runners, including running shoes, insoles, and compression socks. The goal of the quizzes is to help potential customers identify the best products for their individual needs and goals.

Example 2

"You work for a leading personalized vitamin gummies brand that specializes in creating customized gummy supplements, catering to individual nutritional needs and goals. Your task is to create an 8-question online quiz that effectively gathers essential information from individuals. The quiz should be designed to address demographic information, lifestyle habits, nutritional goals, and other relevant information that will help formulate the ideal personalized vitamin gummies."

Example 3

"I run a photography business, and I offer different photoshoot experiences with varying price levels, styles, locations, group sizes etc. Write a 3-message email follow-up sequence to people who completed my quiz funnel but didn't buy a photoshoot experience. The messages should be short, friendly, and focused on adding value rather than hard-selling. Remember, my target audience is people interested in receiving a photoshoot, not photographers."

11

THE HOT DOG COMBO

Tripwire Funnels

When I was a kid, I loved going to Costco with my mom because it almost always meant my sister and I would get hot dogs.

Little did I know that this $1.50 hot dog combo was more than just a cheap meal. It was part of Costco's clever tripwire strategy. By offering such an irresistible deal, Costco was able to entice families like mine to step foot into their stores.

Once we stepped inside, something interesting happened. The exciting atmosphere and the wide variety of products made my sister and me eager to explore further. *Every single time.* It was no accident that the hot dog combo was conveniently placed in the back of the store.

The tripwire did its job, pulling us deeper into the store and tempting us to add snacks that piqued our interest into the shopping cart my mom pulled. T*hat* was the brilliance of Costco's tripwire strategy. They knew that, once we were lured inside, the chances of us making additional purchases were much, much higher.

So what exactly is a tripwire? A tripwire offer is a low-cost, irresistible offer (the $1.50 hot dog combo) that sets you up to make a larger purchase soon after taking advantage of the original offer (adding countless snacks into our cart).

The best part is that creating a successful tripwire offer doesn't require lengthy, complicated sales pages. A concise and persuasive pitch for a product valued between 5 and 20% of the core offer is often enough to seal the deal.

THE FOOT-IN-THE-DOOR TECHNIQUE

The foot-in-the-door technique is a tripwire strategy based on commitment and consistency. It suggests that, when someone agrees to a small request, they are more likely to say yes to a bigger one later.

Two researchers at Stanford University studied this concept further to understand how it can be used in real life.[46] In their study, some people were asked to answer questions about the soap they use (a small request). Then they were asked if strangers could enter their homes and review their soap products (a much larger request).

The researchers discovered that, when the participants were asked questions about their soap usage before being asked to let strangers enter their homes, 76% agreed! But when the soap questions were omitted, that number dropped exponentially.

From this study, the researchers concluded that when making a small request before a bigger one, like asking about soap before entering the house, people are more likely to say yes. It works because people tend to stick to their commitments and stay consistent with what they've already agreed to do. So by offering a tripwire, you can create a psychological commitment in customers that increases the likelihood of them purchasing your upsell offer.

THE STANDARD TRIPWIRE FUNNEL

There are a couple of ways you can set up your tripwire funnel. In this chapter, we'll go over the most commonly used versions. The two main types of tripwire funnels we'll discuss are:

- **Standard Tripwire Funnel** (paid offer up-front): This type starts with the sales page for your tripwire offer, where customers can make a purchase right away.
- **2-Step Tripwire Funnel** (free offer up-front): This type begins with a page where customers can sign up for a lead magnet or freebie. After they sign up, they are introduced to the tripwire offer.

Let's start by looking at the standard tripwire funnel.

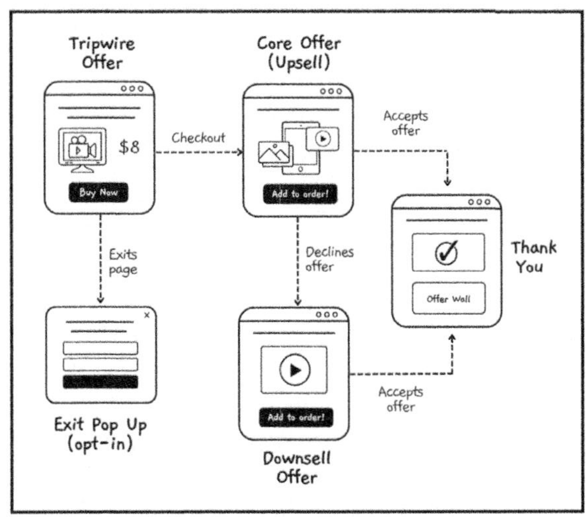

Standard Tripwire Funnel Workflow

The original format for the tripwire funnel is to present the tripwire offer to your prospect right at the beginning of the funnel. This format is especially effective when you have a low-priced tripwire, such as a $1 trial. Here's how this funnel flows:

- Tripwire Offer (with exit pop-up if they decline)
- Check out page
- Core offer upsell (with downsell offer if they decline)
- Thank you page (with an offer wall)

Tripwire Offer

At the first step of this funnel, you introduce your tripwire offer. Typically, you offer a significant discount on one of your existing products or a specially created offer specifically designed for this funnel. You want it to be a low-commitment purchase, so trip offers work best if they are no more than 10% of your core offer cost. When it comes to *where* to place your tripwire, you have a few options.

#1 Separate Sales Page

When you create a sales page specifically for the tripwire offer, it gives customers a clear, straightforward experience. This page includes convincing sales copy, attractive visuals, and an easy process to buy the tripwire offer.

#2 Email Placement

Placing the tripwire offer within an email is a direct and personalized way to engage with your subscribers. By leveraging the existing trust, you can entice subscribers with the tripwire offer.

#3 Embedded in an Existing Page

Embedding the tripwire offer within an existing page, such as an exit pop-up or product page, can leverage the traffic and engagement on your website. This approach eliminates the need for users to navigate away from the existing page, reducing potential friction and distractions.

If the lead decides not to take the tripwire offer, you can still catch their attention before they leave your sales funnel. You can use an exit pop-up that appears when the user tries to close the browser window. This pop-up usually offers a freebie or something valuable in exchange for their contact information. By getting their details, you can continue marketing to them and build a relationship in the hopes of making a sale in the future.

Exit Pop-Up Example.

Check Out

When designing your tripwire checkout page, it's important to include elements that increase buyer confidence and encourage them to complete the purchase. One important part is a guarantee that eliminates buyer risk. By offering a guarantee, like a 30-day, no-questions-asked guarantee, you assure prospective buyers that they can try the product without worrying about losing their money if they're not satisfied.

Pro tip: You can set up an abandoned cart sequence if they don't complete the checkout within a certain time frame.

Core Offer Upsell

Right after someone buys your tripwire offer, you'll show them a sales page for your main product. If possible, try using a video on the sales page. Videos have a powerful visual appeal that is more engaging than plain text.

Your core offer is usually more expensive—it could be an online course, upgraded product, mentorship program, or software with a higher price, like a yearly plan. If your checkout or sales system supports it, make this page an easy one-click upsell, where buyers don't have to enter their credit card information again, making it easier for them to purchase. Think of how Amazon uses one-click checkout. By showing your main product right after the tripwire and offering a one-click upsell, you increase the chances of buyers making the additional purchase.

Not every customer who enters your tripwire funnel will be ready to buy your core offer immediately. To make the most revenue from these customers, you can offer a downsell. A downsell is an offer shown to customers who say "no thanks" to your main offer. It's usually a simpler version of your main offer with a lower price, like your entry-level offer.

You can also try offering a payment plan on the downsell page. This lets customers who can't afford the full price upfront still make a purchase by paying in installments. By having a payment plan option, you have a better chance of converting customers by appealing to different budget ranges.

Thank You Page

The thank you page is where you confirm your customer's purchases and tell them what will happen next. As discussed in Chapter 7, you should always take advantage of the extra space on this page by creating an "offer wall " to encourage them to make more purchases.

THE 2-STEP TRIPWIRE FUNNEL

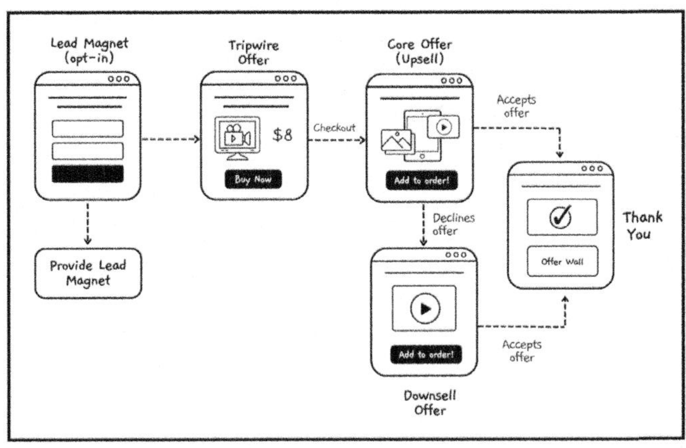

2-Step Tripwire Funnel Workflow

The 2-step tripwire funnel follows a similar structure as the standard tripwire funnel, but there is one key difference: it includes an initial lead magnet page before presenting the tripwire offer.

By adding the lead magnet, visitors must sign up to become subscribers before they can access the tripwire offer. This approach helps improve the conversion rate by ensuring that only qualified leads move on to the next step of the sales funnel. Using a 2-step tripwire funnel also allows you to focus on leads that are more likely to convert, improving the overall conversion rate. Here are the main stages in a 2-step tripwire funnel:

- Lead Magnet Page
- Tripwire Offer (with exit pop-up if they decline)
- Check out page
- Core offer upsell (with downsell offer if they decline)
- Thank you page (with an offer wall)

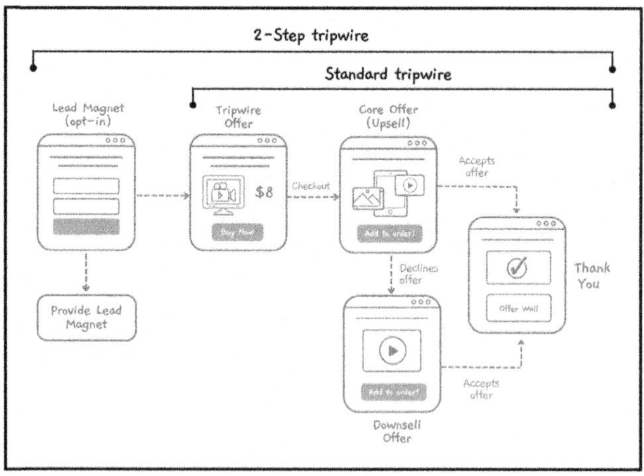

2-Step Tripwire vs. Standard Tripwire

The structure after the lead magnet step is exactly the same in the 2-step tripwire funnel as the standard tripwire funnel mentioned earlier. The only difference is that, once they click "submit" to access the free offer, you immediately redirect them to the tripwire offer. Alternatively, you could include the tripwire offer in the email containing the freebie.

Adding the extra lead magnet step helps turn cold and warm traffic into leads as soon as they enter your website. To make your lead magnet page effective, the free content should relate closely to your tripwire and upsell offers.

CRITERIA OF POWERFUL TRIPWIRE OFFERS

Low Barrier to Entry

A great tripwire offer shouldn't make it hard for customers to get started. This is often called a low barrier to entry. It should be affordable, simple to understand, and require minimal effort to participate.

When the barrier to entry is low, more people are likely to take advantage of your offer. For example, if you're selling an online course, setting a low price point or offering a discounted trial period can attract a larger number of potential customers, who might be hesitant to invest in a higher-priced course.

A low barrier to entry also reduces the risk for leads. It allows them to try your product or service without a big financial commitment. This can be especially effective when you offer a money-back guarantee or a free trial period. Customers feel more comfortable taking the leap when they know they can check out your offer's value before fully committing.

Targeted Offer

A great tripwire offer should be designed specifically for your ICAs. It should address their unique needs, interests, and preferences. Generic offers *will not* grab their attention.

When your tripwire offer is targeted to your ICAs, it focuses on what your audience truly wants. For example, if you're targeting busy parents who want easy dinner recipes, creating a tripwire offer with a collection of quick, healthy meal ideas specifically for families would be appealing and relevant. Customers are more likely to be interested in your tripwire offer when it matches their needs because it shows that you understand their specific challenges and have a solution for them.

Having a targeted tripwire offer keeps your sales funnel consistent because it creates a logical pathway for the customer. For instance, if your tripwire offer is a guide on stress management, it would make sense to follow it with a core offer that provides a comprehensive stress reduction program. This consistency enhances the overall customer experience and opens intuitive opportunities for upselling and cross-selling.

High Perceived Value

Having a high perceived value is crucial for a powerful tripwire offer. It's not just about making it *look* valuable, but about *actually providing* something valuable to your customers. You earn future deals and build long-term relationships by over-delivering on this offer. Think of it as a "sample" of your main product. It should leave customers impressed and wanting more!

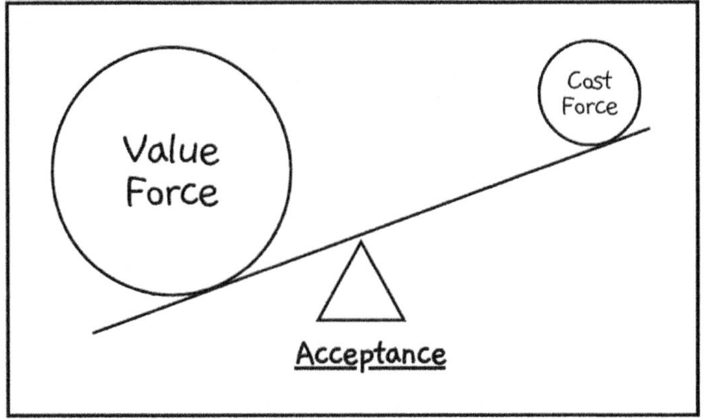

When customers believe they're receiving more value than what they're paying for, they are more likely to accept the offer. The "Value Force" being greater than the "Cost Force " means that, when customers believe they will receive high value, they are much more inclined to justify the cost.

Useful But Incomplete

By strategically designing an incomplete tripwire offer, you can effectively drive customer engagement and encourage further purchases.

For instance, let's consider an example where you're selling an online course. As the tripwire product, you could offer the first few modules of the course for free or at a low cost. This provides immediate value to customers as they gain knowledge and insights from those initial videos. But the content is incomplete, so they want to access the remaining modules to benefit from the course.

TYPES OF TRIPWIRE OFFERS

The $1 Trail

$1 trials are highly effective for subscription-based products. They allow customers to experience your product for a limited period, usually 30 days, at a low cost. You can offer a time-limited trial, typically lasting 7 to 10 days, at a low price point (such as $7 for 7-day access). This encourages customers to explore and use all the features of your digital product, training course, or membership site.

Disney Movie Club is an excellent example of a tripwire funnel in action. They allow customers to select four movies of their choice for just $1 to encourage membership enrollment. Once they become a member through this offer, Disney requires them to purchase five additional movie titles at the regular price over the course of two years, which more than compensates for the low cost of the tripwire.

The A to C Offer

Many companies provide a limited version of their main product as a tripwire offer. One effective approach is to create a "quick start" guide that focuses on addressing a specific need and offering it at a discounted price. Unlike your core offer, which covers the entire A to Z process, the quick start guide offers a streamlined path from point A to point C, providing valuable information along the way.

Bonus Content

Consider providing exclusive content as special bonuses that are only available to customers who purchase your tripwire offer. Jay Abraham coined this technique as the "ethical bribe."[47] The key is to make sure these additional resources have a high perceived value. The tripwire offer should be relevant and enhance the customer's experience. By offering valuable bonus content, you can ethically bribe customers to take advantage of the tripwire offer and increase their overall engagement with your business.

Free + Shipping

Offering a "Pay Only the Shipping Cost" deal effectively attracts price-conscious individuals who are interested in your product. With this type of tripwire, you provide a physical product at no charge, requiring customers to pay only for the shipping fees.

For instance, you can offer a free physical book while charging only for the cost of shipping. (Recall this tripwire offer uses the consumer psychology principles from Chapter 7.)

Consultations

Consultations where you provide a 15-minute personalized session via phone, chat, or email can be a valuable tripwire offer. To implement this strategy, begin by offering a lead magnet to attract potential customers and capture their email addresses. Once you have built a list of interested individuals, you can then pitch the tripwire offer that includes the opportunity for a one-on-one consultation.

It's crucial to consider the limitations of offering consultations as a tripwire. Since consultations rely on your time and availability, it may not be feasible to offer them unless you have enough resources and can accommodate the demand. If you're limited on time and can't scale live consultations, then focus on the automated tripwire tactics.

CHAPTER RESOURCES

Action Items

1. Develop a precise tripwire offer that directly targets a specific pain point or desire of your ICA. Use ChatGPT if you need help and refer to tripwire approaches we explored in this chapter, like low-cost trials, A to C offers, bonus content etc.
2. Set the price of the tripwire between 1% and 10% of your core offer and make sure it delivers clear value.
3. Consider incorporating an exit pop-up for visitors who navigate away from your website without purchasing the tripwire offer.
4. Strategically integrate upsells (core offer) and downsells (entry-level offer) during the checkout process.

RELEVANT TOOLS

General tools to get you started:

- **SamCart** optimizes checkout with features like order bumps, 1-click checkout, and pop-up checkout for smooth tripwire transactions.
- **Thrivecart** is a more advanced e-commerce tool that lets you design a customized checkout experience for your tripwire strategy.

- **Builderall** is an all-in-one marketing and funnel-building platform with a suite of over 40 tools, including a funnel builder and Smart Checkout, which are perfect for creating a tripwire.
- **ConvertFlow** is an e-commerce funnel builder with dozens of templates, including cart upsells and downsells for your tripwire strategy.
- **GetResponse** is a marketing suite with a conversion funnel tool that includes features like customizable order forms and one-click upsell pages.
- **Justuno** uses intelligent data-driven upsells and cross-sells to improve user experiences and boost the average order values.
- **Order Bump** is an upsell tool designed to add upsells to the checkout page seamlessly without replacing the entire checkout process.
- **Rebuy** is a comprehensive Shopify app that provides options to upsell, downsell, customize shopping carts, and create post-purchase offers.

While there aren't currently AI tools specifically designed for tripwires or checkout optimization, you can use the following AI tools to enhance your tripwire funnel:

- **Jasper.ai, Copy.ai,** and **Copymatic** are AI writing tools that can help you craft compelling messaging for your tripwire funnel.
- **TurboSite** uses AI to analyze user behavior and offers real-time suggestions to help you create a smoother tripwire funnel.
- **Magic Design by Canva** is an AI-powered tool that can help you design appealing visuals or graphics for your tripwire offer

ChatGPT EXAMPLE PROMPTS

Example 1

"Brainstorm 5 unique, creative tripwire offer ideas for my video and podcast editing business. These offers should be priced at $29 each and designed to be passive sales, requiring no additional work on my part once they are set up. The goal is to add value to potential clients and make them excited about potentially working with me. Each idea should be explained in detail and include the specific benefits it offers."

Example 2

"Generate a table that outlines the 5 tripwire offer ideas you brainstormed above and their associated perceived value enhancements. For each tripwire offer, provide three distinct perceived value ideas in separate columns." *This prompt is a follow-up prompt from Example 1.*

Example 3

"You operate a virtual language tutoring business. Your lead magnet is a free personalized language learning assessment for French, Spanish, Chinese, or Arabic to help website visitors determine their current language proficiency level. Based on this lead magnet, which of the following tripwire offers would be most effective for converting potential clients through a two-step tripwire strategy? Explain your reasoning. [Insert list of tripwire ideas here]"

12

OSCAR THE COW

Email Funnels

In one of his interviews, marketing coach and entrepreneur Terry Dean gave an example of a story he sent to his audience via email that became a story people would remember for decades.[48] Terry explained:

"I wrote an email way back in 2000 about how the internet allowed me to work from anywhere. I chose to live way out in the country, where my nearest next-door neighbor was a cow named Oscar. The cow was owned by the neighbor and regularly came up to the fence to eat the grass on our side of the fence. I sent one email about that. I've had dozens of people ask me about Oscar over the years. When speaking at conferences, people who were on my list way back then still ask about the cow..."

But why was Oscar the cow so memorable all those years later? Because our brains interpret stories differently than informational text. In one fascinating study, researchers discovered that, while factual content only activates the language processing part of the brain, storytelling engages several areas of our brains.[49]For instance, vivid metaphors activate the sensory cortex associated with the five senses, while words describing motion stimulate the motor cortex responsible for movement and coordination.

In another study, neuro-economist Paul Zak found that stories release oxytocin, a chemical that promotes a sense of safety and trust in our brains (the same "trust hormone" we discussed in Chapter 4).[50]

Storytelling is an *incredibly* powerful tool. So, you might be wondering how all of this relates to emails… After all, emails are typically expected to be concise and straight to the point. Stories, on the other hand, are often associated with longer narratives.

Can storytelling really be effective in emails? Yes and no. While it's true that your emails probably shouldn't be a 2,000-word saga, there are ways to incorporate storytelling in your emails to make them as impactful (and high-converting) as possible.

EMAIL FUNNEL ANATOMY

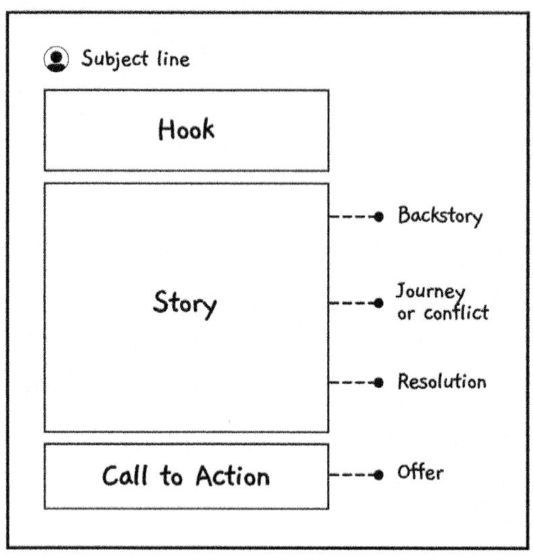

The anatomy of an email in this funnel follows a 3-step approach: Hook, Story, and Action.

So far, we've discussed two types of email: Nurture Emails from Chapter 5 and the Abandoned Cart Sequence from Chapter 7. But how should you communicate with customers who already know and love your brand?

That's where your general email funnel comes in. It's like an ongoing conversation that guides your customers to enter your other funnels and ultimately ascend your value pyramid. Unlike the nurture and abandoned-cart messages that are very concise, your email funnel is designed to engage deeper with customers. In this case, you provide storytelling, educational, and behind-the-scenes content because, at this point, you have a hot/loyal audience that wants to connect deeper with your brand.

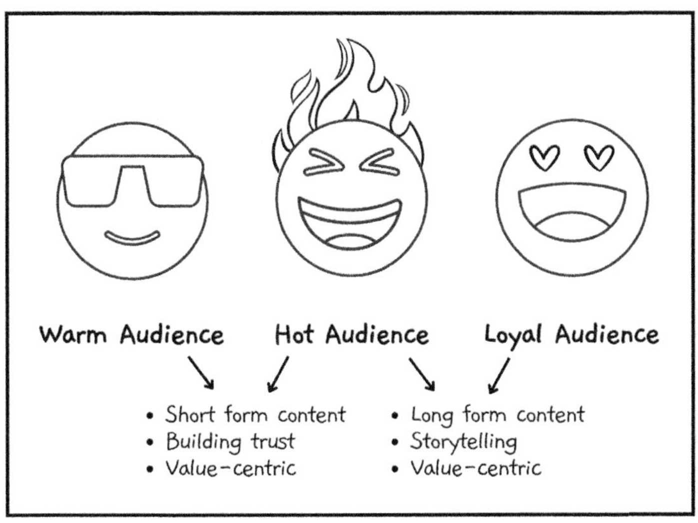

Type of communication format depending on your audience

BEGINNING OF THE EMAIL

HOOK

We've discussed how to write a strong hook in the context of website headings (refer to Chapter 6), but when it comes to email, the book looks pretty different. Instead of focusing on your value prop, your email hook generates emotion through storytelling.

Let's look at a handful of hook templates to get you started. Keep in mind, this isn't a comprehensive list, and you can use many other creative hook structures. Don't be afraid to experiment and find the ones that resonate best with your audience.

#1 The Emotional Hook

Starting with an emotional hook is a great way to grab people's attention and make a connection with them. An emotional hook can be something that makes people curious, excited, or nostalgic.

In a world where people have short attention spans, and there's a lot of competition in peoples' inboxes, starting with an emotional hook is a way to stand out. By making people feel something, you can leave a lasting impression and create a stronger bond with your audience.

Remember, your window for hooking someone is very small. So get right to the action. Don't write lengthy backstories for context; this isn't Harry Potter fan fiction. For example, let's look at this hook:

> I was MORTIFIED the first time I was asked to set revenue goals.
>
> The standards I found for graphic designers online were confusing and unrealistic. I had no previous data to rely on. I had absolutely *no clue* what the "normal" level of success was for graphic designers like me... and I was about to be held accountable to some wild number I conjured out of thin air.

Curiosity: This emotional hook is fantastic because the emotionally-charged word "mortified" instantly grabs the readers' attention and makes them want to hear more of the story. Then at the end of the hook, the mention of being held accountable to a self-determined "wild number" creates anticipation. It opens a loop in the reader's mind, leaving them wondering how the story will unfold.

Relevance: The hook is relevant because it addresses a problem that many freelance graphic designers face, trying to set revenue goals without having enough experience or clear benchmarks.

Value: The author openly admits to having "no clue" how to determine a revenue goal. This sets the stage for the rest of the email, which provides helpful information and solutions. The reader can expect to gain insights and guidance on how to set their own goals effectively.

#2 The Compelling Statistic

Another easy way to make your readers curious is to begin with a mysterious set of numbers. Suddenly, your mind is filled with questions like, "What do these numbers mean?" "Why are they important?" "How do my numbers compare to them?" For example:

> 168. That's how many hours there are in a week, and if you've just launched your business, you probably feel like this isn't enough.

Curiosity: The email opens with the statement that there are only 168 hours in a week, implying this might not be sufficient for running a business effectively. However, it doesn't immediately provide a solution or answer. It leaves the reader eager to learn more about how they can overcome time constraints and make the most of their business journey.

Relevance: The hook directly relates to people who have recently started a business. It acknowledges the challenge of limited time. This makes the hook highly relevant to their situation. They can easily relate to it.

Value: The hook suggests that, inside the email, the reader will find useful information or solutions to help them manage their time better.

#3 Ask A Question

Using a question as a hook works well because it makes the reader stop and think about what you're asking. It's not just about reading a story—they're now part of the story. Also, questions can make readers curious, especially when they're surprising or different. Let's look at an example that uses an unexpected question in the hook:

> Do you know what websites and tape have in common?
>
> Websites stick in people's minds, and tape, well, it sticks to just about anything.
>
> So the real question is, how can you make your website as sticky as tape so your visitors don't just bounce?

Curiosity: The hook sparks interest by using the open-loop method, creating an unexpected comparison between websites and tape. The reader is wondering about the connection between these two seemingly unrelated things, encouraging them to continue reading to find the answer.

Relevance: The hook is highly relevant to any reader who has a website or is considering creating one. The problem of visitors leaving or "bouncing" from a website is a common challenge that many website owners face.

Value: The hook clearly hints at the value that will be provided in the subsequent content. It promises to deliver a solution to make the reader's website more engaging or "sticky" like tape. This implies that the reader will learn how to keep visitors on their site longer, which could lead to better user engagement, increased conversions, and ultimately, improved website success.

#4 The Controversial Hook

Try saying something surprising or controversial if you want more people to notice your writing. It may spark conversations and get people talking about your content.

But be careful not to take extreme positions or make harmful statements. Doing so can damage your reputation and have negative consequences for you and your client. Even if you see a short-term increase in traffic and sales, it's not worth the potential long-term problems. Consider this playful example for a recipe app:

> Get out of the way, pineapple!
>
> Figs have taken your spot as the best fruit to put on pizza.
>
> But how did this unassuming fruit rise to claim the coveted spot on the pizza topping hierarchy?

Curiosity: The hook stirs curiosity by introducing a novel idea about pizza toppings, which creates an open loop that encourages the reader to continue. The question at the end suggests that, by reading the rest of the content, the reader will discover a fascinating narrative about how figs became a popular pizza topping.

Relevance: This hook is highly relevant for readers of a recipe app. It's about pizza, a universally beloved dish. The introduction of figs as a new popular topping creates a controversy, drawing in the reader's personal preferences and possibly prompting them to try a new recipe.

Value: The hook implies that the email will provide an interesting story about food trends and possibly even a new recipe to try. This adds value for the reader who uses the app for cooking inspiration.

MIDDLE OF THE EMAIL

Storytelling

Including a story in the email body is a powerful way to engage your audience and boost conversions. By crafting compelling stories, you can create an emotional bond that connects readers to your brand and products.

Create a Journey

As we discussed, emotions play a huge role in storytelling. When crafting a story-based email, the goal is to evoke a specific feeling in your readers. Whether it's laughter, joy, or even a touch of sadness, the key is to captivate them through the experiences of your main character.

A simple rule applies, no matter what emotion you want to convey: you need to include *some type of conflict* in your story. It doesn't have to be a big issue—a small clash or awkward moment works fine. Here's an example:

> As I type this email from a small hostel in Paris, my mind can't stop replaying the rather...*eventful* dinner Alex and I just came back from.
>
> You see, we had finished an extremely long day exploring the streets of the city. My hair looked like a rat's nest. I smelled like French blue cheese.
>
> On top of that, my stomach was growling, and I could feel the hangry mood starting to set in.
>
> In my state of hunger-induced desperation, I didn't put

much thought into choosing a place to eat. I simply spotted a nearby restaurant, made a hasty reservation, and off we went.

Little did we know that this impulsive decision would turn out to be a **DISASTROUS mistake.**

"Bonsoir, monsieur et madame!" the waiter greeted us. "Welcome to the most elegant and expensive restaurant in all of Paris!"

"Elegant? I think we may be in the wrong pl—" Alex started to object.

"Let me pour you a glass of our 1966 champagne..." the waiter interrupted, trying to impress us.

"Oh! No thank y-" I attempted to decline, but he swiftly guided us to our table.

"The madam doesn't like champagne? Chloé!" he called out to another waitress. "Bring the 1986 Burgundy, one of our finest reds."

With a swift pop of the bottle, we sat there, utterly in shock by what was unfolding before us.

As the evening went on, it all became a blur...that is, until we received the eye-watering bill. It was at THAT moment that I realized an important lesson for every freelancer.

The email goes on, but let's look at why this story works:

Show, Don't Tell

The email uses vivid descriptions to create an immersive experience for the reader. Through carefully chosen words, the reader is transported to a small hostel in Paris, where they can visualize the author's disheveled appearance, with hair resembling a tangled rat's nest, and detect a distinct scent reminiscent of French blue cheese.

In general, effective storytelling harnesses sensory words to describe smell, sight, taste, and touch. Rather than simply recounting events, the use of descriptive language allows the reader to imagine the scenarios and sensations vividly, evoking a stronger emotional response.

Write Conversationally

By using interjections like "Yay," "Oh," and "Ugh," or sound effects like "CREAK!" and "BAM!", you can make your story feel more alive. We use these expressions when we talk to someone face-to-face, and including them in your storytelling adds a sense of authenticity.

Dialogue is another great tool that makes your story feel more conversational. Instead of just telling the reader what happened, dialogue allows you to showcase the characters' interactions, emotions, and reactions.

Relatable Situation

When your audience can relate to the experiences, emotions, or challenges described in the story, they become more engaged and invested in it. This keeps them reading until the end (to your offer), and it will create trust and further humanize your brand.

Rising Tension or Conflict

In the example, as the story progresses, tension builds as the hero realizes that this is not the restaurant where they were expecting to eat. Their attempts to decline the champagne and their redirection to the table heighten the suspense, leaving the reader eager to know what will happen next. This conflict motivates the reader to continue reading and invest *emotionally* in the narrative.

Stories are all about overcoming adversity, even the most absurd ones, like your toast catching on fire. Without a problem to solve, there's no emotional journey for the readers to experience. In the business world, brands often hesitate to share any difficulties they've faced, fearing it might damage their reputation. But nobody can relate to perfection because life isn't perfect. Some examples of adversity in daily life could include:

- I was trying to assemble my new office chair, but the instructions were missing a crucial step.
- As I left to go on a date, I realized I had locked myself out of the house.
- I was in a really important meeting, but then my dog started barking like crazy.

Universal Lesson

Towards the end of the story, the author sets up a takeaway to connect the dining experience to her audience. Having a universal lesson in your email is essential. It provides relevance that the readers can apply to their own lives or situations.

END OF THE EMAIL

Action

Once you have successfully captured your readers' attention and engaged them with your storytelling, the last step is to guide them toward the action you want them to take. This action could vary depending on your goals, whether it's to make a purchase, subscribe to a service, direct them to a tripwire, or download a resource.

A strong CTA starts with a word that tells your readers what to do. Words like "call," "contact," "click," "download," or "read" make them feel like they should take action right away. It's also important to communicate clearly to your audience *why* they should take the recommended action.

What benefits or value will they gain from taking action? Will it help them solve a problem, achieve a goal, or enhance their lives in some way? By explicitly stating why they should take action, you provide a persuasive argument and address the "what's in it for me" question.

STORYTELLING FOR OTHER EMAIL TYPES

Although the examples we've looked at are for a standard newsletter email, you can use storytelling for other types of emails as well.

Product Launches

When it comes to product launches, storytelling can be a powerful tool to engage subscribers and create excitement around your offerings. Instead of simply providing facts and details about the product, use the storytelling methods covered in this chapter to describe the story *behind its creation*. Share the challenges, inspirations, and journeys that led to the development of the product.

Success Stories

Sharing success stories can be a highly effective way to inspire and motivate your audience. Whether it's your personal journey, the story of your brand, or a testimonial highlighting the success of a particular product, storytelling can bring these narratives to life. For example, you could include details about the adversities the client faced, the strategies they used, and the ultimate result they achieved.

Behind the Scenes

Use storytelling to take your subscribers on a journey and show them the inner workings of your company. Share anecdotes, interesting facts, or personal experiences to make the behind-the-scenes narrative engaging and relatable. This approach helps customers understand the value and quality of your products and services, which makes them more likely to choose your brand.

Promotional Emails

Promotional emails can sometimes come across as pushy or annoying. By incorporating storytelling elements into your promotional emails, you can create a more engaging and compelling message. Instead of simply listing the features and benefits of your product or service, tell a story that relates to the needs or desires of your audience. Focus on the problem your product solves or the transformation it brings and tell the story through the lens of a relatable situation.

CHAPTER RESOURCES

Action Items

1. Start by determining the high-level goal of your email funnel, keeping your product/service and ICAs in mind. Do you want to engage your audience through humor, relatability, education, or something else? This decision will set the tone for the type of relationship you build with readers.

2. Once you understand your goal, you can begin writing emails. Start by creating an outline for the email, including the main story and key takeaway.

3. Then add more details to your outline, such as potential hook ideas, the central conflict, lesson/takeaways, and CTA.

4. The last step is to turn this outline into an engaging email. You can either do this on your own or use an AI writing assistant (or ChatGPT) to help you turn the outline into a coherent and compelling message.

RELEVANT TOOLS

General tools to get you started:

- **Hemingway Editor** is a free tool that improves the readability of your emails by highlighting complex sentences, passive voice, and more.

- Your **email marketing tool of choice** like Mailchimp, Brevo, Klaviyo, GetResponse etc. (for a more comprehensive list, refer back to Chapter 5)
- Additional AI-powered tools:
- **Jasper.ai, Copy.ai,** and **Copymatic** are AI writing tools that can help you craft compelling messages for your emails.
- **Grammarly** is an AI-powered writing assistant that can help refine your email content for grammar, spelling, and style, ensuring your storytelling is polished and error-free.
- **tinyEmail** is an AI email marketing platform that helps you create personalized emails, generate optimized copy, and easily segment your audience.
- **Writecream** uses AI to help you generate marketing copy, audio, and images in seconds.

ChatGPT EXAMPLE PROMPTS

Example 1

"You run a drone videography business that specializes in providing aerial footage for events. Your primary audience is people who are interested in getting drone footage for their events but are not drone pilots. Your task is to brainstorm 15 engaging and informative email ideas that you can send to your subscribers. These topics should include stories, situations, lessons, and tips that showcase the potential of drone footage and how it can capture their special moments."

Example 2

"You are a senior marketer with expertise in copywriting, working at a custom 3D merch company. Draft 10 short bold and engaging hooks for an email about unexpected, yet ingenious, requests the company has received from clients. The hook should be 1-2 sentences and pique curiosity. Use these example hooks as a reference: [Example 1], [Example 2], [Example 3]."

Example 3

"Based on the outline below, write an engaging 250-word email for a data analysis and visualization bootcamp. The tone should be friendly yet knowledgeable.

The structure of the email has a hook, story with a minor conflict, key takeaway, and call to action. Avoid jargon or complex vocabulary. Email outline: [Insert outline]."

13

TEN PERCENT

Webinar Funnels

For more than a century, researchers have been studying how well people remember new information and, more importantly, how much they forget. They came up with a concept known as the "forgetting curve," which suggests that, when we don't actively try to retain information, we tend to lose it over time.

The forgetting curve follows an exponential pattern, which means that in the first days following exposure to new information, we forget a lot of it, possibly up to 90% according to some studies.[51] Even memories that initially seem strong are destined to fade away over time.

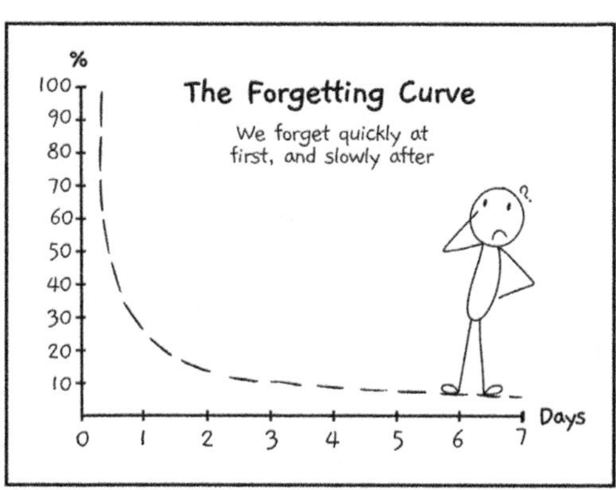

As days pass, the percentage of information we remember decreases until we are left remembering only 10%

Although we tend to forget information that our brain considers irrelevant, there's still a good chance that roughly 10% of your message will stick with your audience. As you prepare your webinar, take a moment to reflect on the core idea or concept you want your audience to retain. In other words, what's your 10% message? Here are some examples of 10% messages from this book:

- Without enough traffic, your business won't get far.
- Humanized brands build stronger relationships.
- Streamline your website to prevent decision fatigue.

The problem is that people remember very little, and what they do remember is often *random*. If you don't control the 10% message, it'll be left to chance.

Cognitive scientist Dr. Carmen Simon confirmed this concept of random memory in a study she conducted in 2013.[52] She had 1,500 people look at a PowerPoint with 20 slides, each containing one message.

After 48 hours, she asked them what they remembered. On average, people remembered four slides. To get even more information from the study, she segmented the participants into different groups. The control group, which saw the decks without any modifications, remembered information from four random slides. Dr. Simon and her team then presented the same PowerPoint to other groups with a crucial difference: four specific slides were modified.

For instance, in one version, the modified slides had a different background color, while in another version, the modified slides consisted mostly of pictures with only a few words.

Participants still remembered only four slides overall, but the modifications had a noticeable effect. Specifically, participants remembered the messages on the four slides that were specifically modified. In other words, Dr. Simon's study demonstrates that you have the power to control the 10% message that people remember.

TACTICS TO MAKE YOUR 10% MESSAGE MEMORABLE

What can we take away from this study, and how can it help improve your webinars? Dr. Simon's research provides some valuable insights to make your webinars more memorable. By using these findings, you can make your 10% message stick with your audience.

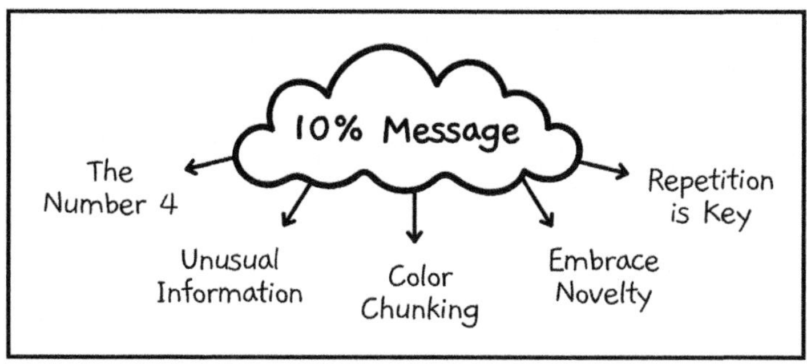

Ways to increase the recall of your 10% message

The Magic Number Four

Research, including Dr. Simon's study, suggests that people have limited capacity in their short-term memory. They can only hold around 4 or 5 items at a time. This means that, during your webinar, you need to be strategic about what information you want your audience to remember. Focus on key points, essential details, and actionable takeaways rather than overwhelming them with too much content.

Unusual Information Stands Out

When you create a webinar, the way you present your content matters. If everything in your webinar is overloaded with intense colors, flashy graphics, or overwhelming visuals, participants may feel confused and overloaded. On the other hand, if your webinar is filled with plain text, monotonous bullet points, and lacks engaging elements, it might fail to make a lasting impression on your viewers.

Use Colors as Memory Aids

Organizing your slides by color coordination or "chunking" related content together can improve memory recall. You can do this by using the same color scheme for related content or using distinct images to represent different sections. When making your webinar, don't overload your audience with too much information. Treat your webinar like a sneak peek of your main offer. This will create interest, so your viewers want to learn more. To do this, focus on creating clear connections between different "chunks" of your webinar. This will help your audience understand and retain the information better and increase the likelihood of them converting down the line.

Embrace Novelty

Using novelty as an attention-grabbing tool can be highly effective during webinars. People naturally gravitate toward new and surprising information.

To ensure your audience remains engaged and retains your 10% message, try incorporating unique elements into your webinar, like fresh insights, unexpected anecdotes, or innovative approaches to familiar topics. By adding these unique elements, you'll capture your audience's interest and create a more memorable and impactful webinar experience.

Repetition

Repetition is a powerful technique to reinforce key messages in your webinar. By repeating essential words or phrases throughout your presentation, you can anchor the information in your audience's memory. Studies have shown that audience attention is greatest at the beginning and end of presentations and webinars.[53] So, introduce your core message at the start and repeat key points at the end to ensure your audience retains that crucial 10% of the information.

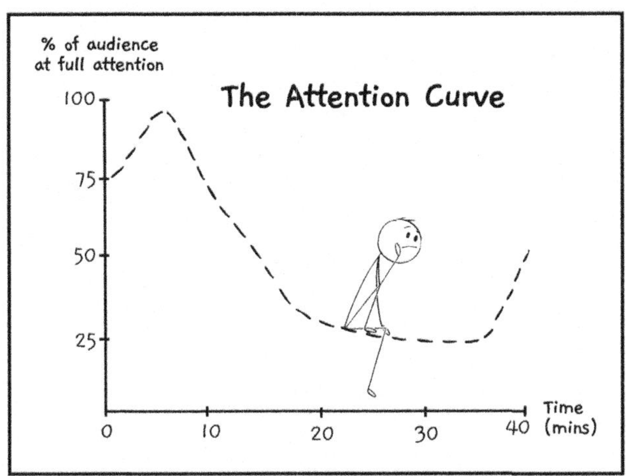

Attention is highest in the beginning, lowest in the middle, and medium at the end.

Create a Roadmap Before Starting

Having a clear and organized structure for your webinar is essential—it's like creating a map to guide both you and your audience. Research shows that people remember structured information 40% better than unstructured information.

To make your webinar effective and easy to remember, use structures that are intuitive and easy to follow. For instance, if you're explaining steps or sharing information, go with a simple order, like "first, second, third" or "past, present, future." When you want to convince your audience, follow the "problem-solution-benefit" approach. This means first talking about the problem, then providing your solution, and finally, highlighting the benefits.

WEBINAR USE CASES

Webinars are a versatile, effective tool for various types of offers. Below, we'll cover some different use cases for both live and pre-recorded webinars.

Bootcamps and Courses

Live webinars are a great way to engage your audience directly, providing valuable insights into the content and structure of your educational programs. On the other hand, pre-recorded webinars offer the advantage of flexibility, allowing participants to access the content at their convenience. Use interactive features, like Q&A sessions and polls, in live webinars or incorporate engaging elements, like quizzes and on-screen interactions, in pre-recorded webinars to keep participants actively involved and interested.

Group Coaching and Masterminds

For group coaching and mastermind programs, webinars offer a unique opportunity to foster a sense of community and collaboration among participants. In live webinars, you can bring your members together, facilitate group discussions, and encourage the sharing of experiences and ideas in real-time. For pre-recorded webinars, you can create discussion forums or community platforms where participants can interact and exchange insights at their convenience.

Done-for-you Services

Webinars are also an ideal way to showcase your "done-for-you" services and illustrate how your service can solve the client's problem. In live webinars, use case studies and real-life examples to demonstrate successful projects and interact with the audience. For pre-recorded webinars, craft compelling stories and testimonials to showcase your expertise in providing tailored solutions. Whether live or pre-recorded, address potential clients' pain points and offer solutions, positioning yourself as a reliable and trustworthy service provider.

Membership Programs

Live webinars for your program can offer members access to exclusive content and insights, fostering engagement and connection. For pre-recorded webinars, create a series of valuable content that members can access at their own pace. This will reinforce the ongoing benefits and value of your ongoing programs. Whether live or pre-recorded, webinars increase the amount of value you provide in the program and can enhance member loyalty.

1:1 Coaching Programs

Personalized webinars, delivered either live or pre-recorded, are an effective way to attract clients for your 1:1 coaching programs. For live webinars, tailor your presentations to address viewers' individual needs and answer questions in real-time. In pre-recorded webinars, customize the content to suit the client's unique requirements, allowing them to access valuable insights at their convenience.

LIVE WEBINAR FUNNEL

Webinars provide an excellent opportunity to connect with your prospects, subscribers, and customers more effectively. However, it's crucial to avoid turning the webinar into a dull sales pitch. Instead, focus on delivering genuine value to your audience, like you would with a lead magnet or freebie. Consider your webinar as a "test drive" for your value pyramid. If your attendees find the content valuable and enjoyable, they will likely be interested in learning more and, as a result, more receptive to your upsell page's offerings. So, ensure your webinar offers real value, making your audience eager to learn more about your products or services.

The ultimate goal is to automate your webinar funnel so that it's not dependent on your time. We'll discuss how to do that shortly. But in the beginning, live webinars can be a great tool to assess how leads respond to your content and help you refine your messaging before you transition to a pre-recorded webinar funnel.

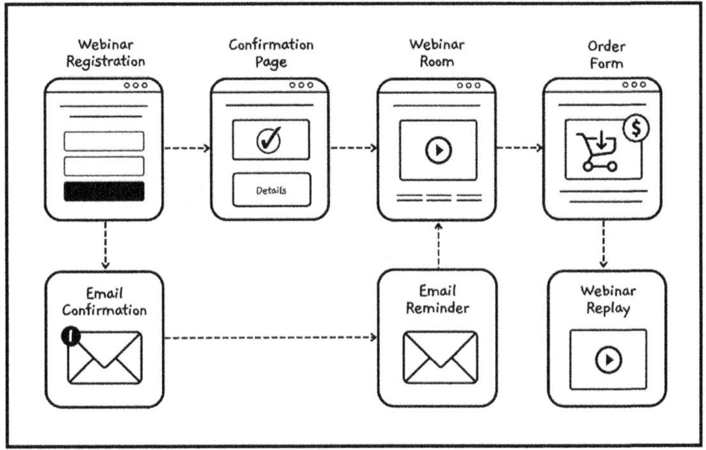

Live Webinar Funnel (note you can send the confirmation via text instead)

Registration Page

The webinar registration page serves as the entry point, playing a critical role in attracting potential attendees and encouraging them to reserve a spot. A successful registration page has a compelling headline, a concise and engaging description of what participants will gain from the event, and key details such as the date, time, duration, and presenter's credentials. It's crucial to emphasize the unique value of the webinar and why it's a must-attend event.

The page also has a simple, user-friendly registration form, collecting only necessary information, like name and email address. Long forms can deter people from completing the sign-up process. Optionally, you can include space for attendees to share specific questions about the webinar, which you can address once it goes live.

Confirmation Page

After someone signs up for your webinar, they will see your confirmation page. Its main job is to confirm their registration and remind them of the webinar details. A good confirmation page should be easy to understand and visually pleasing, giving attendees confidence that their registration went through. Make sure to repeat important information like the date, time, and link to join the webinar.

The truth is, not every registered attendee will remember to show up for your webinar. That's why it's a good idea to send a friendly reminder email 24 hours before the webinar starts. This email should remind people what they will learn from the webinar and give clear instructions on how to join. Encourage them to add the event to their calendar, so they don't forget.

Webinar Room and Order Form

During the webinar, you'll share valuable information, emphasize your 10% message, and interact with the audience in a virtual webinar room hosted on platforms like Zoom or GoToWebinar.

After the attendees finish watching the webinar, you'll guide them to an order form with a relevant upsell. This step takes advantage of their interest and engagement, since they've just seen the webinar's value, with the opportunity to learn more. By offering an upsell that complements what they've learned, you create an easy way for interested attendees to take action and continue ascending your value pyramid.

Replay Page

Even if you remind people 24 hours before the webinar, many of them (up to 60-80%) may not attend. That's why having a webinar replay page is crucial. You can send registrants the access link to this page, usually with a countdown of 48 or 72 hours before it gets taken offline to create urgency. On the replay page, you can post a recording of the webinar with the attached offer, allowing you to reach those who registered but missed the live event. This gives you another chance to close more sales and engage with your subscribers who might have been interested but couldn't attend.

AUTOMATED WEBINAR FUNNEL

Once you've perfected the live webinar, you can smoothly switch to the automated webinar funnel to save time. Automated webinars are pre-recorded yet designed to appear as live events, using specialized software, like GoToWebinar, Livestorm, or Builderall. With this software, you can upload your pre-recorded webinar, and it will be scheduled to run at specific times and dates. The software can also handle email notifications and reminders for your registered subscribers. While you can use Zoom, it's easiest when the components of your webinar funnel are ALL in one place (i.e. integrate opt-in pages, create event automation etc.). Zoom works great for live events, but it doesn't have innate funnel capabilities, so you would have to integrate it with another platform.

You can run automated webinars frequently, since they don't require live hosting. Another possibility with automated webinars is that you can provide the option for attendees to watch an instant webinar as soon as they register.

The structure of your automated webinar funnel follows the same path as a live webinar funnel. It begins with a webinar registration page where visitors can subscribe to reserve their spot for the event. The only difference is that, when people register, you have two choices: give them instant access or delayed access.

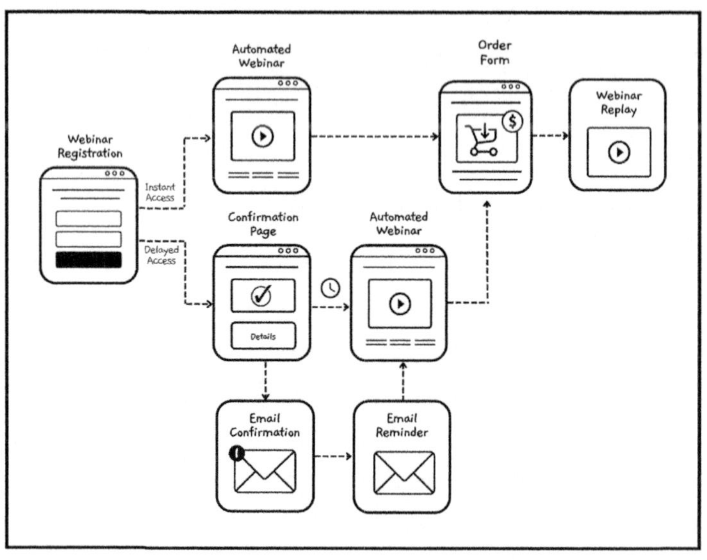

Automated Webinar Funnel Workflow

OPTION 1

Instant Access

When people sign up for the webinar, they are immediately directed to the webinar room to watch the pre-recorded webinar. This option provides instant gratification because they can access the content immediately after registration. This technique can increase engagement and reduce the chances of no-shows. The simplicity of this approach, with fewer steps and no separate confirmation page, can make it easier for attendees to navigate the process.

Pros:

- Instant access to webinar content: Attendees can start watching the webinar immediately after registration, increasing engagement and reducing the chances of no-shows.
- Simplicity and ease of use: By eliminating the need for a separate confirmation page, the registration process becomes more streamlined and user-friendly.
- Higher probability of attendance: Since attendees get instant access to valuable content, they may be more motivated to attend the session.
- Cons:
- Lack of a "live webinar" experience: Because the webinar is pre-recorded and attendees get immediate access, it might lack the interactive and personal touch of a live webinar experience, which can make it feel somewhat automated and less engaging.
- Less anticipation: With instant access, attendees do not experience the build-up of anticipation that delayed access can provide, potentially reducing excitement and curiosity.

OPTION 2

Delayed Access

With this option, after users register for the webinar, they are redirected to a confirmation page. On this page, all the essential webinar details, such as the date, time, and webinar room link, are confirmed, just like in the live webinar funnel. This means that attendees have to wait a certain amount of time before they can access the webinar room.

Pros:

- Increased anticipation: By creating a short waiting period of time between registration and access to the webinar, attendees may become more excited and eager to participate.
- Simulates a "live webinar" experience: The specific time and date for access give the webinar a more interactive and time-sensitive feel, even though it's pre-recorded.

Cons:

- Risk of forgetfulness or scheduling conflicts: A delay in access may lead some attendees to forget about the webinar or encounter scheduling conflicts, resulting in lower attendance rates.
- Potential loss of interest: If the waiting period between registration and the webinar is too long, attendees might lose interest or get distracted by other things, decreasing the likelihood that they will show up.
- Longer registration process: Having a confirmation page and a delayed access system adds more friction to the registration process, potentially leading to a drop-off in sign-ups.

CHAPTER RESOURCES

Action Items

1. Identify the 10% message you want attendees to remember. This will be the cornerstone of your webinar content.

2. Plan the sequence of your webinar's components carefully. Use memory recall techniques, like repetition, color coordination, and visuals, to help participants remember the content better.

3. Craft a compelling registration page with a clear headline and concise description of the webinar's benefits, using a user-friendly form to collect attendee information.

4. Start with a live webinar funnel, gauging engagement and addressing participant questions. Use this feedback to refine your message and delivery.

5. Once you're confident about the live webinar's 10% message, slides, and delivery, you can then scale your efforts by automating it. For automated webinar funnels, you can choose to provide instant or delayed webinar access, depending on your goal.

RELEVANT TOOLS

General tools to get you started:

- **GoToWebinar, Livestorm, ClickMeeting,** and **EasyWebinar** are webinar software tools that let you create live and automated webinars with either integrated or redirected order forms.
- **Builderall** is an all-in-one marketing and funnel building platform with a suite of over 40 tools,

including a webinar builder with integrated video, chat, and sales features.

- **GetResponse** is a marketing suite with a conversion funnel tool that includes a comprehensive live/automated webinar builder.
- Additional AI-powered tools:
- **Beautiful.ai** and **Gamma** help you design visually appealing and engaging slide decks in minutes.
- **Presentations.ai** is a ChatGPT-powered tool for presentations. Just type your idea, as you would for a ChatGPT prompt, and it outputs a custom slide deck.
- **Tome** helps users easily generate entire narratives or stories from documents to create cohesive and memorable presentations.
- **Simplified** uses AI to improve presentation content for clarity to make sure you are communicating effectively.
- **Jasper.ai, Copy.ai,** and **Copymatic** are AI writing tools that can help you craft better copy and scripts for your webinar funnel.
- **Steve AI** and **Pictory** are AI-powered video editing tools that help you easily edit pre-recorded videos for your automated webinar funnel.

ChatGPT EXAMPLE PROMPTS

Example 1

"You are a popular social media influencer, and you want to create a 20-minute webinar that teaches aspiring influencers how to create a strong personal brand. The key takeaway of the webinar is that creating value-centric, authentic content is the best way to attract your tribe. The beginning and middle of the slide deck should focus on education and adding value.

Make sure to repeat the key takeaway at the start and end of the presentation so participants retain that message. The CTA should encourage participants to buy your Personal Brand Media Kit, which they can get for 30% off."

Example 2

"Based on the slide deck outline above, write a script that takes around 20 minutes to speak. Include the estimated speaking time for each slide. Make sure at least 5 slides are actionable and provide clear tips/strategies that can help participants. The tone should be relatable, friendly, and authentic. Avoid jargon or complex vocabulary."

Example 3

"Generate a concise, engaging webinar registration page for a business that provides financial education to college graduates and young professionals. The webinar is about teaching the basics of personal finance. Include a compelling heading, subheading, and a list of 5 key benefits that registrants will learn from the webinar."

14

THE APPLE WAY

Product Launch Funnels

It was the 2020 pandemic, and there I was...lounging in my pajamas and eating too much sourdough bread as I scrolled through the news.

Little did I know that my feed would soon be flooded with headlines about the upcoming release of the iPhone 12. From "iPhone 12 Release Date: Launching in 5 Days!" to "How to Secure an iPhone 12 Pre-Order Ahead of the Release Date," the excitement was palpable.

Now, I wasn't *planning* on buying a new phone, but the buzz was contagious. Previews and rumors about the latest iPhone were spreading like wildfire across the internet, and I couldn't help clicking on articles to see what all the fuss was about.

And that's because Apple is the MASTER of product launches. They don't just release a new product and slap on a price tag. No, long before the actual launch date, they rope in expert bloggers, news outlets, and notable personalities to join the hype. They create a whirlwind of anticipation, building curiosity and leaving everyone guessing about what the big reveal will be.

THE 2-PHASE FUNNEL

There are several different ways to set up a product launch funnel. We'll go over three common types. Most brands do a combination of them, since different funnels can reach your audience in different ways. In general, each product launch funnel has two main categories.

#1 The Teaser Phase

The teaser phase is when you offer sneak peeks and teasers about your upcoming product through social media posts, email newsletters, and original content (like blog articles). Give your audience a taste of what's to come to create curiosity.

#2 The Release Phase

After building anticipation and excitement during the teaser phase, it's time to officially launch your product. During the release phase, the goal is to incentivize as many early customers as possible to purchase the product. You can do this by offering limited-time promotions or discounts to encourage customers to make a purchase during the launch period. Now let's take a closer look at the funnels.

SOCIAL MEDIA LAUNCH FUNNEL

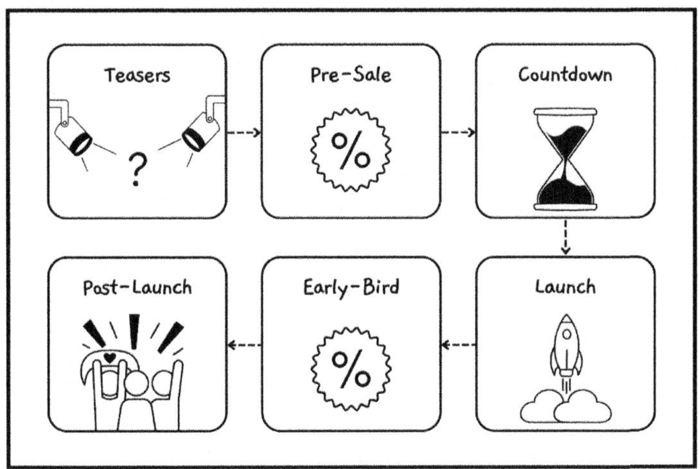

Social Media Post Order

When it comes to creating anticipation and excitement for your product launch, using the power of social media can be a game-changer. Your social media platforms can be a goldmine for connecting with your existing loyal followers and potential clients who are eager to explore your new offering. If you have a larger budget, you can also consider partnering with influencers to increase the reach of your new product.

To make the most of social media for your product launch, you'll want to craft engaging posts in four different categories: teaser posts, countdown posts, launch posts, and post-launch posts.

The Teasers

In teaser posts, provide subtle hints and glimpses of the product or offer you've been developing. Be careful not to reveal too much information at this stage. Think of it as a friend teasing you with the promise of "big news" they can't wait to share. This approach builds curiosity and intrigue among your audience, leaving them eagerly awaiting more details. A few examples of teaser posts include:

- **Behind-the-scenes**: Take your audience behind the scenes with posts that show them the fascinating process of developing your product. People love to see what goes on behind closed doors, which will create anticipation for the official launch.
- **Feature excited clients**: Think of these posts as playful client interviews. You can create posts that showcase their positive experiences with your existing products and ask them what they're most looking forward to with the upcoming product.
- **Product sneak peeks**: These posts offer glimpses of your upcoming product without revealing everything. This strategy keeps your social media followers curious and eager to find out more.
- **Guessing games**: These types of posts are interactive and get your followers to guess what your new product is. You can use quizzes, riddles, or games to start conversations and increase engagement with your community. For example, sharing partial product shots can spark curiosity and encourage discussions among your followers.

Pre-Sale Offers (Optional)

Offering your followers exclusive pre-sale discounts, bonuses, pre-orders, or special deals can be a powerful incentive to encourage early interest and purchases. Make sure these posts emphasize the limited-time nature of the offer, generating a sense of urgency that motivates people to seize the attractive deal.

Countdown Posts

Once you've teased your product on social media, it's time to announce the much-anticipated launch date. You can create excitement by sharing a series of countdown visuals, displaying the remaining days and/or hours until your product officially hits the market.

Launch Day

On the day you launch your product, you want your post to be *scroll-stopping.* Use bold colors, big letters, clear pictures, and eye-catching visuals to stand out on social media. Show your product clearly and explain what makes it special. Make sure your audience knows they can't miss out on this amazing new offer.

Post-Launch + Early-Bird Offers

Following the launch, you can continue the momentum by offering early-bird discounts and post-launch content.

- **Early-bird discounts**: Offer special discounts for early customers to create excitement and encourage immediate purchases.
- **Highlight product benefits**: Showcase why your new product is worth getting. Use social media carousels or videos to explain its advantages in more detail, without overwhelming your audience.
- **Show the product in use**: Share quick videos to demonstrate how easy and enjoyable it is to use your product. This helps your audience understand its benefits better.

- **Partner with influencers**: Collaborate with industry influencers or celebrities to promote your product. Their endorsement can expand your reach and attract a new audience.
- **Share user feedback**: Encourage customers to share their experiences with your product. Sharing positive feedback on social media can pique interest and build trust among potential buyers.

Whether users click on the links in your pre-launch, launch, or post-launch social media posts, you need to direct them someplace. When people click the link in your post, they should be taken to your sales page; from there, they can make their purchase through a simple order form.

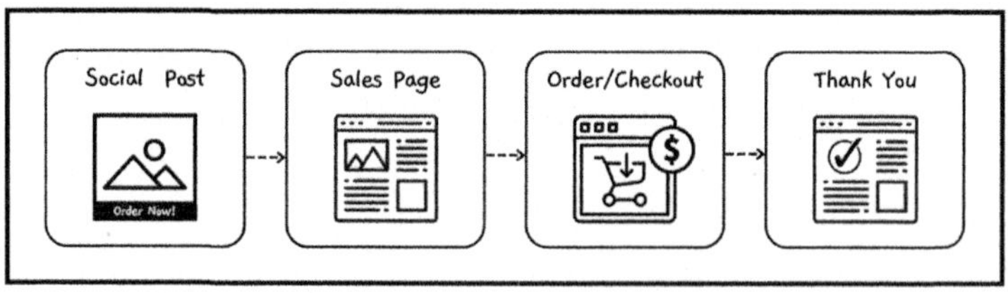

Social Media Launch Funnel Workflow

CONTENT MARKETING LAUNCH FUNNEL

Content marketing is a good way to build a launch funnel, but it takes time and consistency to do it well. Even if your product launch isn't for a few months, you should start content marketing as soon as possible. Creating valuable content, like blog articles, will help you attract and engage potential customers.

If you are using organic content to drive traffic and generate leads, why not take advantage of that existing audience when it's time to launch your product? You can create a funnel that uses your organic content to guide potential customers through the sales process.

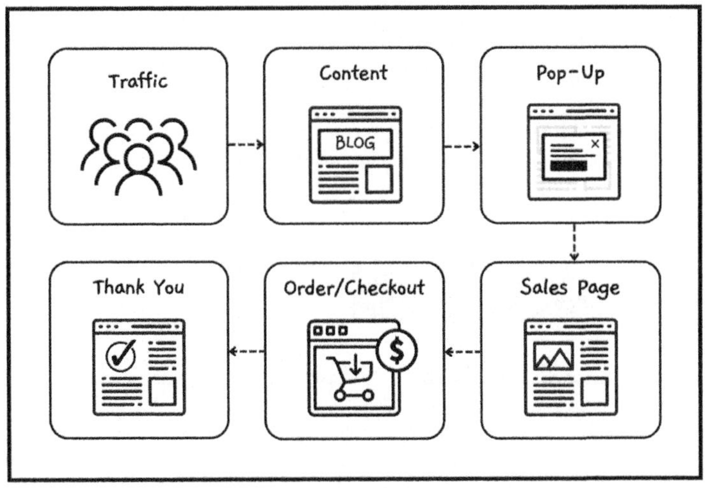

Content Marketing Funnel Workflow

The main difference between a content launch funnel and a social media launch funnel is that, instead of generating anticipation and launching through social media posts, you will do it through your organic content.

The first step is to publish informative and engaging content, such as articles on your blog, to attract and educate your audience about your product or industry. Then, as people engage with the content, you want to create a pop-up that offers pre-orders or early-bird discounts.

To add a sense of urgency to your pop-up, consider using a countdown timer. The main purpose of the pop-up is to introduce your visitors to the product, educate them about its problem-solving capabilities, and guide them to a sales page for more details.

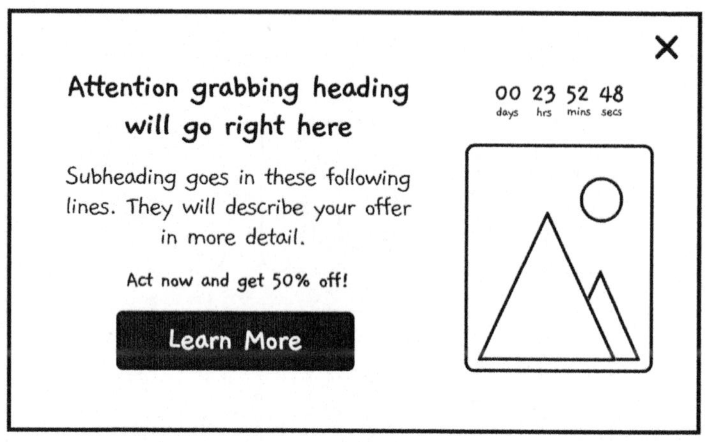

Anatomy of an urgency pop-up: includes a heading, subheading, limited discount, CTA, countdown timer, and image.

The sales page, order form, and order confirmation that we explored in the social media launch funnel can also be applied to this funnel. If you choose to create several types of launch funnels, you only need to make adjustments at the *beginning* of each funnel. The good news is that you can reuse the same sales pages and order forms, saving time and effort. For example, you can create a hybrid funnel that combines the two we've discussed:

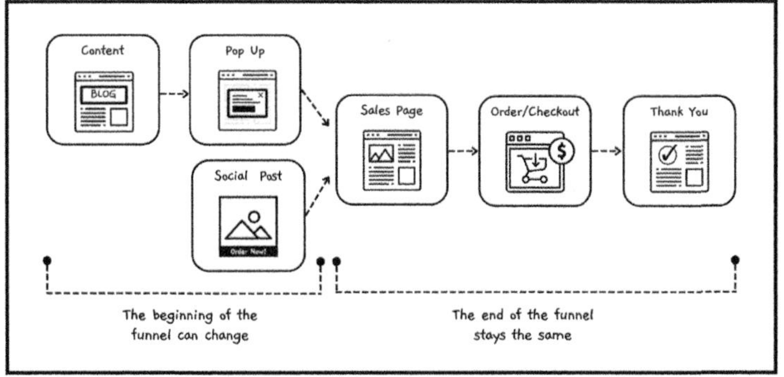

Example of a hybrid funnel that combines social media and content marketing to generate traffic to the second half of the funnel.

EMAIL/TEXT LAUNCH FUNNEL

Let's dive into the email/text launch funnel, an incredibly effective approach you shouldn't overlook. Let's look at how to approach this launch sequence using the list of subscribers who are either past customers or qualified leads. Typically, email/text launch sequences consist of around messages (though of course, you can adjust this as necessary).

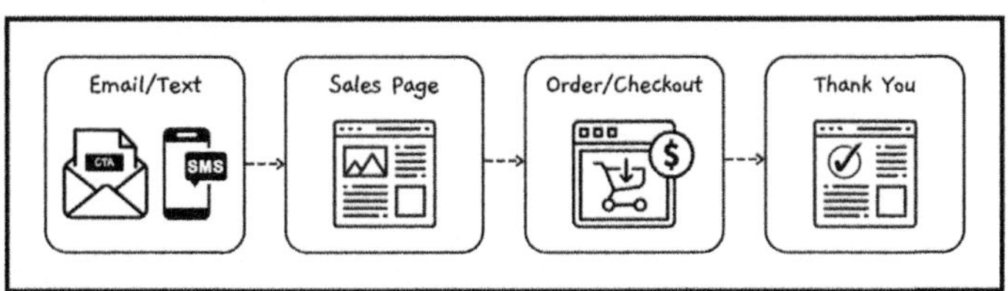

Note: you can replace the sales page with a pre-sale page if you haven't launched the offer/product yet.

MESSAGE #1

Introduction and Teaser

In this first message, *tell a story* about a common problem your audience faces (if you need a refresher on storytelling, visit Chapter 12). Show that you understand their struggles and goals. Towards the end of the message, mention that you've developed a solution and offer a brief tease of the product.

Keeping the details brief is essential. This will generate excitement and curiosity in this first message. Encourage your readers to learn more by visiting a pre-sell page where they can find more information about your product and place pre-orders. This way, you create urgency and set the stage for a series of engaging emails leading to a successful product launch and sales.

MESSAGE #2

Educate About the Problem

In this message, you'll go deeper into the problem your customers are facing. Share relevant statistics or case studies of others who have experienced similar challenges. The goal is to educate your customers about the problem in a more detailed and informative way.

By presenting these facts, your customers will realize *that they are not alone*—which creates a sense of solidarity and reinforces the importance of a solution.

After highlighting the problem, transition to sharing your solution. To learn more and take action, direct them to the pre-sell page for pre-orders. The sales page should give them more details and convince them to make an order.

MESSAGE #3

The Solution and Emphasize the Pre-Sale Offer

This message comes before your official product launch. Instead of focusing on problems, it's *all about excitement.* Highlight the benefits of your product. How will it help them? Why is it something they can't live without? What makes it better than the competition?

Then, offer a special discount for clients who purchase the product before the official launch date. Pre-orders can help build anticipation and revenue for your company. In this email, direct your audience to the pre-order sales page that addresses any concerns they might have.

MESSAGE #4

Product Launch

This message is a celebration of your product's official launch. You're thrilled with the results. Share positive feedback from private product testing, and if you've sold out from pre-orders, let your audience know.

This email should radiate excitement and convey the message: *The product is finally here, and it's amazing! Customers love it, and you will too.* Then, guide your readers to a sales page where they can purchase your product.

MESSAGE #5

Final Call

One to two days after launch day, send a follow-up message to remind your customers that your product is available. This time, create a sense of urgency, depending on your product.

For example, if it's a physical product, you can mention that it's selling fast and won't be available for much longer. For digital services, you might offer a special discount for those who sign up before midnight.

WAITLIST LAUNCH FUNNEL

So far, we've looked at launch funnels that mainly focus on products or services that are ready for launch. But what about offers that are still in the development phase? That's where the waitlist launch funnel comes in. Rather than scrambling to generate buzz just weeks or days before the launch, a waitlist funnel allows you to create anticipation. Once your product or service is complete, you can then easily transition your waitlist into an email/text launch funnel.

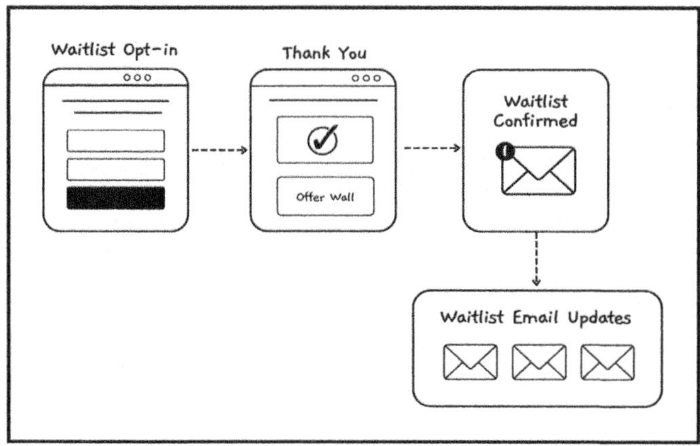

Your waitlist funnel starts with an opt-in page (meaning, a page where people choose to receive email or text communication). Think of this page as a mini landing page, where you have a strong above-the-fold (ATF) section, and you highlight the main benefits of your upcoming product/service. The goal is to persuade visitors to take action—in this case, to get updates about the new offer.

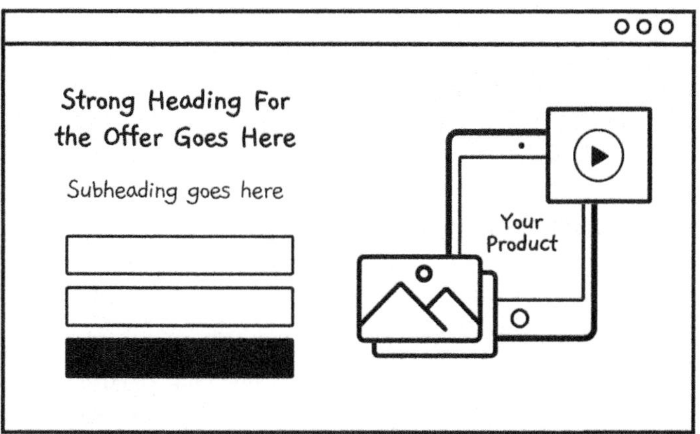

Waitlist Opt-in Example (ATF)

After subscribing, they land on a thank you page, where you confirm their early access registration. In addition to confirming their registration, you have two options for your offer wall:

1. Encourage customers to pre-order the product/service at a discounted rate for early-bird access. This helps you generate pre-launch revenue to fund the final development stages.
2. Provide a discount that they can redeem when the product launches.
3. Provide a beta trial: If your product is in its beta phase, selling discounted early access (and even offering the first handful of spots/products for free) helps you gather critical customer experience data and testimonials.

Once people have successfully subscribed to your waitlist, it is crucial to stay in touch with them. Without regular updates, their excitement for your product may dwindle before it even hits the market. You can maintain their interest through emails by offering them glimpses of what's to come, special content, or routine updates.

ROBINHOOD'S HYBRID FUNNEL

Who *doesn't* want to get people interested in their product before it's officially available? Few have been as successful as the notorious fin-tech startup, Robinhood. They managed to generate 1 million sign-ups for their waitlist while their mobile app was still being developed.[54]

While offering a commission-free stock trading platform was a big deal, what really got people excited was their clever waitlist strategy that built up hype for a whole year before the app launched.

Robinhood's Waitlist Opt-in Hero Section

Robinhood's sign-up page was straightforward, focusing on the sign-up button and encouraging users to act quickly. The waitlist sign-up process was hassle-free, only requiring the user's email address. After signing up with their emails, users received a Thank You message informing them of their position on the waiting list.

Here's where things get interesting. Once users completed the waitlist process, the Thank You page immediately encouraged them to enter the referral funnel. This merging of two funnels, creating a seamless experience for the user, is known as a hybrid funnel.

Thank you!

We have added your email address to the signup queue.

327,648 People ahead of you

This reservation is held for yourname@gmail.com Is this not you?

Interested in priority access?

Get early access by referring your friends. The more friends that join, the sooner you'll get access.

Or share this unique link:
www.robinhood.com/referral-link123

Robinhood's Thank You page has two elements: 1) the number of people ahead of you and 2) the referral funnel that promises to bump up your spot on the waitlist.

Robinhood's referral funnel was incredibly straightforward. To move up the waitlist and get earlier access to the platform, users needed to refer the platform to their family and friends. The more people joined using their referral links, the higher they climbed in the line for platform access upon launch.

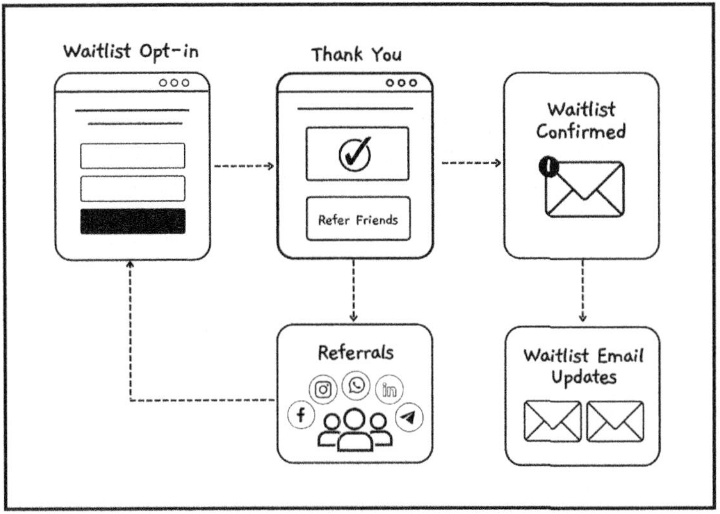

The hybrid approach of Robinhood's waitlist and referral funnel acted as a catalyst for their exponential growth. By adopting some of Robinhood's strategies, you can set up your waitlist funnel for success. Let's break down why Robinhood's waitlist funnel was so successful.

Viral Growth

The Robinhood case centered on having their registrants promote the product FOR them. Math tells us that, if each person refers more than one individual (and then those people do the same), the growth is exponential.

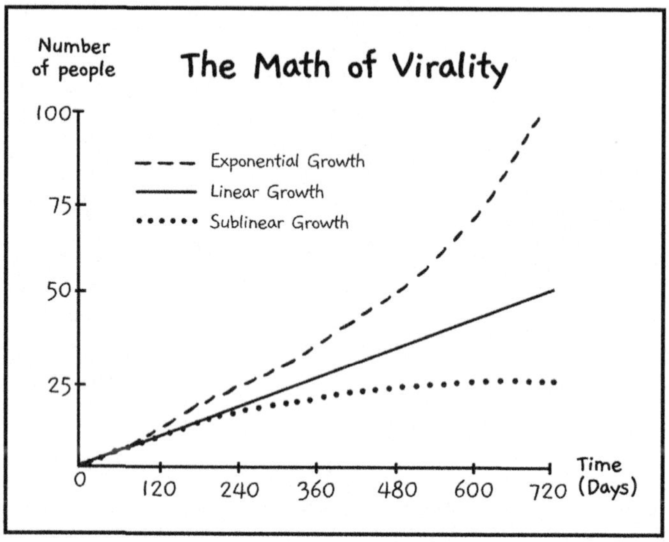

In this chart, we can see three types of growth. The dashed line shows exponential growth, where each new user, on average, brings in more than one additional user (and that new user brings in another one and so on). The bold line represents linear growth, which means the user count increases at a steady rate because every new user, on average, brings in one more user. The dotted line illustrates sublinear growth, indicating that the user count doesn't increase much on its own because each new user, on average, doesn't manage to bring in a new user.

The math behind exponential growth is precisely why Robinhood's growth went viral. To incentivize people to jump the queue and refer others, they needed to create a sense of scarcity by offering "priority access."

If you want to create a waitlist funnel that experiences viral growth in anticipation of your product/service launch, you need to incentivize referrals. In Robinhood's case, they provided priority access. Other methods could include:

- Limited Editions: Offer a limited edition or special version of the product to referrers.
- Discount Tiers: Create different discount levels based on the number of referrals made.
- Exclusive Features: Provide exclusive features or benefits to those who refer others.
- Referral Bonuses: Give monetary rewards or credits for each successful referral.
- Leaderboards: Display a referral leaderboard, publicly recognizing top referrers.
- Early Beta Testing: Allow referrers to participate in beta testing and provide feedback.

CHAPTER RESOURCES

Action Items

1. Determine your audience's preferred communication channel—text, social media, email, blogs, video tutorials etc. Pick one channel for now.
2. Based on the chosen communication channel from Step 1, pick the most effective launch funnel strategy for your business (i.e. social media launch funnel, text launch funnel, etc.)
3. If your product is still in the development phase, consider setting up a waitlist funnel. If you want a referral-based waitlist, pick an incentive, like limited editions, early access, or bonuses.

4. If you plan to offer monetary rewards or a prolonged discount period, create a clear budget. Questions to think about include: How much can you give in referral bonuses? What is the highest discount you can offer while staying profitable?
5. Define the timeframe for your launch funnel. Establish the duration of the waitlist, pre-sale, early-bird, and post-launch period.
6. Once you've identified your launch funnel, budget considerations, and time constraints, you're ready to build the funnel. Use the launch funnel tips and diagrams from the chapter to support you.

RELEVANT TOOLS

General tools to get you started:

- **OptinMonster** helps you create pop-ups to redirect website visitors to a sales page or create opt-in forms for your waitlist.
- **Hello Bar** lets you create eye-catching notification bars, alerts, and pop-ups for your launch funnel.
- **Wheelio** allows you to gamify the opt-in process by offering website visitors a chance to spin a wheel for exclusive offers or waitlist access.
- **ConvertFlow** is a funnel builder that lets you create scheduled promotion funnels, personalized opt-in forms, expiring countdowns, pop-ups, and more.
- **Builderall** is an all-in-one marketing and funnel-building platform with a suite of over 40 tools, including a launch tool, email/text messaging, and social media post scheduling.

- **ReferralCandy** lets you create referral programs that motivate existing users to refer friends, which can help you build your waitlist launch funnel.
- **Later** is a social media planning tool to help you schedule and plan content for your social media launch funnel.
- Your **email/text marketing tool of choice,** like MailChimp, ManyChat, SendPulse etc. (for a more comprehensive list, refer back to Chapter 5) to send pre-launch, launch, and post-launch messages to your subscribers.

Additional AI-powered tools:

- **TurboSite** uses AI to analyze user behavior and offers real-time suggestions that can help you create more effective website pop-ups, sales pages, and waitlist pages.
- **aiCarousels** simplifies the design and writing process of creating engaging carousel posts.
- **Creasquare**, **Ocaya**, **Practina** are all-in-one AI platforms for creating, writing, and scheduling social media content.
- **Writecream** uses AI to help you generate marketing copy, audio, and images in seconds.
- **Jasper.ai, Copy.ai** and **Copymatic** are AI copywriting tools that can help you write your website, email, blog, and social media copy in a fraction of the time.

ChatGPT EXAMPLE PROMPTS

Example 1

"Generate 10 detailed short-form video ideas for Instagram Reels and TikTok that provide a sneak peek of our upcoming nourishing hair-growth oil. Each video concept should be creative and unique, designed to excite viewers about the product. Provide specific descriptions of the type of shots and content that should be included in each video, focusing on engaging visuals and storytelling to highlight the product's benefits and use cases. The goal is to create content that resonates with our audience and builds anticipation for the product launch."

Example 2

"Brainstorm 5 incentive strategies that encourage individuals to join the waitlist for an upcoming AI investment course and motivate them to refer their friends. Make sure these incentives do not involve monetary rewards. After listing the strategies, explain which one you believe would be the best for generating referrals and explain your reasoning."

Example 3

"Come up with 3 unique and engaging early-bird campaign ideas for promoting our new hands-on educational science kits for kids. The campaigns should highlight the kits' key features and encourage purchases during the first week after launch. The kits include topics like astronomy, biology, chemistry, and invention. Incorporate elements like limited-time discounts, bonus items, and exclusive online tutorials in the early-bird campaigns."

15

JUST LIKE HABITS

Funnel Sequencing

In his best-selling book "Atomic Habits," James Clear introduces the concept of habit stacking, a strategy for adding new habits into your routine by stacking them on top of existing habits.[55] For example, if you make a cup of coffee every morning and you want to start reading more, you can stack these habits. Every time you finish making your coffee, sit down to read for ten minutes.

This concept of habit stacking parallels beautifully with the concept of funnel sequencing. With funnel sequencing, you are essentially stacking, or sequencing, funnels that naturally progress from one funnel to the next. In the same way that habit stacking uses the power of existing habits to introduce new ones, funnel sequencing uses the momentum from one funnel to propel them into the next.

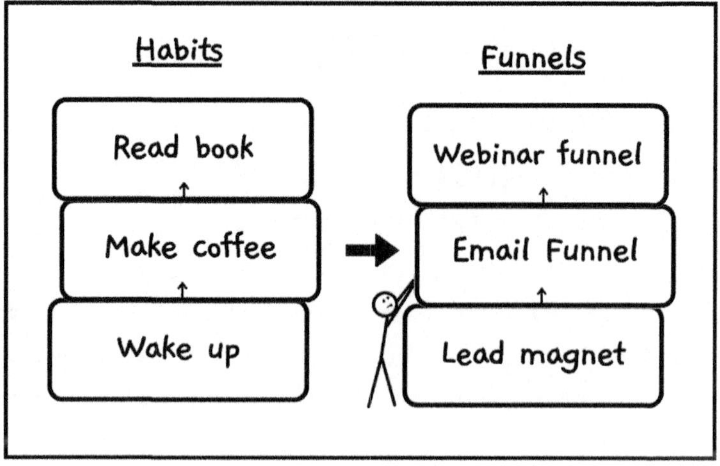

While this book shares 12 core funnels, that doesn't mean you should rush to build all 12 of them for your business. Start by picking one funnel for each phase of your value pyramid. By creating one funnel for each phase, you can guide customers through a sequence of funnels to progress seamlessly up your value pyramid.

For example, you might send someone from your lead magnet to a tripwire funnel to your email funnel and later to a launch funnel. Or maybe you send someone from a bridge funnel to a quiz funnel to a checkout upsell and, finally, to a webinar funnel. Of course, you can choose different funnels for each level in your value pyramid; there's no strict order to move your customers through the funnel sequence. Funnel sequencing is more about transitioning customers to more advanced offers as they continue to engage with your business.

HOW TO CREATE A FUNNEL SEQUENCE

Your value pyramid is like a multi-tiered structure, with each level representing a progressively more expensive offer. Now, consider your funnels as a series of interconnected steps or pathways leading the customer up this pyramid. Each funnel represents a specific stage in the customer journey, beginning at the base of the pyramid, moving upwards, ultimately leading to your core offers.

The idea is to make this journey as smooth and intuitive as possible for the customer. One efficient way to do this is to place the first step of your next funnel on the last page of your previous funnel. Let's break this down further. Imagine a customer has just completed a funnel; maybe they just made a purchase or signed up for your newsletter. At this point, their engagement with your business is at its peak, and they are primed for the next step.

Instead of leaving them to navigate to the next level of the value pyramid on their own, you can guide them by presenting the first step of the next funnel on the final page of the current funnel.

This method harnesses the customer's engagement momentum, guiding them seamlessly into the next funnel without losing their interest or commitment. It creates a logical progression that caters to the brain's preference for structured information and processes.

Now, let's look at some examples of funnel sequences and how to connect them.

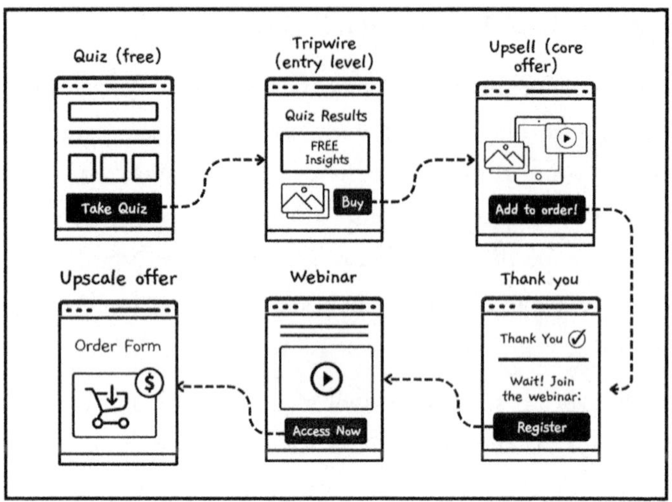

In this example, the sales funnel process starts with a quiz funnel that's designed to draw potential customers toward your main product or service. After participating in the quiz, users are directed to a results page, where they are offered complimentary content. This might include a personalized checklist, a document, or other useful information.

At the bottom of the quiz results page, there is a tripwire offer with a compelling call-to-action. If a lead clicks on this CTA, they are entered into the tripwire funnel, where an upsell opportunity is presented during the checkout phase.

Once they complete the purchase, a "thank you" page appears, featuring a CTA that guides them to the next funnel: a webinar. Here, the user can register and attend the webinar or watch a replay. The webinar room also gives them the opportunity to purchase the upscale offer.

Notice how this funnel sequence is designed to transition potential customers smoothly from one stage to the next, creating a streamlined journey toward purchase offers higher up on your value pyramid.

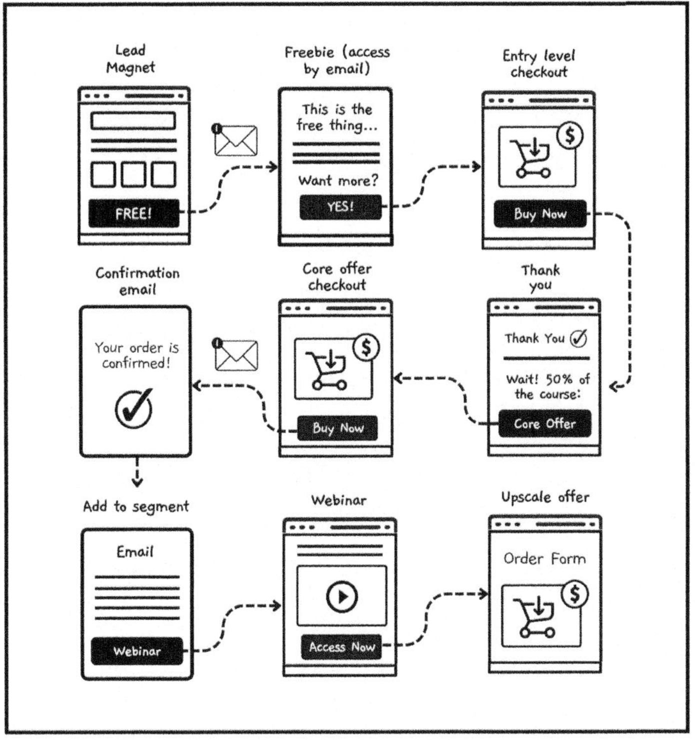

In this more advanced scenario, the journey starts with a lead magnet displayed on the homepage. When users choose to receive this magnet, they are sent an email with the free offer. Either within this email or on the last page of the free offer, there's a call to action, nudging them to explore and purchase the entry-level offer. Remember that the free offer should be partially incomplete, which creates their desire for more value, leading them to make the first purchase.

After the customer purchases the entry-level offer, they are directed to a "thank you" page that presents a one-time promotion for your core offer. The limited availability of this offer creates a sense of urgency, nudging them to make a purchase.

Once they've purchased the core offer, they are added to a specific email funnel. This funnel segments them as promising leads for your upscale offer, given their previous purchases. They are sent nurturing emails with CTAs, encouraging them to register for your webinar. This webinar serves as a platform to create rapport while providing more details about the upscale offer. The webinar room should always include a link to the order form, allowing interested customers to make immediate purchases.

These are just two examples. There are an infinite number of variations of funnel sequences. The key is to create a funnel sequence that works best for 1) what you're selling and 2) what your customers prefer.

Your funnel sequence should be built around your products or services. Each step in your sales funnel should highlight the value of what you're selling, helping to draw in your customers and move them to the next step.

The second important consideration is to make your funnel sequence considering your customers' preferences. To do this, you need to know what your customers want, what they like, and what encourages them to buy something. For example, if your customers enjoy learning, you could use webinars or free resources as a main part of your sales funnel. If they like exclusive offers, then limited-time deals could work well.

CHAPTER RESOURCES

Action Items

1. Make a list of your offers at each level of your value pyramid, from free offers to upscale offers.
2. Based on your products/services and your ICAs, pick a specific Power Funnel for each level of your value pyramid.
3. Create a visual representation of how each funnel links together using the Funnelytics free funnel mapping tool. This could include adding a specific CTA button, sending a sequence of texts/emails, etc.
4. Once you've designed your funnel sequence, make a list of any frictions that people might face while transitioning between funnels (i.e. filling out forms, lengthy checkout, unclear CTAs etc.)
5. Choose at least one friction from step 4 to tackle. Over time, work towards reducing as much friction as possible to create smooth transitions between funnels.

RELEVANT TOOLS

General tools to get you started:

- **Funnelytics** is a funnel mapping and tracking tool that also offers a free drag-and-drop funnel mapping tool. Use this tool to help visualize your funnel sequences more easily.

- **Deadline Funnel** can help create urgency in your funnel sequence by adding countdown timers to limited-time offers.
- **Builderall** and **Simvoly** are website and funnel builders that are easy to use and offer templates specifically designed for different funnel stages.
- **Convertflow** is a funnel builder that integrates with email marketing software, Google Analytics, and e-commerce platforms.
- **SamCart** is a platform that specializes in high-converting checkout pages, order bumps, upsells and more
- **Canva** and **Youzign** are free graphic design tools that can help you create images, banners, and visuals for your funnel pages.
- **Hotjar** and **Crazy Egg** provide heatmaps, scrollmaps, A/B testing, and other visual analytics to understand user behavior and optimize funnel pages.

Additional AI-powered tools:

- **ABtesting.ai** simplifies A/B testing with AI-generated suggestions for headlines, copy, and call-to-actions for your website to make your funnel sequence more effective.
- **TurboSite** uses AI to analyze user behavior and offers real-time suggestions to help you create a smoother funnel sequence.
- **VisualEyes** is an AI-driven user testing tool that simulates eye-tracking studies and preference tests to create better web pages within your funnel sequence.

- **MarbleFlows** is a no-code funnel builder, including AI-generated forms to capture leads for your free or paid offers within your funnel sequence.
- **SmartLead** is an AI-powered email marketing tool that helps you personalize emails, create follow-up sequences, and implement auto-rotating accounts.
- **Jasper.ai**, **Copy.ai** and **Copymatic** are AI copywriting tools that can help you write high-converting copy in a fraction of the time.

ChatGPT EXAMPLE PROMPTS

Example 1

"Create a seamless funnel sequence for my public speaking coaching business that guides users from a lead magnet download to the referral program. The last step/page of one funnel should smoothly connect to the next. Provide step-by-step details for each stage: Lead magnet > SMS nurture > SMS quiz funnel > (Option 1) Checkout (Option 2 if they don't buy) Offer a tripwire 5 days later > Once they are customers, join the referral program. Each step should feel like a logical progression and create a smooth experience. Give example CTAs for each step."

Example 2

"Based on the funnel sequence outlined above, list possible frictions in the customer journey. Develop a plan to address potential frictions in the customer journey and identify the highest priority friction. Then provide a list of action items to minimize/eliminate that friction that can be completed in 5 days." *This prompt is a follow-up prompt from Example 1.*

Example 3

"I am currently working on the home page and sales pages of my website. I want to use a heat map tool, like Hotjar, to optimize my website user experience so I can seamlessly guide potential customers through a funnel sequence. Write a detailed guide on how I can use this tool and what metrics to focus on (including what percentages I should aim for) to maximize website presence."

16

ONE HUNDRED MILLION

AI in Your Funnel

As I write this, ChatGPT is achieving remarkable growth, becoming the fastest-growing tech platform in history with a staggering 100 million users in just two months.[56] To put this in perspective, it took Netflix a decade, Twitter five years, Instagram two and a half years, and TikTok nine months to reach comparable user numbers.

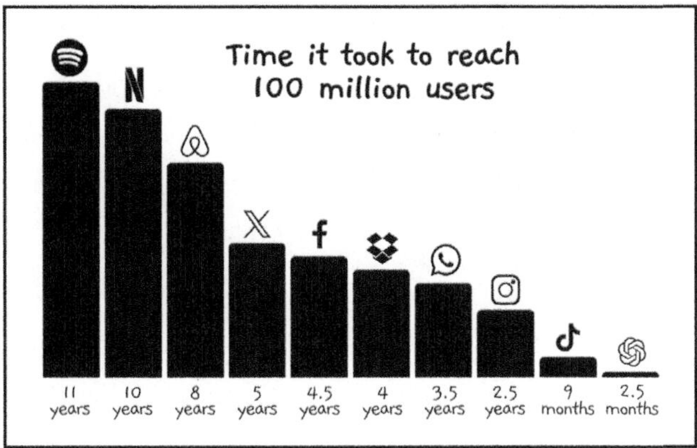

The two key factors for ChatGPT's explosive growth are its usefulness and versatility. OpenAI didn't just create something people wanted to use—they created an all-purpose tool that almost anyone could find valuable. This is largely because the AI-powered chatbot is trained on trillions of parameters, allowing it to have diverse use cases.

So, if you could master only *one* AI tool for your business, it should be ChatGPT. Not only can it optimize different areas of your business, but it's free. That's why the first part of this chapter focuses on laying the groundwork for you to use ChatGPT for your Power Funnels. In the second part of this chapter, we'll look at other relevant AI tools for your business. For the sake of space, we won't cover every single tool, but the end of this chapter will point you to several AI directories so you can explore the up-to-date and relevant tools for your business.

CHATGPT ESSENTIALS

ChatGPT is designed to understand and generate human-like text, so it has a wide range of business uses, including:

Idea Generation

ChatGPT isn't just a chatbot—it's an idea powerhouse. By feeding it prompts or questions, ChatGPT can help you brainstorm new product ideas, marketing strategies, or operational improvements.

Market Research

You can use ChatGPT to analyze market trends, industry reports, or customer feedback. By asking the right questions, you can also get deeper insights into your target audience, competitors, and potential opportunities in the market.

Content Creation

With ChatGPT, you can easily produce a wide variety of written content, like blog posts, social media posts, marketing copy, product descriptions, or templates for emails/text campaigns.

By providing specific instructions, or "prompts" (we will cover how to do this shortly), you can create high-quality content in a fraction of the time.

SEO

As we touched on in Chapter 3, ChatGPT can be incredibly powerful for keyword research and producing SEO-optimized content. AIRPM is an excellent ChatGPT Chrome extension that provides thousands of prompts to help you master SEO like: *Outrank the competition on Google with an in-depth, SEO-optimized article based on [YOUR COMPETITOR URL].* We'll look at other ChatGPT Chrome extensions later in this chapter.

Process Streamlining

With ChatGPT, you can identify and address inefficiencies within your existing processes, whether it's related to inventory management, customer onboarding, content creation, or any other operational aspect. You can describe or provide relevant data about the process you want to optimize. ChatGPT's analysis can then reveal inefficiencies and offer suggestions on how to streamline your methods.

Customer Support

ChatGPT can integrate with chatbots for customer support systems, so your business can give fast and personalized service to customers. This can help reduce wait times and improve customer satisfaction.

Task automation

ChatGPT can be used to automate simple, yet time-consuming tasks, like summarizing reports, managing to-do lists, or writing emails. By automating repetitive tasks, you can spend your time on more strategic areas in your business.

PROMPT BASICS

Now that we've touched on a few different ways to use ChatGPT for your business, let's look at the specifics of crafting effective prompts. In ChatGPT, a "prompt" is the command you write to the model that will generate a response.

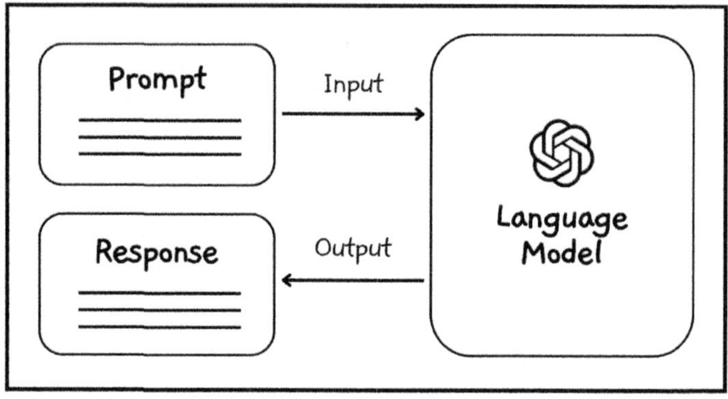

While theoretically, you can write any prompt and get a response from ChatGPT, some prompts are more effective than others. That's where the concept of prompt engineering comes in. Prompt engineering is the process of strategically writing prompts to generate more accurate, relevant, and useful responses. Before we look at prompt engineering techniques, it's important to understand the core types of ChatGPT prompts.

Explanation Prompts

These prompts ask ChatGPT for explanations of concepts, processes, or ideas. For example "Explain [concept] as if I'm a beginner" or "How does [product/service] work?"

INSTRUCTION PROMPTS

These prompts guide ChatGPT in providing instructions or written tutorials. For example, "Provide step-by-step instructions to [complete specific process]" or "What are common mistakes to avoid when [performing specific tasks]?"

Prediction Prompts

These prompts ask ChatGPT to forecast outcomes or trends. For example: "Predict how [specific product/innovation/trend] will reshape [industry] over the next [timeframe]" or "How will [industry] adapt to changing consumer preferences over the next [timeframe]?"

Scenario Prompts

These prompts ask ChatGPT to provide a response based on the context of a particular situation. For example: "How do you recommend fixing a conflict between team members about [topic]?" or "What would you do if customers repeatedly complained about [problem]?"

Comparative Prompts

These prompts ask ChatGPT to compare two or more options. For example: "Analyze the pros and cons of [option 1] and [option 2] in the context of [industry]" or "Which of the strategies mentioned above is more effective? Explain your reasoning."

Ranking Prompts

These prompts ask ChatGPT to rank options based on your criteria or preferences. For example: "Rank these [payment methods] from the most preferred to the least preferred by online shoppers" or "Which [market research methods] do you think is most reliable for gathering insights about customer preferences and behaviors?"

Feedback Prompts: These prompts ask ChatGPT for feedback or suggestions. For example: "Do you have any suggestions on how to improve this [product listing description] to make it more compelling?" or "What feedback do you have for our [social media strategy] to increase engagement?"

Open-Ended Prompts

These prompts cause ChatGPT to provide a wide range of responses. For example: "Brainstorm a webinar script outline about [topic]" or "Design a game-changing product that could disrupt [industry]."

TECHNIQUE #1

Role-playing

Now that we've looked at the basic ChatGPT prompts, we're ready to look at the first prompt engineering technique—role-playing. This method involves telling the AI to adopt a specific persona or expertise. Your prompt could start with "Write in the style of Trevor Noah" or "You are an experienced technical writer with expertise in machine learning." Prompt engineering with role-playing improves ChatGPT's ability to provide contextually accurate and informed responses. Let's look at what a *complete* role-playing ChatGPT prompt might look like:

> You are an expert [role/profession]. Create a 10-step guide to [task]. Explain each step in detail and avoid technical language or jargon. Provide a time estimate for each step then suggest a 1 week schedule for completing the task. Also include a section at the end on the most common mistakes that beginners make when attempting this task and how to avoid them." Notice how this prompt starts with defining the role and continues by providing a specific task and clear constraints to instruct the AI model more effectively.

TECHNIQUE #2

Tone Analysis

If you're using ChatGPT to write content like articles, social media posts, or website copy, it's important to help it use the right style. By default, ChatGPT has a relatively formal tone and sometimes comes across as outdated. To make sure ChatGPT's writing voice matches the tone you want, you can use the second prompt engineering technique.

For tone analysis, you need to provide ChatGPT with samples of writing that have the style you're aiming to recreate. Then ask ChatGPT to analyze the tone of those samples. This helps you create a description of the style and tone you're looking for that you can use in future prompts. Just **copy and paste** the following prompt:

> You are a tone analyzer. Analyze and then describe the writing style and tone of [text], so I can recreate that style. Don't take any context from the "text" below. The text shared in this prompt is only for tone analysis.
>
> Example: The author's writing style in this text is friendly and concise, and they use a conversational tone. They use transitional phrases to connect ideas throughout the text. They use clear and easy language.
>
> Text = [insert here]

The text you insert in this template can be your own writing or writing from a source whose writing style you admire. Once you have ChatGPT's tone analysis result, you can then paste it at the end of all your copywriting prompts.

TECHNIQUE #3

Priming

The priming technique involves giving the AI examples to provide additional context. This guides the AI's response in a specific direction, much like handing ChatGPT a map with clear directions. If you skip priming, you'll still get a response, but it will be more generic. The best part about priming is that it streamlines your process by cutting down the time you spend on iterations and fine-tuning. Priming can be broken down into three categories:

No priming: "Write 10 messages for my SMS marketing campaign about [topic]."

Priming with one example: "Write 10 messages for my SMS marketing campaign about [topic]. Here's an example: [Insert example here]."

Priming with several examples: "Write 10 messages for my SMS marketing campaign about [topic]. Here are 3 examples: [Example 1] [Example 2] [Example 3]."

As you've probably guessed, the more examples you give, the more accurate the results will be.

TECHNIQUE #4

Temperature

You can control ChatGPT's creativity using the "temperature" setting on a scale of 0 to 1. A lower score makes the AI less creative and will output consistent responses when given the same prompt. A higher score increases creativity and generates different responses for the same prompt (which can be especially helpful for brainstorming and idea generation).

- **Low temperature (0 to 0.3):** More focused, coherent, but less creative outputs.
- **Medium temperature (0.3 to 0.7):** Good balance between creativity and coherence.
- **High temperature (0.7 to 1):** High creativity and variety of responses but less coherent.

While the default of 0.7 works well for most use cases, feel free to experiment! To adjust the temperature, simply add it at the end of your prompt, like this: "Brainstorm a list of 10 [topic] ideas. Adjust the temperature to 0.1"

TECHNIQUE #5

Mega Prompts

So far, we've looked at relatively short- to medium-length ChatGPT prompts, but sometimes they don't fully capture what you want. For example, using a one-sentence prompt like "give me a checklist of what I need to be a successful solopreneur" will not generate the detailed response you're looking for. That's because AI tools like ChatGPT don't have the implied understanding to generate the granular output you intended—unless your prompt is very specific. That's where mega-prompts come in. These are longer instructions that explain your intentions.

There are 5 key components that go into a mega prompt:

1. **Define ChatGPT's Role:** Clearly outline the persona and characteristics ChatGPT should adopt while generating responses.
2. **Your Goal:** Specify the main goal you want ChatGPT to help you achieve.
3. **Context:** Provide enough information to help ChatGPT generate relevant/personalized responses.
4. **Task Description:** Break down the specific tasks or steps you want ChatGPT to help you achieve.
5. **Constraints & Formatting:** Lay out any guidelines, restrictions, or formatting preferences for ChatGPT's responses.

Now, let's look at an example of a ChatGPT mega-prompt:

Role: You are a Business Automation Advisor, a professional who specializes in helping small business owners automate various aspects of their operations. As my advisor:

- You prioritize cost-effective methods because you know I have a tight budget.
- You always include unconventional and often overlooked automation tactics for solopreneurs.
- You are specific, actionable, and don't use wordy sentences.

Goal: You are my virtual Business Automation Advisor for today. You will help me identify areas in my business that I can automate that will save me time.

Context:

- My business: I provide actionable marketing resources for early stage drop-shipping businesses (1:1 programs and video courses).
- My value proposition: Drop-shipping business owners can learn how to market their brand and products more effectively.
- My target audience: Early stage drop-shipping businesses that sell to the US market.
- Product portfolio: My products range from $49-$699, and most of them are self-paced.
- My current stage: I generate $6,000 in monthly revenue, and I pay a part-time virtual assistant.

Structure of Today's Tasks:

1. Based on the context above, you will return a list of 15 potential areas in my business that I can automate.
2. I will choose one area to focus on.
3. You will generate 10 high-level automation tactics to address the chosen area.
4. I will pick one tactic to use.
5. You will develop a detailed, actionable plan with key steps to implement the selected tactic.
6. You will provide a checklist of all the action items I need to complete at the end.

Constraints & Formatting:

- I will let you know when we can proceed to the next step. Don't continue without my confirmation.
- You will rely on the context of this brainstorming at every step.
- Your answers should be in bullet point format, with subheadings to separate different ideas.

TECHNIQUE #6

Response Correction

Getting the right response from ChatGPT is an iterative process. Once you have a draft, you can then refine the output with Response Correction prompts. For example, you could ask ChatGPT to adjust its response for length, clarity or tone. All you have to do is provide instructions on how it can improve its previous response. For example:

- **If the response is too long**: "Rewrite the article above but be more concise" or "Cut down the length by 30%" or "Reduce repetition and excess prose."
- **If there's mission information**: "Elaborate on [insert specific topic]" or "This time provide a more detailed guide" or "Use quantifiable metrics for each point."
- **If the tone is off**: "Rewrite it in a more enthusiastic tone" or "Avoid jargon and advanced words" or "Don't use cliche phrases and exclamation points."

Help with Prompts

While we've covered the basic types of prompts and discussed five key prompt engineering techniques, there are still many prompt styles and templates to explore. The good news is that there are several tools to help you craft prompts, including:

- **Hugging Face** shares prompts for nearly everything
- **PromptPal** is a prompt directory
- **SnackPrompt** provides curated prompts
- **GPTHero** auto-generates custom prompts
- **Learn Prompting** provides a free and comprehensive guide for AI prompting

Best ChatGPT Google Chrome Extensions

- **AIRPM For ChatGPT** provides over 3,000 curated prompt templates to your ChatGPT interface. It's a compilation of the best prompts for SEO, marketing, copywriting, and more.
- **ChatGPT File Uploader Extended** lets you upload PDFs, spreadsheets, images, and other files to ChatGPT so you can write prompts that reference specific data.

- **WebChatGPT** increases the relevance of ChatGPT's results by using the most up-to-date information online (and can even reference URLs). This extension is helpful because one of ChatGPT's biggest shortfalls is that its knowledge base is limited to 2021.
- **Merlin** gives you direct access to ChatGPT across your browser by clicking Cmd+M. This means you can easily summarize articles, generate emails, and so much more.
- **ChatGPT Writer** lets you use ChatGPT to write emails/messages on any website and supports all languages.
- **Promptheus** turns ChatGPT into a voice assistant, letting you speak prompts instead of typing them. Just hold down the spacebar and talk with ChatGPT.
- **YouTube Summary with ChatGPT & Claude** generates quick summaries of YouTube videos and web articles. For a text-specific Chrome extension, **Summarize** works well.
- **SuperPower ChatGPT** has many features (i.e. search chats, view prompt history etc.), but the standout feature is its ability to make folders for organizing your chats. Just title your folders then drag and drop relevant chats into them.

Now that we've finished exploring ChatGPT fundamentals, prompt engineering, and helpful resources, let's look at other AI tools that can streamline tasks across your Power Funnels. AI is a bottomless pit, so the following sections in this chapter will curate the AI tools that are the most relevant, time-saving, and intuitive tools when it comes to your online business.

More AI Tools: A Cheat Sheet

Design

- Midjourney
- DALL-E 2
- IconLab AI
- Plurana
- Exactly.ai
- Blend AI Studio
- PhotoShoot.ai
- Pebblely
- Magic Design by Canva

Website

- TurboSite
- ABtesting.ai
- VisualEyes
- MarbleFlows
- MarketMuse
- Hexometer
- Yuspify
- MontereyAI
- Aidaptive
- Moda

Nurturing

- tinyEmail
- SmartLead
- AIAssist
- Writecream
- Maverick
- Gan.ai

Presentations

- Beautiful.ai
- Gamma
- Presentations.ai
- Simplified
- Tome

Market Research

- VenturusAI
- GapScout
- BetterFeedback
- CrawlQ AI
- Insight7
- Wayyy

SEO/Ads

- Surfer SEO
- SEOdity
- GrowthBar
- Scalenut
- Adzooma
- Adcopy
- Adcreative.ai

Social Media

- Practina
- Ocaya
- Creasquare
- aiCarousels
- InfluencerMarketing.ai
- Lately.ai
- Trimmr
- ClipBuddy
- Devi
- Flowjin

Productivity

- Motion
- Trevor AI
- Otter.ai
- MyMap.ai
- MonitUp AI

Video

- Steve AI
- Hour One
- DeepBrain
- HeyGen
- VidIQ
- Pictory
- VideoGen
- Teach-O-Matic

Writing

- Jasper.ai
- Copy.ai
- WriteSonic
- Copymatic
- Quillbot
- Grammarly
- Copysmith.ai
- TeamAI

Customer Support

- WebWhiz
- HappyChat
- Robofy
- SiteSpeakAI
- Lyro AI
- RealFeedback
- Rep AI
- Manifest.ai

AI FOR WRITING

Using AI writing tools as you build your Power Funnels can be a huge advantage, given our in-depth exploration of copywriting in this book. You can take the copywriting concepts we've covered and accelerate your writing process with the following AI tools.

- **Jasper.ai** is an advanced AI writing platform that helps you write nearly anything. It can turn single pieces of content into full-scale campaigns, write SEO-optimized articles, and write with a consistent writing tone. It has 50+ templates to save you time.
- **Copy.ai** is another powerful AI writing tool that writes in your brand voice, allows team collaboration, provides up-to-date information, and offers dozens of templates. It also has a free AI writing generator if you want to play around with the AI first.
- **WriteSonic** and **Copymatic** are ChatGPT-powered platforms that help you generate high-quality written content. They have templates for blog posts, website copy, product descriptions, and more.
- **Quillbot** is an AI writing editor with a variety of features, like rephrasing, grammar checker, plagiarism checker, summarizer, and more.
- **Grammarly** is another AI writing editor that corrects grammar and spelling errors, improves sentence structure, and offers tone suggestions to polish your writing.
- **Copysmith.ai** provides a suite of AI-powered tools, including **Rytr** for marketing copy, **Describely** for product content, and **Frase** for optimized Google ranking.

- **TeamAI** is like ChatGPT but specifically designed for teams. It offers a variety of collaboration tools, a built-in prompt library, supports file uploads, and much more.

AI FOR DESIGN

AI-generated art has a broad range of uses for your online business. You can use these tools to create blog graphics, social media illustrations, mockups, product packaging ideas, website wireframes, icons, logos, and so much more.

- **Midjourney** is one of the best generative AI platforms. Similar to ChatGPT, you need to provide detailed prompts, and in response, it will generate captivating AI-generated images or graphics. If you need help with writing your Midjourney prompts, MJ Prompt Tool is a great resource.
- **DALL-E 2**, similar to Midjourney, uses AI to generate images from text prompts.
- **Exactly.ai** lets you train your personal AI model to generate images in your unique brand style using text-based descriptions.
- **Plurana** generates high-quality SVGs with patterns, prints, and social media designs.
- **IconLab AI** uses AI to design custom icons and logos with just one click.
- **Blend AI Studio, PhotoShoot.ai,** and **Pebblely** use AI to improve the lighting, composition, and background of your product images.
- **Magic Design by Canva** helps you create design graphics and marketing materials with AI-suggested layouts.

MARKET & CUSTOMER RESEARCH

By using AI tools for market research and customer insights, you can make more informed decisions when building your Power Funnels. These tools can help you identify market gaps and trends, gather data patterns, predict niche preferences, and more.

- **VenturusAI** analyzes the feasibility of your business idea and helps you identify target audiences from demographic data.
- **GapScout's** AI-driven market research tool finds gaps, opportunities, and key themes in the market through custom review analysis and competitor research.
- **Wayyy** uses AI to create surveys that help you gain deeper customer insights.
- **CrawlQ AI Audience Research** does predictive niche research based on the seed inputs you provide about your target audience.
- **Insight7** is an AI-powered customer insights tool that extracts patterns from data, prioritizes action items, and visualizes insights for faster decision-making.
- **BetterFeedback** uses AI to streamline data analysis and user feedback so you can gain deeper insights and improve the customer experience.

AI FOR SEO AND ADS

As we discussed in Chapter 3, AI can be especially helpful for technical or time-consuming tasks, like SEO. In seconds, you can get AI tools to draft high-opportunity keywords or write SEO-optimized copy for your niche. AI also goes a long way when you need to write tight yet attention-catching copy for ads. The following tools can streamline that process and save you hours of time.

- **Surfer SEO** uses AI to streamline your content creation process by taking care of keyword research, writing, and optimization.
- **SEOdity** offers a variety of AI-powered SEO features, like keyword research, competitor ranking analysis, SEO content editor, team collaboration, Google integrations and more.
- **GrowthBar** helps you and your team plan and write long-form blog content optimized for SEO.
- **Scalenut** offers an AI-powered marketing platform that helps with SEO analysis, content marketing, social media management, and email marketing.
- **Adzooma** optimizes online advertising campaigns with AI insights, suggestions, and performance improvements.
- **Adcopy** uses AI modeled after your niche to craft high-converting ads, generate instant ad variations, lets you control the creativity level of the AI, and more.
- **Adcreative.ai** is an AI-powered tool that helps you develop more effective ads, write high-converting headlines, and provides real-time insights into your ad performance.

AI FOR SOCIAL MEDIA

Having a social media presence is non-negotiable in today's digital environment. Millions of potential customers spend their time there, so it's essential to educate and engage with them there. Whether you manage the social media content or delegate it to a team, these AI tools exponentially boost productivity.

They generate content and automate tasks, allowing your social media accounts to grow in the background while you concentrate on high-impact tasks.

- **Practina** is an AI-powered social media management tool that generates, schedules, and publishes posts. It integrates with Instagram, Facebook, YouTube, LinkedIn, and more.
- **Ocaya** is a ChatGPT-powered social media management platform that helps you design and write content in a fraction of the time. It offers templates, collaborative workspaces, and real-time analytics and integrates with 30+ platforms.
- **Creasquare** lets you design content, generate captions with AI, and schedule social media posts.
- **Devi** is an AI social media assistant that streamlines lead monitoring, outreach, content creation, and scheduling.
- **aiCarousels** simplifies the design and writing process of creating engaging carousel posts.
- **Lately.ai** is a social selling platform that learns your brand voice and turns your content into targeted, engaging social media posts.
- **InfluencerMarketing.ai** helps you find influencers, manage campaigns, and easily track performance insights.
- **Trimmr, ClipBuddy** and **Flowjin** extract valuable content from videos or podcasts to create social media clips, so you can quickly and easily repurpose content.

AI FOR VIDEO

There are countless ways to provide value for your audience, but one very effective way is through video. Whether you want to create long or short-form videos, using complex editing software can be overwhelming (and time-consuming). With these AI video creation and editing tools, you can create high-quality content without the hassle.

- **Steve AI** simplifies the video creation process by offering script writing, voiceovers, video generation, music composition, cover image design, and more.
- **Pictory** is an AI video-editing tool that can extract highlights from longer videos/recordings, convert blog posts into engaging videos, auto-generate captions, and more.
- **DeepBrain** and **HeyGen** are AI-powered text-to-video generators. Just enter your text, and it will output a video with photo-realistic AI avatars.
- **Hour One** is an AI-powered video generator that creates professional videos within minutes, using text-to-video tech, templates, virtual presenters, and collaboration tools.
- **VidIQ** uses AI to optimize video content to increase visibility on platforms like YouTube.
- **Teach-O-Matic** is an AI text-to-video tool that generates how-to videos from prompts.
- **VideoGen**'s AI quickly generates videos with copyright-free assets, background footage, and lifelike voiceovers.

AI FOR YOUR WEBSITE

With AI, you can optimize your website's performance, messaging, and customer experience to stay ahead of competitors. The following AI tools offer a range of features that help you optimize website content, increase engagement, and personalize product recommendations.

- **TurboSite** uses AI to optimize your website's performance by analyzing user behavior and providing real-time suggestions.
- **ABtesting.ai** simplifies A/B testing with AI-generated suggestions for headlines, copy, and call-to-actions to maximize conversions.
- **VisualEyes** is an AI-driven user testing tool that simulates eye-tracking studies and preference tests to help you create more effective web pages.
- **MarbleFlows** is a no-code funnel builder and includes AI-generated forms to capture leads for your free or paid offers on your website.
- **MarketMuse** uses AI to optimize website content by suggesting keywords, topics, and improvements based on search engine trends and competition.
- **Hexometer** is an AI website monitoring tool that proactively identifies issues across availability, performance, user experience, SEO, security, and more.
- **Yuspify** uses AI to analyze customer behavior on your website and automatically offers personalized product recommendations tailored to individual preferences.
- **Monterey AI** creates automated feedback channels and then analyzes both qualitative feedback and quantitative data to increase website engagement.

- **Aidaptive** is a Shopify app that uses AI to predict visitor preferences, customize web experiences based on real-time behavior, and adjust product placements accordingly.
- **Moda** is an AI Shopify extension that automatically segments your website traffic, optimizes email/SMS campaigns, and provides real-time insights across workflows.

AI FOR NURTURING

Some areas of your online business, like communicating with your audience, are ideal to automate. Whether your preferred communication is email, SMS, or WhatsApp, these AI tools can lighten your workload.

- **tinyEmail** is an AI email marketing platform that helps you create personalized emails, generate optimized copy, and easily segment your audience.
- **SmartLead** is an AI-powered email marketing tool that helps you personalize emails, create follow-up sequences, and implement auto-rotating accounts.
- **AIAssist** is a ChatGPT-powered tool that automatically answers customer emails and inquiries within seconds.
- **Writecream** uses AI to help you write emails and marketing content in seconds.
- **Maverick** and **Gan.ai** are both AI-powered tools that craft personalized video messages to nurture customer relationships through channels like email and SMS.

AI FOR CUSTOMER SUPPORT

One guaranteed way to kill the customer experience is having poor customer support. That's why incorporating AI-driven customer support tools that offer real-time conversations and personalized guidance can dramatically boost customer satisfaction.

- **WebWhiz** lets you train ChatGPT on your website data and create an AI chatbot capable of instantly answering customer questions.
- **HappyChat, Robofy** and **SiteSpeakAI** are AI-powered chatbots that you can train using your website data so it can answer questions more accurately.
- **Lyro AI by Tidio** is an AI-driven chatbot that engages website visitors in real-time conversations and handles up to 70% of common customer questions.
- **RealFeedback** is a ChatGPT-driven chatbot that engages users conversationally to collect valuable insights to help you improve the customer experience.
- **Rep AI** is an e-commerce chatbot that combines behavioral AI and conversational AI to deliver personalized shopping experiences to customers.
- **Manifest.ai** is a ChatGPT-powered shopping assistant for Shopify stores that helps visitors find the products they're looking for.

AI FOR PRESENTATIONS/WEBINARS

Whether you're looking to capture leads, deliver memorable webinars, or impress potential investors, the resources below will help you create presentations that leave a lasting impression. The tools range from designing slides to generating scripts.

- **Beautiful.ai** is an AI-powered presentation software that helps you design engaging, on-brand slide decks.

- **Gamma** helps you create presentation outlines and then uses AI to auto-format the content into eye-catching slides. It also offers built-in analytics to measure engagement.
- **Presentations.ai** is a ChatGPT-powered tool for presentations. Just type your idea, as you would for a ChatGPT prompt, and it outputs a custom slide deck.
- **Simplified** uses AI to improve presentation content for clarity to make sure you're communicating effectively.
- **Tome** helps users easily generate entire narratives from documents to create cohesive, memorable presentations.

AI FOR PRODUCTIVITY

Using AI for personal productivity can be another way to give you and your team an edge. Whether it's organizing your schedule, streamlining tasks, or managing to-do lists, these tools help you work smarter, not harder.

- **Motion** is an intelligent calendar that uses AI to optimize your schedule, meetings, tasks, to-do lists, and activities for more efficient time management.
- **Trevor AI** is a smart scheduler that increases your productivity by managing your to-do list, creating time blocks, and integrating with third parties, like Google and Todoist.
- **Otter.ai** automatically transcribes and summarizes conversations, which can be helpful for internal or client-facing meetings.
- **MyMap.ai** is a mind map tool that uses AI for chat-based mapping and concept mapping so you can easily visualize your ideas.

- **MonitUp AI Time Tracker** boosts your productivity by analyzing your computer usage and then optimizing your time and task management.

Discover More AI Tools

- AI Tools Directory
- Toolspedia.io
- AI Scout
- TopAI.tools
- Future tools
- OpenTools
- Supertool

Conclusion

You've reached the end! I'm so thrilled you spent the time learning about Power Funnels so you can apply them to your business. Remember, this book isn't meant to be read once and forgotten. It's an operating manual meant to help you as you start to build your own digital funnels. Think of this as your marketing assistant, reference document, and occasional source of inspiration—all in one.

Before you start applying the techniques we've covered, let's review the main steps for building powerful funnels in your business, with the goal that you (hopefully) remember 10% of this book's message.

STEP 1

Define Your Ideal Customer Avatars

Identify your ideal customers (ICAs). Understand where they spend time online, what their needs or desires are, and how you serve them with your offers. Doing this first can save you a lot of time and money in the long run—just look at Burger King's satisf...ailure if you need a reminder.

STEP 2

Choose Your Traffic Strategies

It's incredibly difficult to sell even the best product or service if people don't know you exist. Once you've defined your ICAs (and where they spend their time online), pick the traffic generation strategies that make the most sense for your niche. If you know your dream clients love scrolling through TikTok, use that platform to target them. If they hang out in online communities, then use those channels to get traffic. Regardless of the method, remember that every funnel starts with traffic.

STEP 3

Create Your Value Pyramid

Draft the various offerings, products, or bundles you'll present at each level of your value pyramid. If you're unsure where to start, begin with your core offer and expand it vertically. This means stripping down your core offer to create your entry-level offer or enhancing your core offer with added benefits to create your upscale offer. As your business grows, the value provided at each level will gradually become more distinct. In general, this step is key for your funnel strategy because it is a clear progression for your customers, guiding them naturally toward the highest value you can offer.

STEP 4

Design Your Funnel Sequence

Once you've created your value pyramid, the next step is deciding which funnel to use at each level and how they will seamlessly lead to the next. Remember, the secret to funnel sequencing is to place the first step of your next funnel on the last page of your current one.

STEP 5

Nurture, Nurture, Nurture

Not every lead will be ready to buy right away. Many people will need time to think about their choices, learn more about what you're selling, and develop trust with your brand. That's why it's crucial to have a plan that gradually nurtures these leads to become buyers. One of the best ways to nurture leads is to humanize your brand through a welcome sequence and nurture funnels.

STEP 6

Optimize the Sales Process

Your funnels won't convert if the sales process is unintuitive, long, or complex. Audit your website to make sure the navigation is easy, your pages are simple, and your titles are compelling. Most people only scan website text. They pay the most attention to headings, subheadings, calls to action, and images. If you nail those, you've won half the battle.

STEP 7

Leverage Loyalty

After you've successfully converted leads into customers, it's important to encourage them to continue their journey with your brand. At this point, you can leverage the principles of loyalty psychology, implementing loyalty programs to promote repeat purchases, referrals, and ultimately guide them up your value pyramid to upscale offers.

STEP 8

Expansion Time

Once your initial funnels are performing great and driving sales, you can add more funnels to your business to create multiple pathways for customers to ascend your value pyramid. In other words, you're giving customers more ways to start buying from you and to keep buying more over time.

FINAL NOTE

As you set up your initial funnel, be prepared for a journey of continuous refinement. You're simply discovering how your unique audience responds to your funnel. Embrace this learning process, because it's a fundamental part of the beginning.

Investigate, for instance, what your dream customers value the most and weave that into your lead magnet. Test different email styles to find out which one resonates most with your ICAs. Every lesson you learn from creating your first funnel will fuel the improvement of the ones that follow.

From this process of crafting your first funnel, remember that every step, every tweak, and every discovery brings you closer to perfecting your strategy. Patience, persistence, and a willingness to learn are your greatest allies in this process.

Your success isn't measured by the perfection of your first funnel but by the progress you make with each iteration. The secret to any Power Funnel is always found in its maker's ability to adapt.

So, design, implement, refine, and above all, *grow*. Grow until you're not just building funnels but building lasting relationships. And with that, I leave you to start this exciting journey.

Cheers,

Ylva Bosemark

Acknowledgments

To be honest, I'm not quite sure where to begin these acknowledgments. This book exists thanks to the contributions of so many people. I'm eternally grateful to every single person who shared their ideas with me, honed my skills, and provided their support. Without all of you, this book would not be possible:

To Rob Markovich, not just for your brilliant foreword, but for understanding me, my business, and this book since day one. I'll always be grateful for the phone call that forever changed my life. Thank you, thank you, thank you.

Endless gratitude to my superstar editor, Daniel—how can I ever thank you enough for all your help? I'm so honored I got to work with you.

To Adnan Iftekhar for being my first mentor, role model, and cheerleader when entrepreneurship felt like a distant reality. I cannot tell you how grateful I am that our paths crossed all those years ago.

Thank you Meggin Kearney for seeing my potential to partner with Google when no one else did. You're the reason I fell in love with the endless possibilities of technology.

To Amaya Rivera and Maria Patterson—you have no idea how much you've helped me grow as a writer (though maybe this book offers some proof). I wish there were more teachers like you.

Thank you Scott Galloway for inspiring me to think boldly and to tell better stories. You've helped me realize that life is so rich.

I'd like to thank Colleen Phillips for supporting me through all my highs and lows and to whom I owe a debt I can never repay.

Thank you Tressa Thomas for bringing my MVP to life. You make me proud to be a process-obsessed, optimization geek.

I'm also grateful to the experts in cognitive and behavioral sciences—the remarkable doctors, scientists, and professors who are far more qualified than I am to make the arguments presented in this book.

I owe a huge thank you to my parents for giving me that initial shove out the door, for teaching me to dream bigger, and for never telling me I was too young to work with the big guys. A warm hug to my friends and my sister Elsa for your unwavering support. And to the love of my life, Santi—you give me a reason to wake up every morning.

To my readers: thank you for making this journey magical. Thank you for all your messages and for spreading the word about this book. You make the long hours and hard work absolutely worth it.

About the Author

Ylva Bosemark is a serial entrepreneur who launched her first business while in high school. She sold laser-cut, eco-friendly corporate merchandise to clients like Google, Salesforce, VMware, VitalHD, and many more. In college, she founded a drone e-commerce store, offering ready-to-fly kits, drone parts, and repair services. Remarkably, she successfully sold the business just two years later.

Having experienced the challenges of entrepreneurship firsthand, Ylva understands how demanding startups can be when resources and time are scarce. While there's an abundance of business information available online, oftentimes, the methods are inefficient or outdated—especially for individuals of her generation.

To address this gap, Ylva has meticulously curated proven strategies and adapted them to our contemporary, increasingly tech-driven landscape. The result of her dedication is this book: a guide written by a digital native for digital natives and aspiring future makers. Throughout these pages, Ylva shares her experiences, insights, and a roadmap for harnessing AI in our ever-evolving business world.

References

[1] Hill, Andrew, et al. "Earliest homo." *Nature*, vol. 355, no. 6362, 1992, pp. 719–722, https://doi.org/10.1038/355719a0.

[2] Cosmides, Leda, and John Tooby. "Evolutionary Psychology: A Primer." *Center for Evolutionary Psychology UC Santa Barbara*, 1997, www.psych.ucsb.edu/research/cep/.

[3] Qumer, Syeda Maseeha, and Benudhar Sahu. "Burger King's Satisfries: The Failed French Fry." *The Case Centre*, 2016, www.thecasecentre.org/products/view?id=137324.

[4] Godin, Seth. *Purple Cow, New Edition: Transform Your Business by Being Remarkable*. Penguin Publishing Group, 2009.

[5] Tuvenvall, Julius. *Spam by Oatly*, 2023, juliustuvenvall.se/Spam-by-Oatly.

[6] Ibid

[7] Cook, Jodie. "How Gymshark Became a $1.3 Billion Brand, and What We Can Learn." *Forbes*, Aug. 2020, www.forbes.com/sites/jodiecook/2020/08/17/how-gymshark-became-a-13bn-brand-and-what-we-can-learn/?sh=7c730b6b76ed.

[8] Zak, Paul J., et al. "Oxytocin Increases Generosity in Humans." *PLOS ONE*, Nov. 2007, journals.plos.org/plosone/article?id=10.1371%2Fjournal.pone.0001128.

[9] Ratey, John J, and Richard Manning. *Go Wild: Free Your Body and Mind From the Afflictions of Civilization*. Little Brown & Co, 2014.

[10] MacInnis, Deborah J, and Valerie S Folkes. "Humanizing Brands: When Brands Seem to Be Like Me, Part of Me, and in a Relationship with Me." *Journal of Consumer Psychology*, 11 Jan. 2017, www.sciencedirect.com/science/article/abs/pii/S1057740816301061.

[11] Arora, Nidhi, et al. "The Value of Getting Personalization Right-or Wrong-Is Multiplying." *McKinsey & Company*, McKinsey & Company, 12 Nov. 2021,

www.mckinsey.com/capabilities/growth-marketing-and-sales/our-insights/the-value-of-getting-personalization-right-or-wrong-is-multiplying.

[12] Pemberton, Chris. "Tap into the Marketing Power of SMS." *Gartner*, 3 Nov. 2016, www.gartner.com/en/marketing/insights/articles/tap-into-the-marketing-power-of-sms.

[13] Iyengar, Sheena S, and Mark R Lepper. "When Choice Is Demotivating: Can One Desire Too Much of a Good Thing?" *Journal of Personality and Social Psychology*, June 2000, faculty.washington.edu/jdb/345/345%20Articles/Iyengar%20%26%20Lepper%20(2000).pdf.

[14] Scott, Edward. "Make Product Categories the Top-Level Navigation Items on Mobile Sites (33% Don't) ." *Baymard Institute*, Jan. 2023, baymard.com/blog/main-navigation-product-categories.

[15] Melina, Remy. "How Advertisements Seduce Your Brain." *LiveScience*, 23 Sept. 2011, www.livescience.com/16169-advertisements-seduce-brain.html.

[16] Bull, Peter N., et al. "Decision Making in Healthy Participants on the Iowa Gambling Task: New Insights from an Operant Approach." *Frontiers of Psychology*, 19 Mar. 2015, doi.org/10.3389/fpsyg.2015.00391.

[17] Mahoney, Manda. "The Subconscious Mind of the Consumer (and How to Reach It)." *Harvard Business School Working Knowledge*, 13 Jan. 2003, hbswk.hbs.edu/item/the-subconscious-mind-of-the-consumer-and-how-to-reach-it#:~:text=The%20Subconscious%20Mind%20of%20the%20Consumer%20(And%20How%20To%20Reach%20It),-by%20Manda%20Mahoney&text=Harvard%20Business%20School%20professor%20Gerald,place%20in%20the%20subconscious%20mind.

[18] Draper, Alan. "New Outbrain Study Says Negative Headlines Do Better Than Positive." *Business 2 Community*, Mar. 2014, www.business2community.com/blogging/new-outbrain-study-says-negative-headlines-better-positive-0810707.

[19] Gallo, Carmine. "What I Learned Watching 150 Hours of TED Talks." *Harvard Business Review*, 28 Apr. 2014, hbr.org/2014/04/what-i-learned-

watching-150-hours-of-ted-talks?utm_source=medium&utm_medium=article&utm_campaign=caelanhuntress.

[20] Chernev, Alexander, et al. "Choice Overload: A Conceptual Review and Meta-analysis." *Society for Consumer Psychology*, Aug. 2014, myscp.onlinelibrary.wiley.com/doi/abs/10.1016/j.jcps.2014.08.002.

[21] Hendricks, Kent. "The Decoy Effect: Why You Make Irrational Choices Every Day (without Even Knowing It)." *Kent Hendricks*, 7 Feb. 2018, kenthendricks.com/decoy-effect/.

[22] Ibid

[23] Berger, Jonah. "How to Change Anyone's Mind." *Wharton Risk Management and Decision Processes Center*, 7 May 2020, riskcenter.wharton.upenn.edu/labs/howtochangeanyonesmind/.

[24] Gneezy, Uri, et al. "The Uncertainty Effect: When a Risky Prospect Is Valued Less than Its Worst Possible Outcome." *The Quarterly Journal of Economics*, 1 Nov. 2006, doi.org/10.1093/qje/121.4.1283.

[25] Knutson, Brian, et al. "Neural Predictors of Purchases." *Neuron*, 4 Jan. 2007, www.ncbi.nlm.nih.gov/pmc/articles/PMC1876732/.

[26] "Spend 'til It Hurts." *Carnegie Mellon University Press*, 2007, www.cmu.edu/homepage/practical/2007/winter/spending-til-it-hurts.shtml.

[27] Zellermayer, Ofer. "The Pain of Paying ." *Research Gate*, Jan. 1996, www.researchgate.net/publication/280711796_The_Pain_of_Paying.

[28] Prelec, Drazen, and George Loewenstein. "The Red and the Black: Mental Accounting of Savings and Debt ." *Marketing Science* , 1999, www.jstor.org/stable/193194.

[29] Kumar, Vineet, and Timothy Derdenger. "The Dynamic Effects of Bundling as a Product Strategy." *HBS Working Knowledge*, 22 Feb. 2012, hbswk.hbs.edu/item/the-dynamic-effects-of-bundling-as-a-product-strategy.

[30] Anderson, Chris. *Free: The Future of a Radical Price*. Random House Business, 2010.

[31] "Consumer Trends Report | Q2 2023 Quarterly Changes in Consumer Trends." *Jungle Scout*, Jungle Scout, 20 July 2023, www.junglescout.com/consumer-trends/.

[32] "49 Cart Abandonment Rate Statistics 2023." *Baymard Institute*, 2023, baymard.com/lists/cart-abandonment-rate.

[33] Ibid

[34] Ibid

[35] Ibid

[36] Mansfield, Matt. "Customer Retention Statistics - the Ultimate Collection for Small Business." *Small Business Trends*, 29 Dec. 2022, smallbiztrends.com/2016/10/customer-retention-statistics.html.

[37] "Targeted Online Marketing Programs Boost Customer Conversion Rates." *McKinsey & Company*, www.mckinsey.com/capabilities/growth-marketing-and-sales/how-we-help-clients/clm-online-retailer. Accessed 31 July 2023.

[38] Wu, Chin-Shan, and Fei-Fei Cheng. "The Joint Effect of Framing and Anchoring on Internet Buyers' Decision-Making." *Electronic Commerce Research and Applications*, 20 Jan. 2011, www.sciencedirect.com/science/article/abs/pii/S1567422311000032.

[39] "Red Bull NPS & Customer Reviews ." *Comparably*, www.comparably.com/brands/red-bull. Accessed 31 July 2023.

[40] Beatty, Sharon, et al. "The Involvement-Commitment Model: Theory and Implications." *ResearchGate*, Feb. 1988, www.researchgate.net/publication/223632342_The_involvement-commitment_model_Theory_and_implications.

[41] Gutman, Jonathan. "Means–End Chains as Goal Hierarchies." *Wiley Online Library*, 7 Dec. 1998, onlinelibrary.wiley.com/doi/abs/10.1002/%28SICI%291520-6793%28199709%2914%3A6%3C545%3A%3AAID-MAR2%3E3.0.CO%3B2-7.

---

[42] Festinger, Leo. *The Theory of Cognitive Dissonance.* Row, Peterson and Company, 1957.

[43] Hull, C. L. "The Goal-Gradient Hypothesis and Maze Learning." *American Psychological Association,* 1932, psycnet.apa.org/record/1932-01362-001.

[44] Nunes, Joseph C, and Xavier Drèze. "The Endowed Progress Effect: How Artificial Advancement Increases Effort ." *Journal of Consumer Research,* 1 Mar. 2006, academic.oup.com/jcr/article-abstract/32/4/504/1787425.

[45] Brafman, Ori, and Rom Brafman. *Sway: The Irresistible Pull of Irrational Behavior.* Crown Business, 2009.

[46] "Compliance without Pressure: The Foot-in-the-Door Technique." *American Psychological Association,* 1966, psycnet.apa.org/record/1966-10825-001.

[47] Abraham, Jay. *Money-Making Secrets of Marketing Genius Jay Abraham and Other Marketing Wizards: A No-Nonsense Guide to Great Wealth and a Person Fortune.* Abraham Publishing Group, 1994.

[48] Kreitman, Adam, et al. "Why Storytelling Is the Key to Selling with Email." *The Daily Egg,* 15 Feb. 2014, www.crazyegg.com/blog/storytelling-in-email/.

[49] Paul, Annie Murphy. "Your Brain on Fiction." *The New York Times,* 17 Mar. 2012, www.nytimes.com/2012/03/18/opinion/sunday/the-neuroscience-of-your-brain-on-fiction.html.

[50] Zak, Paul J. "Why Your Brain Loves Good Storytelling." *Harvard Business Review,* 28 Oct. 2014, hbr.org/2014/10/why-your-brain-loves-good-storytelling.

[51] Finkenbinder, E O. "The Curve of Forgetting." *The American Journal of Psychology,* Jan. 1913, www.jstor.org/stable/1413271.

[52] Simon, Carmen. *Impossible to Ignore: Creating Memorable Content to Influence Decisions.* McGraw-Hill Education, 2016.

[53] Mills, Henry R. *Teaching and Training: A Handbook for Instructors.* Macmillan, 1977.

[54] Mazarakis, Anna, and Alyson Shontell. "How Two Founders Got Nearly 1 Million Users for Their App before It Even Existed." *Business Insider,* 11 July

2017, www.businessinsider.com/free-viral-marketing-how-robinhood-got-1-million-users-before-launch-2017-7.

[55] Clear, James. *Atomic Habits: Tiny Changes, Remarkable Results: An Easy and Proven Way to Build Good Habits and Break Bad Ones.* Penguin Random House, 2018.

[56] Rao, Pallavi. "How Long It Took for Popular Apps to Reach 100 Million Users." *Visual Capitalist,* 13 July 2023, www.visualcapitalist.com/threads-100-million-users/.

Printed in Great Britain
by Amazon

37641538R00205